BT
710
.S65
1985

INTERRELIGIOUS EXPLORATIONS SERIES

Society and Original Sin

Society and Original Sin:
Ecumenical Essays on the Impact of the Fall

EDITED BY
DURWOOD FOSTER
AND
PAUL MOJZES

A NEW ERA BOOK

PARAGON HOUSE
New York

Published in the United States by
Paragon House Publishers
2 Hammarskjold Plaza
New York, NY 10017

A New Ecumenical Research
   Association Book

ISBN: 0-913757-15-2 (Softbound)

All rights reserved. No part of this book
may be reproduced in any form without
permission, unless by a reviewer who
wishes to quote brief passages. © 1985.

Library of Congress Cataloging in Publication Data
Main entry under title:

Society and Original Sin.

   Includes index.
   1. Fall of man—Addresses, essays, lectures.
2. Sin—Addresses, essays, lectures. I. Foster,
Durwood. II. Mojzes, Paul.
BT710.S65   1984   233'.14   84-25406
ISBN 0-913757-15-2 (pbk.)

Contents

1. The Human Prospect in the Light of the Fall—
   HANS SCHWARZ 1
2. The Fall: Its Factual Acceptance and Practical
   Meaning in Contemporary Society—MAURICE BOUTIN 13
3. Satan: Reality or Symbol?—YOUNG OON KIM 21
4. The Fall and Misogyny in Justin Martyr and
   Clement of Alexandria—SARAH PETERSEN 37
5. The Islamic Concept of Sin—SULAYMAN S. NYANG 52
6. Some Reflections on the Unification Account of the Fall—
   JONATHAN WELLS 62
7. The Fall in *Divine Principle*—DURWOOD FOSTER 73
8. The Unification Doctrine of the Fall and the
   Problem of Evil—GENE JAMES 86
9. A Good Thing Spoiled: Reflections on the Personal and
   Social Dimensions of Sinfulness—J. DEOTIS ROBERTS 100
10. The Cracked Mirror: Understandings of the
    Myth of the Fall—PAUL MOJZES 106
11. The Response to Suffering—THOMAS WALSH 119
12. Original Sin and Human Value—LLOYD EBY 133
13. Sin and Society—M. DARROL BRYANT 149
14. The Opposite of Sin is Love—CARL SKRADE 164
    About the Authors 183
    Index 187

Preface

The following essays were initially written for a seminar convened by M. Darrol Bryant in Nassau, in February 1983, under the sponsorship of the New Ecumenical Research Association. Participants representing a wide range of backgrounds and perspectives were invited to exchange views regarding original sin or the fall, particularly how these notions might illuminate perennial problems of society. As the dialogue proved unusually evocative, it seemed eminently desirable to present the papers to a larger audience. It is our conviction that neither frantic alarm over the world's crises, nor the many prescriptions for their cure, can have much point apart from a clear diagnosis of what is fundamentally wrong with the human condition. In the Judeo-Christian and Islamic traditions at least, no notion has functioned as pivotally and inclusively in pointing to the core of human derangement as has sin. To inquire after the source of sin is, however, to raise the question of original sin, an idea that has in fact always been inseparable from the web of human interrelationships.

A neglect of the problem of original sin and sin in general can be noted in recent decades as people tended to explain the problem of evil in human affairs exclusively in terms of social maladjustment, personal mental disorders or faulty societal structures. This neglect led at least one social scientist, Karl Menninger, to ask pointedly, Whatever happened to sin? in his book by the same title. Obviously it is not being suggested that this volume will remedy the situations; other recent books have also turned to a renewed exploration of human sinfulness. It is hoped that this modest contribution to reopening of the discussion of the fall may prompt another fresh look at the issue of the roots of the human malaise not only to clarify Jewish, Christian, Muslim, and Unificationist thought on this problem but to help thinkers in these traditions in their dialogues with people of other orientations as they attempt to communicate their profound convictions and evaluation regarding the human condition.

Regretfully the papers do not represent the entire spectrum of views on original sin. No Jewish, Eastern Orthodox, or Evangelical Protestant writers were present at the conference and there is only one Roman Catholic paper. While this means that the discussion of the subject matter is not inclusive, it is hoped that a sufficient variety of treatments of the fall is present here to be stimulating to the reader.

It goes without saying that no single vision of original sin and society dominates this volume. Although five of the papers are by theologians of the Unification Church, these also are notable for the variety of their approaches. They show that while Unification teaching has indeed contributed a powerful new impulse to serious thinking about the fall, a vigorous diversity of interpretation is at work within that tradition itself. As has happened characteristically in the New ERA process, this diversity mingles productively with the broad spectrum of other views convened in dialogue to generate fresh questions and insights. The only premises for such exchange are complete freedom to speak one's own mind and openness to listen conscientiously to others. The printed papers offered here were written and revised for the purpose of that kind of wider ecumenism. It is our earnest hope that their publication will carry further what the seminar in Nassau experienced as a very fruitful beginning.

Durwood Foster and Paul Mojzes

1 The Human Prospect in the Light of the Fall: *The Biblical Notion of the Fall and the Future of the Human Race*

HANS SCHWARZ

Human betterment is of intrinsic concern to all. Whether one considers humanistic ideas of self-improvement, theological notions of liberation, or political thoughts on revolution, in each instance one notices that humanity is not satisfied with its present condition and intends to improve on it. Yet the history of humanity does not clearly indicate an upward-slanting line of progress toward the better. Though undeniable technological progress has been made, in their innermost inclinations and aspirations, humans today do not differ much from their ancestors who lived thousands of years ago. When theologians assert that we are sinners and justified at the same time, they also seem to indicate that there is no prospect of perfection this side of heaven. Yet those who take the concept of personal sanctification seriously realize too that a saint is never exempt from the possibility of lapsing into sinfulness. All these factors seem to imply that human potential for self-improvement is not one that would, or even could, lead to an ever-improving world. Jesus rightly cautioned that God's kingdom is not of this world, nor will it be built in the human context (cf. Matt. 11:12).

The Biblical Notion of the Fall

The biblical notion of the fall seems to tarnish the human prospect even more. That humans are sinners in need of divine forgiveness, most thoughtful theologians will contend. Yet the biblical account of the fall in Genesis 3 is conspicuously isolated from the rest of the Old Testament.[1] It is not picked up by the psalmist, the prophets, or any other writer in the Old Testament.[2] But we dare not treat it as if it expresses an isolated incident. The fall forms part of humanity's history, and it is only natural to perceive it in its context as the first link of a whole sequence of sinful events. It is immediately followed by the story of Cain slaying his brother, the vindictive attitude of Lamech (Gen. 4), the marriage between the sons of God and the daughters of humans (Gen. 6), the flood (Gen. 6–9), and finally the construction of the Tower of Babel (Gen. 11).[3]

The event depicted in Genesis 3, however, is not just one among many. It is the first sinful event occurring to the first woman and to the first man, whose name, Adam, is understood as a proper name in the latter part of Genesis 3. By talking about Adam as a specific man, the Yahwist wants to show the exemplary character of this event. The sin committed in Genesis 3 is not simply a violation of God's command not to eat from the tree of the knowledge of good and evil. Rather, the distrust of God is at the center of the fall account. While the condition depicted in the Yahwistic creation account is characterized by innocence, "a pure childlike relationship with God, a life also reflected in the relationship between man and woman," the harmony between God and human beings is now broken.[4] The intention of connecting creation and fall so intimately is not to show how the once good creation got so bad. Even after the fall, the world, including humanity, is still God's good creation. The Yahwist wants to demonstrate the reason for our present human predicament.

It has been claimed often that the disruption of the initial harmony is actually beneficial because it leads to the actualization of the human potential. Hegel, for instance, understood sin as the logical necessity to recognize the good, since if the human being "does not know about evil, he also does not know about good."[5] He characterized the fall "as the eternal myth of man through which he becomes man." The German philosopher Friedrich Schiller thought along similar lines and concluded that the alleged disobedience against God's command was: ". . . actually the fall of man from his instinct, which brought moral evil into creation, but only to enable the moral good within creation. Therefore without doubt it is the happiest and greatest event in human history. From this moment onward his freedom is inscribed, here the first and remote foundation was laid for his morality.[6]

This idealistic notion of human sinfulness is affirmed by many psychoanalysts. For instance, 175 years after Schiller, Eric Fromm claimed: "This first act of disobedience is man's first step toward freedom." Man was expelled from paradise and is now able "to make his own history, to develop his human powers, and to attain a new harmony with man and nature as a fully developed individual instead of the former harmony in which he was not yet an individual."[7] Carl Jung was a little more restrained when he wrote: "There is deep doctrine in the legend of the fall: it is the expression of a dim presentiment that the emancipation of the ego-consciousness was a Luciferian deed."[8] Pursuing a different perspective, Teilhard de Chardin also came close to this idealistic notion when he asserted that evil is a necessary by-product of evolution through which nature progresses in manifold errors and trials on its evolutionary course.[9]

The idealistic interpretations of the fall argue on the basis of an evolutionary process, in which the later stages are perceived as more highly developed and therefore better. There are two objections, however, that have to be voiced. First, it is difficult to assert on strictly biological grounds that an evolutionary development toward a higher stage is necessarily better. Biologically speaking, humans are not better than fish, though humanity represents a higher evolutionary development. A highly developed culture is not necessarily better than a primitive one, even if one judges "better" here by moral standards. Second, the account of the fall is not amenable to any kind of evolutionary interpretation. This becomes evident in two ways.

First, the eruption of sinfulness in Genesis 3 cannot be deduced by causal inference from God's good creation.[10] When Adam is questioned by God about his behavior, he attempts such a causal inference, saying: "The woman whom thou gavest to be with me, she gave me fruit of the tree, and I ate" (Gen. 3:12). In other words, he wants to excuse himself by blaming the cause of evil on God. Eve attempts a similar causal inference, though not as daring, when she replies to God: "The serpent beguiled me, and I ate" (Gen. 3:13). Again, the excuse is made that the cause of evil comes from outside. Yet neither of these attempts suffices before God to account for the gravity of the situation. Second, there is no causal connection between this first sin and the emergence of subsequent sins. We concede that the Yahwist demonstrates in the chapters following the account of the fall that evil spread like a forest fire. But he does not mention anywhere that new sin is connected with prior sin. Therefore, the first sin cannot be used to excuse the significance of subsequent sins.

Evil came into the world with the first appearance of man and woman and it continued to erupt with every further appearance of man and woman. It is useful to note here what behavioral psychology states about the phenomenon of aggression. Aggressive drives are present on the animal level. They usually operate to help further the species, not to destroy it. This is true for aggression practiced against other species (defense, hunting, etc.), as well as within the same species (rank and order, mating, etc.). However, as humanity emerged and began to dominate the environment and its own kind through increasingly sophisticated tools and weapons, the aggressive drives became increasingly ambivalent, simultaneously furthering potential good and potential evil. The result has been the extinction of some species of animals, and domestication of others; genocide of parts of humanity, and unification of others through large-scale cultures. As psychoanalysis rightly suggests, the activities of humanity are highly ambivalent—pursuing life and spreading death at the same time.

But the emergence of evil cannot be compared with a fateful decree against which humanity has no choice. It should not be overlooked that it is not a human being but the serpent who is introduced as the tempter in the fall account. It is an exaggerated interpretation of the temptation story to conclude that the woman has more immediate access to the dark sides of life than man because she is seduced first and in turn seduces.[11] What is emphasized, is that the essence of human beings was not sinful from the beginning, and that temptation had to come from the outside. But the cause of evil is not an anti-Godly principle outside of God's creation, such as Gnosticism had suggested. The serpent is explicitly introduced as an animal and as part of God's creation, and not as part of the heavenly court.[12] Why this part of God's good creation becomes the tempter is beyond the interest of the Yahwist, since the solution to this question does not contribute anything to the description of human sinfulness. There are two items, however, that still need clarification: What was the object that tempted humans, and what were the consequences once they succumbed to sin?

The first couple was tempted to be like God: to know good and evil. It is difficult to assume that God had created a creature which was to become his potential challenger, since the human being "carries potential Godhead within himself."[13] While it is also absurd for the Yahwist to surmise that anybody could be like Yahweh, it is much easier for him to suggest that a human being wanted to become like the *elohim*, that it wanted to become divine.[14] When humanity was tempted to know good and evil, it was not just tempted to know the distinction between good and evil, but also to know everything from good to evil.[15] Human temptation was then, and still is, to know everything and to know it better. This attitude challenged any kind of harmonious relationship and should not be confused with the emergence of humanity's inquisitive spirit. It is rather humanity's destructive desire to disallow any "thous" who have their own sphere, and to treat them as "its" who have no secrets. This human hubris effectively destroyed humanity's relationship with God.

However, God did not respond to humanity's sinful pride like an insulted tyrant. Admittedly, the harmonious unity with God was gone, and the couple was sent forth from the garden. But the threat that they would die the day they should eat from the tree of knowledge of good and evil was not actualized once they had sinned (Gen. 2:17). They were only reassured that they would return to dust from which they were taken (Gen. 2:7; 3:19). Almost as if in defiance of the original threat, Adam now dares to call his wife Eve, "the mother of all living."[16] Not even the obligation of work can be understood as the actual curse of the fall (Gen. 2:15). However, once the harmonious relationship with God was broken, the harmonious relationship between humanity and nature, and between man and woman, had disappeared too. Life now, confesses the Yahwist, is drudgery, filled with hatred and passion and longing for harmony. Yet life does not come to an end because "the Lord God made for Adam and for his wife garments of skins, and clothed them" (Gen. 3:21). Instead of lamenting evil, the Yahwist points to signs of grace that are given to the first couple on their wanderings through life, such as the coat of skins and God's help in clothing them.[17] This compassionate act of God could be understood as the first sign of the gospel, rather than a verdict of constant animosity between the snake and humanity.[18]

One would have the greatest difficulty reconciling the third chapter of Genesis with the assertion "that the root of man's sin stems from adultery."[19] Human sinfulness cannot be explained by referring to the lower parts of human anatomy. It was rather the distrust of and aversion to God which put humanity in its fallen state. Since God, as the measure of that which is good, became neglected, humanity was left without a reliable focus for its endeavors. Small wonder that *Divine Principle* now asserts: "The principal cause behind the conflicts and revolutions which constantly take place in human society is the change in the standard of good and evil which occurs, as the purpose sought by man varies."[20] Yet, by nature, the behavior of human beings is not as free and unspecified as we might initially assume.

Humanity in the Context of Divine Preservation

Charles Darwin observed that human moral and mental faculties differ in degree rather than in kind from the capacities of animals. To be human means to act according to certain norms that enable us to live together and further our own species. The explicit forms which these norms assume, however, depend upon the environment in which the social behavior takes place. The trustworthiness of the moral process enacted through the living out of these norms depends on our ability to develop these norms in such a way that standards are established for interacting with the environment. If these norms are not developed in accordance with the changes we encounter and inaugurate, we will become helpless victims of the environmental conditions under which we live.[21] For instance, unless we change our living habits, the crowded conditions in today's anonymous mass society may easily lead to the deterioration of individual partner relationships.[22] This means that, contrary to our obligation of governing this world and subduing it according to the moral norms within us, the world would subdue us and change our moral behavior accordingly.

These insights and conclusions have important implications for our understanding of the traditional theology of orders. Werner Elert is certainly right when he claims that the orders presupposed in the decalogue with words of command and prohibition are orders of God's creation, an order to which we belong as its members. Appropriately, they are called orders of creation.[23] We wonder, however, whether Elert is correct when he asserts that these orders are always orders that are—not orders that ought to be. Truly, the Sixth Commandment does not constitute marriage but presupposes it. Yet adultery was committed through acts that were considerably different in the ancient Israel of King David, the medieval Germany of Martin Luther, or in the Puritan England of the Pilgrim Fathers. Needless to say, in each epoch marriage too was understood quite differently. This does not mean that the underlying norm "thou shalt not commit adultery" loses its binding value. But if we want to maintain the goal of the durable pair relationship which is envisioned in the commandment, the exact interpretation of its normative ought-character must be reevaluated with each changing situation.

Since the moral norms are goal-oriented and are intended to preserve the species rather than to constitute it, it might be good to follow the suggestion of Walter Künneth and talk about orders of preservation instead of orders of creation. Künneth does not intend to diminish the creational character of these orders, but he objects to a static interpretation, and maintains that the creation must be perceived under the aspect of God's conserving activity.[24] This is even more necessary, since we know God's creation only in its fallen condition, under the aspect of preservation. According to Künneth the orders of preservation counteract the tendencies of the destructive anti-Godly powers. They are a sign that God does not want to destroy the world, but wants to conserve it for Christ's sake and turn it toward Christ. The orders of preservation therefore ultimately have eschatological character, for they urge on to an eschatological fulfillment in the new creation.

Since these orders are no longer evident in their original divine creational intention, they assume the character of a law. But as law, they enable and facilitate the living together of people. They express a mutual obligation. Yet they are also susceptible to sinful distortion and can be misused to perpetuate injustice and inequality. Therefore, it is necessary to never divorce them from God, as the originator of these orders. This does not mean, however, that one should go as far as Karl Barth does when he claims that through its sinful existence, humanity is so depraved that it has no possibility of knowing about these fundamental moral laws of nature. Barth insists that these orders cannot be found anywhere, but they are disclosed through Jesus Christ in God's word.[25]

Dietrich Bonhoeffer attempted a similar christomonistic foundation of these orders when he claimed that it is an empty abstraction to talk about the world without relating it to Christ.[26] The relationship "of the world to Christ assumes concrete form in certain mandates of God in the world. The Scriptures name four such mandates: labour, marriage, government, and the Church." The term "mandates" indicates very appropriately the obligatory aspect of these orders. Yet an exclusively christocentric approach to these orders—whether one accepts their foundation in Christ or not—might obscure the fact that the acknowledgement of certain moral norms is a necessary condition for human existence as such.[27] Since they are binding for both atheists and Christians, they are not a source of revelation.

Atheists can recognize these norms of moral behavior as partly inborn and partly handed on by tradition. In the light of God's self-disclosure in Jesus Christ, however, Christians perceive the preserving activity of God in these norms. They realize that through the evolving moral process, God is preserving the human community against self-destruction and against the destructive and seductive tendencies of the anti-Godly powers. Luther has expressed this picturesquely in saying: "If God would withdraw his protective hand you would become blind, or an adulterer and murderer like David, you would fall and break your leg and drown."[28] Through God's self-disclosure in Jesus Christ one is also reminded of the trustworthiness yet transitory character of the moral process. It will find its fulfillment and completion in the eschatological new creation, at which time the moral norms will be unimpaired and self-evident. Then moral behavior will be characterized through complete harmony with God.

The Limits of the Human Potential

During the interim between fall and Parousia, the human prospect is of a rather modest scope. On the one hand we are assured that God's protective hand will save us from ultimate self-destruction. Yet on the other hand people remain both sinners and saints. Even with best intentions one has to admit with Paul: "I do not do the good I want, but the evil I do not want is what I do" (Rom. 7:19). This does not mean that we are schizophrenic. It does mean that we continuously deviate from that which we consider worthy of attaining. Thus any attempt to model the ideal family, the caring community, or the unity of humanity will always fall short of the intended goal. Humanity is basically self-centered, and interested in promoting its own self at the expense of everything and everyone else. Such self-centeredness, however, will eventually cause our own demise, as Immanuel Kant has shown with his categorical imperative. It will invite others to do the same to us as we do to them. Should one then simply give up in despair? It is clear that the human condition neither allows us to save ourselves nor to save the world around us. If the world survives at all and if we are saved, then such attainment cannot come from us or from the world around us. It must come from a power beyond ourselves, i.e., from God. Yet such metaphysical realism does not render us completely inactive.

Again, listen to Paul. While he acknowledges the depth of human depravity, he does not desist from pursuing that which is right, good, and beautiful. He claims: "Not that I have already obtained this or am already perfect; but I press on to make it my own, because Christ Jesus has made me his own" (Phil. 3:12). With this statement he admits that he will pursue his own progress, while also indicating the stimulus for his forward-reaching action. The reason for engagement, he implies, can neither be found in stubbornness nor in the notion that if we try hard enough we will surely succeed. The impetus for our endeavors as well as the vision for the new humanity can only come from the eschatological and at the same time salvific stimulus which Jesus Christ has provided for us. He has overcome the powers of darkness through his sacrificial death and his glorious resurrection. Through our baptism, these benefits have been applied to us. We are new creatures, made new in the prospect of the eschatological completion.

We are continuously admonished to model ourselves according to Christ and to put on the new humanity. All such appeals, however, would be totally futile, if they should simply refer to our own possibilities. They can only be successful because God's sanctifying and directing power dwells in us. As the frequent imperatives in Paul's letters show, this power does not automatically make us into new beings. We can always violate its presence and lapse back into our former sinful states. At the same time, however, the presence of this power, the Holy Spirit, allows us to become new beings, showing forth the grace that is within us, and anticipating something of the new community and the new world that are ahead of us. This kind of proleptic anticipation will lead us toward progress in the face of adversity; it will render us cautious about any utopian dreams of establishing a new Eden on earth; and it will give us confidence and assurance that the future is not bleak or meaningless.

Knowing that the future has already begun in the resurrection of Jesus Christ, we dare to anticipate proleptically this future in which the Christ event inspires us along the way. This process of patient but active anticipation strives for a better humanity, a more just society, and a more humane world. But since it is only anticipation, we are realistic enough to remember our intrinsic alienation from God, the source of all wisdom and all good things. Thus we must reject the illusion that we could ever create a good humanity, a just society, or a new world. Ultimate perfection remains a truly eschatological goal. Undeserved by us, ultimate perfection will be brought about through God's gracious action. Yet the hope which it inspires and the power of God which is active in us provide a mighty stimulus toward this goal.

Notes

1   It is not quite correct to say with Ludwig Köhler, *Old Testament Theology,* trans. A. S. Todd (Philadelphia: Westminster, 1957), 178, that "the priestly writer knows nothing of Paradise, Fall, or cursed ground." While it is true that the priestly writer does not narrate a story of the fall as such, his narrative of the flood depicts the emergence of sin on a global, not an individual scale. For the discussion with Köhler, cf. the perceptive comments by Walther Zimmerli, *Grundriss der alttestamentlichen Theologie* (Stuttgart: W. Kohlhammer, 1972), 153.

2   So Gerhard von Rad, *Genesis: A Commentary,* trans. J. H. Marks (Philadelphia: Westminster, 1961), 98.

3   Cf. for this and the following, Zimmerli, 148.

4   Th. C. Vriezen, *An Outline of Old Testament Theology* (Newton, Mass.; Charles T. Branford, 1970), 414.

5   Georg Wilhelm Friedrich Hegel, *Vorlesungen über die Philosophie der Religion,* vol. 1 of *Sämtliche Werke,* ed. Hermann Glockner (Stuttgart: Fr. Frommann, 1928), 15:285; and *Vorlesungen über die Geschichte,* in *Sämtliche Werke,* 11:413. [Translated by the author.]

6   Friedrich Schiller, *Etwas über die erste Menschengesellschaft. Übergang des Menschen zur Freiheit und Humanität* (1789), in *Gesammelte Werke in fünf Bänden,* ed. Reinhold Netolitzky (Gütersloh: C. Bertelsmann, 1959), 4:103. [Translated by the author.]

7   Erich Fromm, *The Heart of Man: Its Genius for Good and Evil* (New York: Harper & Row, 1964), 20.

8   Carl Gustav Jung, "The Phenomenology of the Spirit in Fairytales," in *The Collected Works of C. G. Jung,* 2d ed., ed. William McGuire, (Princeton: Princeton University Press, 1971), 9.1:230 (420).

9   Cf. Pierre Teilhard de Chardin, *The Phenomenon of Man,* trans. B. Wall, intro. Sir Julian Huxley (New York: Harper, 1959), 301f., where he says: "The involuting universe . . . proceeds step by step by dint of billion-fold trial and error. It is this process of groping, combined with the two-fold mechanism of reproduction and heredity . . . which gives rise to the . . . tree of life." Cf. also p. 310, where he picks up the same terminology in talking about the "evil of disorder and failure" as a necessity in the evolutionary process.

10   Cf. the very instructive comments by Zimmerli, 148f.

11   Cf. von Rad, 87f., in his exegesis of Gen. 3:6, where he presents this interpretation.

12   Cf. Johannes Fichtner, "ophis (Gen. 3)," in *Theological Dictionary of the New Testament,* ed. Gerhard Kittel, trans. G. W. Bromiley (Grand Rapids, Mich.: Eerdmans, 1965), 5:573, who emphasizes the creational aspect of the serpent.

13   This assumption is advanced by Erich Fromm, *You Shall Be As Gods: A Radical Interpretation of the Old Testament and Its Tradition* (New York: Holt, Rinehart and Winston, 1966), 24.

14   Similarly, von Rad, 86, in his exegesis of Gen. 3:4f.

15   Ibid., 86f.; and Henricus Renckens, *Israel's Concept of the Beginning: The Theology of Genesis 1-3,* trans. Charles Napier (New York: Herder and Herder, 1964), 274f.

16   Cf. Zimmerli, 152.

17   So rightly Vriezen, 415.

18   For the interpretation of Gen. 3:15 cf. Fichtner, 5:574f. At this point no indication is made yet that the animosity between the snake and humanity will be overcome. But such animosity will no longer exist in the messianic time. Then the original harmony will be reestablished; cf. Isa. 11:1–8.

19   *Divine Principle,* 5th ed., (New York: Holy Spirit Association for the Unification of World Christianity [HSA-UWC], 1977), 75.

20   Ibid., 87.

21   Wolfgang Wickler, *The Biology of the Ten Commandments,* trans. D. Smith (New York: McGraw-Hill, 1972), 171ff.

22   Ibid., 179.

23   Cf. Werner Elert, *The Christian Ethos,* trans. C. J. Schindler (Philadelphia: Muhlenberg, 1957), 77f.

24   Cf. Walter Künneth, *Politik zwischen Dämon und Gott. Eine christliche Ethik des Politischen* (Berlin: Lutherisches Verlagshaus, 1954), 139f.

25   Karl Barth, *The Doctrine of Creation,* vol. 3.4 of *Church Dogmatics,* ed. G. W. Bromiley and T. F. Torrance, trans. A. T. Mackay et al. (Edinburgh: T. & T. Clark, 1958), 45.

26   Cf. Dietrich Bonhoeffer, *Ethics,* ed. Eberhard Bethge, trans. N. H. Smith (New York: Macmillan, 1955), 207.

27   Immanuel Kant, *Foundations of the Metaphysics of Morals,* in *Foundations of the Metaphysics of Morals and What Is Enlightenment?,* trans. with intro. Lewis White Beck (Indianapolis, Ind.: Bobbs-Merrill, 1959), esp. 38ff., argues on the basis of "pure reason" that there are certain moral norms that, when universalized, will support human existence while others, when universalized, will impede it.

28   Martin Luther, *Predigten des Jahres 1531,* in WA 34 II, 237, 3f., in a sermon on the festival of St. Michael's.

2 The Fall:
Its Factual Acceptance and Practical Meaning in Contemporary Society
MAURICE BOUTIN

The fall and what has been traditionally called "original sin" have had juridical and even biological connotations for a long time. Regardless of whether the fall generates a debt for humankind that no one except God can satisfactorily settle, or whether the fall causes a negative legacy transmitted biologically from generation to generation to each and every human being from the very beginning of his or her own existence—in both cases a relationship to society is implied that shapes the experience of human life.

Juridical and biological categories, however, do not seem quite appropriate for understanding the fall. Indeed, these categories underline the social dimension of original sin, but in a way that might lead one to consider it as a kind of sickness inherent in human nature.

One might be ready to agree that there is a kind of personal sin for which the individual is responsible. But original sin as qualifying human nature—and therefore each and every individual prior to any personal decision and responsibility—is something which obviously needs further clarification.

The point in question is how one can relate sin and society adequately. We are facing here what even radical "demythologizers" like Rudolf Bultmann do not intend to minimize, namely, the very transubjective reality of evil—or, put in more directly anthropological terms, human solidarity for what is happening (beyond personal responsibility) and for what fails to happen in society.

As Kant pointed out in his book on *Religion Within the Limits of*

Reason Alone, the most awkward way to understand the spreading of moral evil and its continuation within human history is to imagine that it comes to us from the first parents through "inheritance."[1] Kant then quotes from the Latin poet Ovid who says: "Human species and ancestors, and what we have not done ourselves—all this can hardly be regarded as our own."[2]

Already prior to Kant, Pascal in his *Pensées* reflects that nothing is more shocking than to say that the sin of the first human ancestors covered with guilt those who stand so far from it that they are likely to be unable to participate in it. "This flowing out [through history]," Pascal says, "seems to us not only impossible, but even very unjust." But he adds: "And yet, without this mystery which is the most incomprehensible of all mysteries, we cannot understand ourselves. The core of the human condition takes its twists and turns in this abyss, so that human being is more unconceivable without this mystery than this mystery is unconceivable to human being."[3]

The understanding of original sin escapes human capacity. What Pascal calls a "flowing out" through history, impossible and unjust as it may seem, remains, however, meaningful. We might recall here Roland Barthes's statement about narratives in which meaning "flees," though his statement does not refer to original sin or to the fall narrative in Genesis. Paradoxically, such narratives are, according to Barthes, most significant for human life.[4]

The doctrine of original sin and the biblical narrative of the fall are attempts to conceptualize daily experience. We are not living in the best possible world. Where does this negative insight come from? Do we still need a so-called "Golden Age" and the loss of innocence at the very beginning of human history to explain it?

I contend that we do not. We should rather focus on basic human needs, as did, for instance, the German theologian Gerhard Freund in his book *Sin in Inheritance.*[5] Among the basic human needs, forgiveness in particular should be emphasized—which Freund has overlooked—for it is indeed one of the main features for a life truly human.

A historical approach to the biblical narrative of the fall is needed. It can be said that the fall in Genesis takes a mythological turn. However, we should not forget that mythology can never be understood merely with reference to mythology. The interpretation would turn out to be merely descriptive, which in turn would generate glaring contradictions, because it attempts to preserve the historical reality over against critical historiographical insights into the biblical narrative of the fall.

Forgiveness transcends the possibilities of the individual. Even self-acceptance is very hard to achieve if it is not somehow rooted in one's acceptance by others. The latter does not depend primarily on an overall concept of human nature as rational. Forgiving may seem "rational" because there can be no real human life otherwise. Yet forgiveness goes beyond the mere cause-effect relationship. Quite often it is anything but rational.

The transcendence of forgiveness takes place in community and society. This is probably the reason why critiques of the traditional understanding of original sin, geared as it is to the concept of human nature, focus instead on the experience of the "world."

From the very beginning of existence we do not stand neutral toward the world into which we are born. The idea of original sin relates to the experience that each human being comes into a world already influenced by the failures and sins of others; a world in which life is a struggle, a struggle that may take place unwillingly; a world in which nobody starts from scratch. As Rudolf Bultmann states:

The traditional mythological understanding of original sin could be criticized in many ways, and one might fancy about an allegedly original good within human being as such. Practically, however, all acknowledge original sin—namely in their own judgment about the concrete individuals they have to deal with as well as in their own behavior: basically we mistrust one another, and mistrust implies refusal of others, closing one's heart to others, hatred.[6]

Through original sin, the individual takes on the current understanding of existence that is prevalent in the world into which he or she is born. Consequently, the individual also shares responsibility for the "spirit of this world" (i.e., that ambiance which one seeks to increase, while being at the same time overwhelmed by it).

This basic state of affairs can be overcome, but only through one's acknowledgement of others. This always involves, to some extent, the reality of forgiveness. It is not to be explained by the very distant past of humankind, even when such explanations claim to be based on the biblical narrative of the fall.

Chapters 1 to 11 of Genesis offer a kind of prophecy concerning the past. This material relates to questions arising from the situation in which the two main literary traditions represented in these chapters happen to be: the Yahwist (J), writing at the end of the tenth century B.C., and the Priestly tradition (P), writing during the Babylonian Exile (sixth century B.C.).

The latter tradition, we may note, makes no mention of the fall. Apparently, contrary to J, P needs no reference to the reality of sin at the very beginning of human history. The reason is probably that P wants to avoid fatalism, inevitable if those exiled to Babylon considered themselves as cursed because of the failures of previous generations. P insists on each generation's responsibility by showing that sin and the break of God's holy commands only intensifies chaos within history.

Genesis 2:4b–25 and 3 both belong to the Yahwist tradition. The major theme is the fall. An old creation narrative is used in chapter 2 merely as a kind of introduction to the fall narrative in Chapter 3. As far as we presently know, J is the first attempt in Israel to theologize about sin as the great calamity which threatens humankind as a whole. J is also the first in Israel to inquire about the origin of the overwhelming power of sin. This builds up the background for J's belief that God is acting in the history of Israel, God's chosen people.

The purpose of the Yahwist tradition is to remind one of God's promises and covenant. These nourish hope in a new salvation, despite the division of the kingdom of David and Solomon into two kingdoms: Israel in the North and Judea in the South.

The Yahwist tradition wonders how it is that David and Solomon showed great failures, although they had done so much for the people and for Yahweh's worship. David did not hesitate to commit adultery and murder because of a woman, Bathsheba. David's sin brought forth in his house rape, fratricide, uprising against him (Absalom), and a brutal rivalry as to who would succeed him on the throne. Solomon, who built a temple for Yahweh, surrounded himself with foreign women who made him tolerate the setting up in the kingdom of places of worship to gods other than Yahweh and thus broke God's covenant.

The Yahwist tradition knows that Rehoboam, Solomon's son and ruler of Judah, disregarded the group called "the Elders" and chose childhood friends as advisors (1 Kings 12:8). These inexperienced advisors persuaded Rehoboam to turn down the Northern tribes' request put to him in Shechem to reduce the various duties imposed upon them by Solomon. Instead, Rehoboam announced still heavier burdens to be imposed upon them (1 Kings

12:1–6). Rehoboam's harshness toward the Northern tribes was the immediate cause for the division of David and Solomon's kingdom in 932 B.C.

The Yahwist tradition knows also that the first king of the Northern Kingdom, Jeroboam, did not oppose Canaanite rites and customs. J is fully suspicious toward what the Northern kingdom borrows from Canaanite traditions. This explains why J is explicitly anti-Canaanite in its commentary on the first command of the covenant (Exod. 34:14–17).

The suspicion of the Yahwist tradition toward the Canaanite rites and toward Solomon's women plays a key role in the qualification of the serpent—a symbol of fertility in the Canaanite religion—in Genesis 3 and in the leading part played by Eve according to the fall narrative. Needless to say, J does not and cannot identify the serpent with a superhuman force called Satan or Lucifer or the like. Such identification takes place within Judaism much later.[7] It will lead for instance in the Targum of Pseudo-Jonathan to construing Cain as conceived by Eve and Samma'el—another name for Satan.[8] This is the background for Jesus' statement about the devil in John 8:44, "He is a murderer from the very beginning" and also for the Book of Revelation, which identifies Satan and the "ancient serpent"—i.e., the serpent of Genesis 3 (Rev. 12:9; 20:2).[9] As to Lucifer as a name for Satan, it results from combining Isaiah 14:12 and Luke 10:18. Lucifer as a name for Satan is found first in Jerome's writings (A.D. 340/350–419/420), although it had been suggested earlier by Eusebius and Athanasius.[10]

The old proverb "The imagination of man's heart is evil from his youth" (Gen. 8:21; 6:5), is not seen by the Yahwist tradition as a satisfactory explanation for the destructive power of sin in Israel's history, and society of the present, and of the recent past. What J needs is a more profound insight into the origin and overwhelming power of sin, which threatens the very existence of God's chosen people. For this, J has recourse to the way its contemporaries explain situations and problems of the present, namely, by referring to the beginning of human history. This leads J to speak of the beginning of human history in terms of a prophecy concerning the past.

In its theological reflection about the origin and power of sin, the Yahwist tradition is guided also by that thinking proper to a society, one which persisted in Israel in spite of the adoption of monarchy and the type of sociopolitical organization attached to it.

The clan is a community of destiny in which all members think of themselves and act in solidarity. The clan acts through the chief or through prominent members. Each member bears the blessings and the curses, the privileges and the punishments inherent in the clan as a whole. Particularly, the clan embodies the ancestors. But the reverse also holds true. What the clan is, does, and experiences can be attributed to its ancestors. Consequently, there is no clear-cut distinction between the ancestors of the clan, the clan itself, the main representatives of the clan, and its members as individuals; all these are more or less one. Social structures, situations, legal claims, and customs of the present are clarified and—if necessary—legitimized by referring to prescriptions, foundations, experiences made by the ancestors and to divine revelations received by them. Therefore, the weakness, misery, and suffering of the present can be understood as caused by the ancestors' attitudes and behavior.

All this explains why the Yahwist tradition transfers its own religious experience and understanding of Israel's history as well as the situation and problems facing God's chosen people at its time to the period of Moses, to the period of the Patriarchs, and even to the ancestors of humankind as a whole. J recounts the course of history in order to keep the meaning of Israel's history alive by focusing on God's covenant with Moses. The word *berit* is not used in the Creation account of Genesis 2. The covenant idea, though, does play a central role in God's command (Gen. 2:17), the observance of which preserves the relationship between man and God and between man and his female partner. This command also has to do with the prohibition of idolatrous practices.

The very first sin, or the fall—and this is of paramount importance for Yahwist tradition—occurs in solidarity. God's command is given to Adam (Gen. 2:16), but Eve's answer to the serpent implies that she too is acquainted with God's command (Gen. 3:2–3). As Eve disobeys, Adam endorses the disobedience as well. By this, J does not want to illustrate that Eve is the first or even the only one responsible for all evil in humankind. Rather, J emphasizes that sin spreads even in such a small community as that formed by the first human couple. Likewise, the consequences of sin have social bearing: the community of love and mutual respect (Gen. 2:23–24) becomes a community ruled by the law of the fittest (Gen. 3–16). Solidarity in love and happiness becomes solidarity in pain and suffering, which might deepen the differences between human beings and cause them to become strangers to one another.

The fall is a breaking up with God, and the consequences of the fall cannot be restored unless God takes the initiative, as for instance in Abraham's blessing (Gen. 12:3). Because of this blessing, humankind may hope for salvation. On the basis of God's covenant with Moses, Israel may expect for the future that God will not abandon God's sinful people to their sad fate.

In the course of history, Israel has been confronted with existential questions awaiting answers, e.g., where do the Patriarchs come from? The God of Israel and of the Patriarchs, Yahweh—is this God not also the Creator of all humankind and the Lord of history? If so, how then is God not acknowledged as such and worshipped by all? How is the origin and the power of sin to be explained?

There are obvious differences between the two traditions represented in Genesis 1 to 11. Only some of those with a more direct relationship to the fall have been noticed for this paper. These two traditions at least evidence an obvious confrontation with questions and problems arising from their own historical situations. The lack of further precision—for instance, on what the first sin consisted of or on the essence of the sinful dimension of human being—shows that these chapters cannot provide us with final answers to central aspects of the fall or of original sin. These chapters of the Bible have, however, permanent relevance. They help keep alive the question of evil that constantly arises from daily human experience.

Genesis 1 to 11 deals with the long period of time from the beginning of the world to Abraham's election by God. The disproportionate length of the narrative pertaining to Israel's history compared with the short account of the much longer period of time from the beginning of human history to Abraham indicates already that the idea of God the Creator is subordinate to the idea of God the Savior in the Old Testament. Therefore, the biblical experience of sin and society is not based on the belief in God the Creator, although it is viewed in that relation by biblical traditions beginning with the Yahwist. The experience of sin and society is rather based on faith in God's salvific action in the history of Israel—and in Jesus Christ as well, for Christians—in which faith in the Creator is, indeed, a central expression that necessarily copes with a real and effective commitment for a better world.

Notes

1 "Wie nun aber auch der Ursprung des moralischen Bösen im Menschen immer beschaffen sein mag, so ist doch unter allen Vorstellungsarten von der Verbreitung und Fortsetzung desselben durch alle Glieder unserer Gattung und in allen Zeugungen die unschicklichste: es sich als durch *Anerbung* von den ersten Eltern auf uns gekommen vorzustellen." Immanuel Kant, *Die Religion innerhalb der Grenzen der blossen Vernunft*, pt. 1, IV, 42, ed. K. Vorländer (Hamburg: Felix Meiner Publishers, 1966), 42, emphasis in the original text. For a critique of Kant's position, see Maurice Boutin, *Relationalität als Verstehensprinzip bei Rudolf Bultmann* (Munich: Chr. Kaiser, 1974), 505–10.

2. "*Genus et proavos et quae non fecimus ipsi, vix ea nostra puto,*" Ovid, *Metamorphoses,* XIII.140 [author's translation].

3 Blaise Pascal, *Pensées,* nr. 434, Brunschvicg ed., 1904), nr. 164, Sellier ed., 1976, established for the first time after Gilberte Pascal's copy of the original manuscript (Paris: Mercure de France, 1976), 90–91 [author's translation].

4 Roland Barthes, *Essais critiques* series "Points," 127 (Paris: Seuil, 1981), 261, 264, 266. See Barthes, *Critical Essays* (Evanston, Ill.: Northwestern University Press, 1972), 264.

5 Gerhard Freund, *Sünde im Erbe. Erfahrungsinhalt und Sinn der Erbsündenlehre* (Stuttgart: W. Kohlhammer, 1979), 156–61.

6 "Man mag an der traditionellen mythologischen Fassung der Erbsünde noch so viel Kritik üben und vom ursprünglich Guten im Menschen fabeln—faktisch erkennt jeder die Erbsündenlehre an, nämlich in seinem Urteil über die konkreten Menschen, mit denen er zu tun hat, und in seinem Verhalten zu ihnen: wir misstrauen einander von vornherein; und in Misstrauen steckt zugleich die Abwehr gegen die anderen, das Sich-verschliessen, der Hass." Rudolf Bultmann, "Der Sinn des christlichen Schöpfungsglaubens," in *Zeitschrift für Missionskunde und Religionswissenschaft* 51 (1936): 1–20, 12. For an analysis of Bultmann's understanding of original sin, see Maurice Boutin, *Relationalität,* 299–305.

7 See, for instance, Book of Wisdom 2:24, first century B.C.

8 *Targum of Pseudo-Jonathan,* on Gen. 4:1.

9 See M. E. Boismard and A. Lamouille, *L'évangile de Jean* (Paris: Cerf, 1977), 238–40.

10 On the issue of "belief in the devil," see H. Haag, *Teufelsglaube* (Tübingen: Katzmann, 1974).

3 Satan: Reality or Symbol?
YOUNG OON KIM

On November 15, 1972, Pope Paul VI spoke forcefully to the crowds gathered in front of St. Peter's Church. According to John A. Hardon, a Jesuit theologian, the Pope admonished the faithful to take note of the existence and power of a personal devil. The devil is very active in the world today, even if many people dismiss him as superstition or nothing but a symbol. The pontiff declared that in our day, as in the apostolic age, the devil is "the treacherous and cunning enchanter, who finds his way into us by way of the senses, the imagination, lust and utopian logic." The pontiff further declared that "those who take him lightly or smile at his existence are the easiest prey of what the apostles called 'the mystery of iniquity.'"[1]

It will be the purpose of my paper to reexamine belief in Satan in the light of its historical context.[2] We shall take account of some theologians who deny the consensus of unbelief regarding Satan in the mainline denominations; and in conclusion, some note will be taken of the *Divine Principle* teaching about the fallen archangel, Lucifer. In brief, I hope to show how necessary the belief in God's personal adversary is in order to understand the fall, original sin, the need for salvation, the work of the Messiah and the eschatological hope.

I also have a more practical purpose. In a recent issue of *The New York Times* book review, T. S. Eliot was quoted to the effect that the Satanism of the French poet Baudelaire was only a back door to belief in God.[3] Similarly, my essay explains the objective reality of Satan and his cunning, malicious purpose to produce more commitment to and zeal for God, the devil's archenemy, and Christ, his dedicated foe.

The Bible has no single, consistent interpretation of the devil from Genesis to Revelation.[4] One should also recall that belief in Satan is largely missing from the oldest portions of the Old Testament, but comes strongly into view after the Persian period—when Zoroastrian dualism was the state religion—and completely permeates the New Testament.[5] So far as I can determine, belief in a personal Satan was as central to Jesus' own faith, as belief in a fatherly God.

The New Testament is filled to overflowing with references to the personal reality of Satan. Only two of the twenty-seven books (1 and 3 John) neglect to mention him, causing Foester to conclude that the New Testament is distinctive in setting Satan totally against God, his absolute antithesis.[6] However, T. Gaster claims that parallels in Jewish literature can be found for every New Testament usage on this matter.[7] The name Satan is used thirty-three times in the New Testament and the term devil twenty-three times. He is also called "the tempter" three times, "the evil one" twice, "the accuser" once, "the enemy" twice, "the plaintiff" once, "the prince of demons" four times, "the ruler of this world" twice, "the prince of the power of the air" once, "Belial" once, and "Beelzebul" six times.

Almost every major incident in Jesus' ministry, according to the Synoptic traditions, contains explicit reference to Satan's opposition. All three gospels say that Satan tempted Jesus after his baptism. Jesus' numerous exorcisms are designed to release men and women *bound* by Satan (Luke 13:16). He teaches his disciples in the Lord's Prayer to pray, "Deliver us from the Evil (one)"—a person, and not abstract evil. When the seventy-two disciples return from their missions and tell Jesus that they exorcised demons, he exclaims triumphantly that he sees Satan fall from heaven (Luke 10:18). Those who do not accept the good news of the imminent kingdom are said by Mark to have had their hearts and ears shut by Satan to God's message (Mark 4:15). When Peter misinterprets the meaning of Jesus' messiahship, he is denounced, "Get thee behind me, Satan" (Mark 8:33). And Luke explicitly condemns Judas' betrayal leading to the crucifixion as an act carried out under satanic domination (Luke 22:3). Thus, as Gaster concludes, Satan invariably appears as "a distinctive personality" and not merely the personification of men's evil deeds and passions.[8]

The Synoptic traditions should clearly demonstrate how central the reality of the fallen angel was for Jesus. However, Herbert

Haag tries to dismiss this element in Jesus' teachings as an unhistorical addition made by the gospel writers and editors. Using Bultmann's radical skepticism, form-criticism and later redaction criticism, Haag attempts to question the authenticity of the Synoptic texts for two reasons: because belief in the devil is an anachronism for present-day Christians, and because he believes Jesus' own message to be singularly free of the satanic concept, an idea imposed upon the text by the later church.[9]

Let me give several examples of Haag's skepticism. Since we have no independent, extra-canonical references to Beelzebul as a synonym for the devil in rabbinic literature, it is doubtful that the Pharisees ever accused Jesus of working cures through Beelzebul's power (Matt. 12:24). Also, there is no clear proof that the word "Evil (one)" in the Lord's Prayer was ever used by first-century Jews as a synonym for Satan. Most importantly, the temptation stories in Matthew and Luke probably represent early Christian meditations on the messianic purpose of Jesus, do not go back to Jesus himself, and at best are mere pious elaborations of the single belief verse in the Markan gospel. Therefore, Haag maintains that since Satan played almost no part in Jesus' original message, we Christians today can reject the notion of the personal devil as an outmoded bit of ancient Jewish folklore.

My reply to Haag would be as follows: I agree with Bultmann and others that much of the original tradition has been reshaped and altered to serve the doctrinal, liturgical, and moral concerns of the post-Easter Christian community. But Satan belongs to the apocalyptic milieu of first century Judaism, the environment of Jesus, and not to a later time. For instance, there is no interest in Satan as such in any of the Greco-Roman philosophies or mystery religions. The devil plays no part in Platonism, Stoicism, Aristotelianism, or the mystery cults of Attis, Isis, or Mithra. If Christians believe in Satan it is because they got the idea from Jesus and his Jewish contemporaries. So, even if some gospel texts occasionally add references to the devil in places where other texts omit them, these still reflect the early Palestinian background of Jesus' ministry and in no case represent a radical transformation of his own views.

According to Haag, only one clear reference to Satan goes back to Jesus. Jesus said, "I saw Satan fall from heaven" (Luke 10:18). Yet this one text is all-important, in my view, as it proves that Jesus himself did believe in an actual personal devil. Note Jesus' exact words, the vividness of his exclamation. He actually saw, he insists, the fall of Satan. This is no symbol, no literary metaphor, but an actual experience for him—as real as Luther's encounter with the devil, or St. Anthony's temptations, or those of many medieval saints. For Jesus, Satan was as objective a reality as God.

Furthermore, if Jesus thought of the devil as a mere symbol for evil, why did he not explain this novel insight to his disciples? In other cases, he was not shy about contradicting conventional Jewish beliefs and firmly-held contemporary religious doctrines. He openly affirmed the notion of the resurrection of the dead in the face of Sadducean disbelief. He forthrightly praised the good Samaritan when most of his Jewish contemporaries were implacably hostile to those heretical, schismatic sectarians. And he clearly repudiated the common faith that the Temple was an inviolable sanctuary which would last forever. Finally, Jesus specifically repudiated certain statements in the revealed Mosaic Law. Why then did he not disavow belief in a literal Satan, if that was his opinion? He did not, one can conclude, because he was convinced of the devil's reality. Thus, in conformity to his belief, the disciples, the four evangelists, Paul, and the later church affirmed the existence of Satan.

With that as background, let's examine the formative stages of Satanology after the death of Paul and before the Nicene Creed. For this purpose, I cite two of many important sources: the Epistle of Barnabas and the Epistles of St. Ignatius. These writings came from different parts of early Christendom—the former from Alexandria, Egypt; the latter from Antioch, Syria. Syrian and Egyptian Christians were as far apart theologically as they were geographically. Antioch was characterized by biblical literalism, Arianism, and Nestorianism; whereas Alexandria was known for Athanasianism, Monophysitism, allegorical exegesis, metaphysical theology, and Nag Hammadi gnosticism. However, on the doctrine of the devil, Syriac and Egyptian Christianity were remarkedly alike, as we shall see.

The Epistle of Barnabas is very important for three reasons: (1) it severely attacks Judaizing Christians in the early Church, (2) it insists on a typological and allegorical exegesis of the scriptures, and (3) it clearly states that God has rejected the Jewish nation as his chosen people and replaced them with the New Israel, the Church.[10] Most importantly, this letter was considered part of the New Testament by Clement of Alexandria and is included in the Codex Sinaiticus of the Bible which some scholars say was given to Emperor Constantine by Bishop Eusebius for the church of Constantinople.[11]

For "Barnabas," the present age is thoroughly evil and is in the firm control of the devil. The devil is prince of this world and Christ will be the Lord of the age-to-come. For this author, the crucifixion and resurrection of Jesus did not destroy the power of Satan. The coming of Jesus weakened the kingdom of this world, but Christ will not become victorious until his second advent in glory.

Like the Dead Sea scrolls, the Epistle of Barnabas emphasizes two ways: the way of light and the way of darkness. The earth is then like a battlefield where the armies of the devil wage war against the children of light. The prince of evil has both fallen angels and wicked men on his side. Each person must choose between the devil and Christ, and that choice determines his final destiny. The road of light leads to heaven, while the opposite road leads to total ruin.

Some have taught that the devil attacks the person from without, as a tempter, or by seizing control of a person's soul (demonic possession). "Barnabas," by contrast, says the devil seeks to "creep into us." An evil spirit gets inside us and lures us to commit sin. Thus, the individual soul becomes a battleground between Satan and Christ.

The Epistle of Barnabas also claims that the literal interpretation of the Bible used by Jews is due to the lying spirit of a fallen angel. True exegesis, in contrast, is the spiritual typological exegesis used so freely by Paul, Barnabas, Philo of Alexandria, and later, Origen.

Outside of the canonical literature, no early Christian writings were more important than the Epistles of Ignatius, seven of which are now considered authentic.[12] Ignatius was the successor of St. Peter as bishop of Antioch and was martyred in Rome (107 A.D.) during the reign of emperor Trajan. Historians of Christian dogma usually commend Ignatius for four teachings: (1) his strong sacramentalism, (2) his defense of episcopal government, (3) his praise of martyrdom, and (4) his stress on the need for Christian unity.[13] It is important to note that every one of these concepts is directly related to the bishop's belief in a personal Satan.

Ignatius wrote of a basic conflict between two aeons: our present age, which represents the kingdom of this world; and the future age, which represents the kingdom of God. The devil is the ruler of this world and has dominated humankind since the fall of Adam and Eve. Jesus Christ was able to shake Satan's rule, but it will not be completely shattered until the Parousia at some undesignated future date.

For Ignatius, this world is not a battlefield, but an arena—like the Colosseum in Rome where so many Christians were killed for amusement. The devil seeks to vanquish every individual Christian. His purpose is to thwart Christ's work of salvation by diverting Christians from their proper goal. Ignatius writes of weeds sown by the devil (Eph. 10:3). He warns, "Flee these evil offshoots, which bear deadly fruit" (Trall. 11:1). This refers to two very different ways the devil schemes to frustrate the purpose of Christ. First, he uses the threat of persecution, torture, and execution to scare Christians into giving up their faith. Second, the devil sows seeds of dissension and heresy in the Christian communities.

Ignatius encouraged Christians to outwit the devil's purpose. He gave encouragement to Christians facing arrest and death. The devil is only prince of this temporal world; the kingdom of heaven belongs to Christ and his reign will last forever. Ignatius stressed that taking the Eucharist guarantees eternal life: "the medicine of immortality," he termed it. Furthermore, if one dies for his faith, he wins a great victory over the prince of evil and death. Like a successful gladiator in the arena, the martyred Christian achieves an everlasting triumph over Christ's foes.

For Ignatius, the heretic and schismatic are as evil as the pagan prosecutor. That is why he emphasized the importance of bishops. The bishop can impose organizational stability and doctrinal orthodoxy. Thus, any Christian who acts without the advice and consent of his bishop is guilty of worshipping the devil (Smyr. 9:1). A heretic is a slave of Satan; a dissenter really adores the prince of evil. On the other hand, Satan's power is greatly weakened when Christians are united and work together harmoniously.[14]

I used Barnabas and Ignatius of Antioch, because after the New Testament period, there was a major change in Christian life and thought. The Church broke its ties with Judaism and became almost exclusively a Gentile faith. Many things changed radically, but the strong New Testament belief in Satan, based on Jewish eschatology, was retained. There were no additions made to Satanology in the patristic age, medieval period, or Reformation. Barnabas' and Ignatius' ideas about Satan were repeated without change by Athanasius, Aquinas, Luther, and Calvin. Not until the Enlightenment was there any serious questioning of belief in Satan. And modern theology's disbelief in Satan originated in this Age of Reason.

In all of the prominent Protestant theologians from Schleiermacher to the Process thinkers, belief in a personal devil is virtually nonexistent. Satan is missing from the cast of characters in the books of Harnack, Troeltsch, Niebuhr, Tillich, Hartshorne, and Bultmann.[15] More recently, a similar situation has taken place among the fashionable Catholic theologians. Let me cite but three examples. Teilhard de Chardin has been a pivotal figure in the refashioning of Catholic doctrine since Vatican II, and Satan obviously plays no role in his theology. Karl Rahner, the dean of Jesuit theologians these days, has published seventeen volumes of *Theological Investigations* whereof only one essay (15 pages) is devoted to "The Sin of Adam" (vol. 11, pp. 247–62), and that one does not mention the devil or Satan even once. Finally, Edward Schillebeeckx, the Dutch Dominican, has two large books entitled *Jesus* and *Christ*. A very important section of the latter is called "Freed from what and for what?" (pp. 512–14). What then are we freed from? At least seventeen different things: from "all kinds of existential anxieties" to "lovelessness" and "panic" or "absence of pleasure." But not once does the learned Dominican mention that the New Testament always defines redemption as liberation from Satan. Like Rahner, he can explain what we are freed from by Christ without referring even once to the prince of this world.[16]

Gustav Wingren, a prominent Swedish scholar and longtime professor of systematic theology at the University of Lund, is an exception to the general rule in regard to his faith in the personal reality of Satan.[17] Although a contemporary of Barth and Bultmann, he strongly dissented from the dialectical system of the former and the radical demythologized existentialism of the latter. His first book was a study of Irenaeus and throughout his career he emphasized the primary importance of God the Creator, the definition of the human being as a creature made in the image of God, and the interpretation of salvation as the restoration of the world to its original status. All of these concepts, Wingren felt, were definitely related to belief in a personal devil.

In his book *The Living Word* he offered a novel contemporary analysis of the biblical message.[18] What is the chief theme of Scripture? Not the fatherhood of God and brotherhood of man, as Harnack maintained. Not the wholly otherness of God, as Barth argued. Not the divine/human encounter, as Brunner claimed. And not theocentric humanism, as Maritain contended. According to Wingren, the Bible's theme is the conflict of God and the devil. God created everything which exists, and Satan represents sinful opposition to the Creator. Thus, creation and sin together fully describe our human situation.

Satan is as real and as personal as God. Their antagonism runs like a scarlet thread through the Bible. Therefore, it is impossible to revive the scriptural message in our generation if we cut away belief in conflict with the devil, the existence of demonic powers, and God's final victory as "too primitive" or "superstitious," Wingren declares (p. 165). God and Satan were both present and active in Adam's temptation and fall, just as both take part right through Israel's outward and inward history until Jesus Christ's crucifixion and resurrection. They are still present in the life of every human today. They will remain in conflict until the end of history. But after that the devil's time is over and God will become "all in all" because sin will be driven out of the creation (p. 166).

The mission of Jesus must be seen in terms of God's resolve to triumph over Satan. When Jesus heals the sick and exorcises demons, the devil is losing control over his dominion and the kingdom of heaven is coming. God's Son took flesh, Wingren asserts, to overthrow the power of the devil and bring his works to naught. All of Christ's activities represent a battle with Satan. Hence, for the New Testament, his crucifixion and resurrection illustrate God's victory over the devil, the release of people who were enslaved in sin, and the coming catastrophe of satanic dominion.

Wingren therefore attacks the privatized spirituality of the pietists who think of the bliss of the devout soul resting in the loving arms of its personal Savior. God is the rightful Lord of all creation. He is not just interested in prayer meetings, hymn sings, evangelistic rallies, and Bible study; He is concerned about the restoration of the entire creation. Similarly, Satan is located in the affairs of every day, and everybody should detect the point in his or her own life where the battle with the adversary is being waged.

From this perspective—God's conflict with Satan—Wingren severely criticizes the theology of Barth.[19] There is in Barthianism no active power of sin, and no tyrannical, demonic power that subjects people to slavery. There is no devil in Barth's system, Wingren complains. The Bible speaks of the conflict between God and Satan. Barth prefers to write about something else—the conflict between God and the human being. So the main problem is not victory over the devil. For Barth, evil has no objective reality. Evil is the Nihil, nonbeing, and not a positive, personal power. For Barth, theology revolves around revelation, the supernatural disclosure of the Wholly Other. God reveals Godself to the human being. That is the essence of Christianity for Barth. However, that is not the biblical faith, for the Scriptures are centered on God's determination to overthrow the rule of Satan and to redeem humankind from demonic bondage.

Another contemporary believer in a personal devil is the German Lutheran theologian, Helmut Thielicke, who is a longtime professor at the University of Hamburg and one of Europe's most popular evangelical preachers.[20] Thielicke was made aware of Satan's power during World War II when the Hitler government deprived him of his professorship, denied him permission to publish his books, and warned laymen not to listen to his sermons. His essay, "The Reality of the Demonic," had to be smuggled out of Germany during the war and was published for use in Allied prisoner of war camps to reeducate captured Nazi soldiers.[21] After peace came, Thielicke returned to university teaching. His three-volume *Evangelical Faith* contains a section on the problem of the devil.[22]

According to the latter book, Satan's existence has been widely denied for three reasons. First, the idea of a personal devil is thought to be out-of-date. To this allegation, Thielicke points out that Satan's reality is affirmed by such famous modern intellectuals as the novelist Thomas Mann and the dissident Marxist philosopher Leszek Kolakowski.[23] Second, Satan cannot be objectified and is beyond the scope of rationalistic philosophy. He hides behind those who are tempted and disguises his true nature. Third, we do not recognize the devil's presence because human sinfulness blinds us. He is not outside us but deeply embedded inside us, our society, and the spirit of our times.

What then are Satan's characteristics?[24] For one thing, he is an invisible spirit and not a material object like a rock or a chair. For another, he manifests himself as a power inside each of us, a power that seizes each individual by the throat, so to speak. Also, there is within every person something which attracts Satan and offers him a hospitable dwelling place. Finally, the devil always appears incognito. He never says, "I am Satan, the enemy of God, and I want you to do evil." No, he comes as a defender of freedom, pleasure, self-realization, hidden truth, and useful power.[25]

Having experienced the terrors of World War II and the evils of National Socialism, Thielicke stresses the demonic characteristics of the modern, omnipotent state.[26] Hitler (or any dictator who holds the reins of power over a whole people) easily becomes an agent of Satan. By encompassing all the agencies of a culture—army, police, legislature, judiciary, education, media, etc.—the all-powerful leader denies the higher sovereignty of God and thereby serves the cause of the devil, as the German churches learned. Of course, Thielicke's teaching on this point is nothing new; he is merely reaffirming the lesson in the book of Revelation: Satan uses Caesar to persecute Christ. But unlike many contemporary theologians, Thielicke does not favor dialogue with or accommodation to the collectivist ideal.

The most convincing proof of Satan's existence is experiential. Those who have become possessed by demonic spirits and those exorcists who have successfully liberated them from bondage are the best authorities on such a subject. Christian history contains many accounts of the devil's temptations and assaults. And this actual experience of Satan's presence continues to the present day. For instance, *Hostage to the Devil* (1976), by former Jesuit theologian and priest Malachi Martin, reports in detail five cases of contemporary demonic possession and their successful cures. After reading Martin's vivid and personally investigated accounts, even the most doubtful should be persuaded that the demonic realm exists.

One such victim is a young priest who gradually loses his faith in traditional Catholic doctrine and becomes fascinated by the need to demythologize it. This thought so obsesses him that soon he feels directed "by remote control." He uses his days off and vacations secretly founding a new religion in Greenwich Village, a faith for Light-bearers conducted in the Shrine of the New Being. Meanwhile, as a parish priest, he feels increasingly driven to alter the language of his Mass. Instead of baptizing in the name of the Father, Son, and Holy Ghost, he changes the Latin to baptism in the name of the Sky, Earth, and Water. Or in place of absolving penitents who confessed repentance for their sins, he prays to "confirm them in their natural wishes." Finally, in July 1967, while celebrating Mass, the priest is overcome by a violent seizure. He suddenly starts swaying, groaning, and weeping. The altar boys can not dislodge his grip on the altar. Then, rigid with paralysis, he loses control of himself and urinates on the altar, defiling the sanctuary. Finally, the priest falls backward, tumbles down the altar stairs, and is knocked unconscious. After investigating these strange events, the bishop requests the priest's resignation. However, he still conducts services in the Greenwich Village shrine he had established. In time, unusual happenings begin to occur at the Shrine of the New Being, finally causing the priest to agree to exorcism. The final blow falls when he is conducting a marriage at the beach for two of his followers. Suddenly, he is "possessed," grabs the bride, drags her into the waves, and tries to drown her. Fortunately, a seminary professor friend is present at the ceremony and hurriedly makes arrangements for help. An official Catholic rite of exorcism is conducted later, liberating the possessed priest of his demonic captor.

A second case involves a brilliant and successful professor who gets deeply involved in psi (parapsychic) investigations without realizing there are dangerous spiritual powers as well as good ones. As a result of his experiences he turns from a professor into a guru, experiences out-of-the-body travels, and becomes convinced he is a reincarnation of an ancient Roman Christian named Petrus. He had made contact with a destructive spirit who is lying to him and flattering his ego in order to possess him. The demon, promising to reveal what original Christianity was like, encourages the psychologist to visit an old shrine in Italy. While there with some of his followers, the psychologist suffers a strange seizure and collapses into unconsciousness. He reaches a condition from which he cannot return to normal. A former student of his, who is also a professional Catholic exorcist, volunteers to help. The rites are successful and the professor returns to his university teaching.

Now, to exorcise a demon is seldom easy and is often dangerous. The priest must recite special prayers, force the spirit to identify itself, lure it out of its human victim, and then banish it. On its part, the demon is sly, clever, powerful, and determined to retain its hold on its victim. So exorcisms are usually violent struggles with many frightening accompaniments. For example, during the rites, all the books on the library shelves may suddenly be hurled to the floor. Or attendants who are present to help the priest and hold the victim down may be driven from the bed by piercing screeches. Or sometimes when the demon gets excited, he suddenly rips off the wallpaper from the ceiling to the floor in an outburst of fury. Furthermore, an enraged demon can attack his victim, the exorcist, or anyone else in the room who is vulnerable.

A third episode is of this more shocking type. R.R. is 33 when he agrees to submit to exorcism. From an early time he has felt thoroughly androgynous by nature. But he meets an attractive girl and marries at age 25. However, when they try to mate she is so upset by his feminine nature that she sues for immediate divorce. Of course, this is equally troubling to R.R. and he decides to undergo a sex change operation. Soon afterward, as a woman, he is initiated into a sex cult and engages in relations on the altar with a Satanist priest as part of a Black Mass. Such traumatic events, one piled on top of another, open up R.R. to complete demonic possession.

Shortly thereafter, he becomes subject to peculiar fits. Also, trouble breaks out wherever he appears: if he enters an office, the secretary immediately starts to make strange mistakes in her typing, or if he joins a group, the members begin to argue with one another. Soon R.R. loses his job. In desperation his parents ask the local Catholic priest for help, and he introduces them to an exorcist.

It should be clearly noted that the author does not ascribe every sexual disorder to demonic possession. Furthermore, R.R.'s successful exorcism does not cure his problem of sexual identity. In this case, the sexual confusion of R.R. simply provides an opening for the demon to make his entry.

R.R.'s liberation is costly, especially for the priest-exorcist. During the rite and in the presence of several witnesses, the provoked and angry demon makes a brutal assault on the priest. Recognizing that the exorcist is a lifelong celibate and totally innocent of sex, the demon suddenly comes out of R.R., with invisible hands rips the clothes off the priest, and sexually attacks him with such violence that the priest suffers a heart attack, later causing his premature death. Once the surprised attendants recover from shock, they place the priest on a stretcher and rush him to the hospital. The priest requires physicians to repair his intestinal wounds and psychiatric attention to restore his emotional balance.

Seemingly, the demon has won. However, when the exorcist recovers he realizes that he must continue and complete his rites. If he does not, R.R. will face the terrors of lifelong possession. Furthermore, since the priest has been assaulted by the demon, he too is forever liable to future attacks and possible possession. With his doctors' and bishop's consent, the exorcist once again confronts R.R. This time the ritual accomplishes its goal.

The above incidents are striking contemporary experiences which parallel many examples of satanic possession from New Testament times through the medieval period. Since Jesus instructed his disciples to cast out demons, for many centuries the Catholic Church has designated priests in every diocese to serve as official exorcists. Thus, an eminent Thomist theologian like Reginald Garrigou-Lagrange, a French Dominican and professor at Pontifical

University in Rome for over fifty years (1909–1960), devotes several pages to possession in his classic study entitled *The Three Ages of the Interior Life*. For those who are adept in spirituality—from St. Anthony in the Egyptian desert to the Curé d'Ars in nineteenth century France—Satan is real, personal, and very much a constant threat to humankind.[27] The title of Hal Lindsey's book, *Satan Is Alive and Well on Planet Earth* (1972), may very well say it all.

In conclusion, let me briefly indicate some of the distinctive aspects of Unificationist teaching about the devil.[28] Satan is not co-eternal with God, as in dualistic philosophies. Satan was not created by God. When the Archangel Lucifer seduced Eve and fell, he became Satan. Satan is not to be identified with the realm of matter. Nor is he the cause of the sexual impulse. He used the power of misdirected love, and caused original sin. Ever since the fall of Adam and Eve, Satan has ruled as prince of this world and subjected all humanity to the bondage of sin. Jesus came as the Messiah to liberate humanity from satanic dominion, but his mission was cut short before completion. Hence, from apostolic times Christians have recognized that Satan still needs to be subjugated before Jesus' "Lord's Prayer" can be realized. This implies that a new Messiah is required to continue and complete Jesus' mission of breaking the power of the devil, redeeming human beings by cleansing them of original sin, and inaugurating the kingdom of God on earth. Like millenarians throughout Christian history, Unificationists believe that God intends to restore sovereign rule in a material as well as a spiritual way, which means that Satan must surrender to God.[29]

Notes

1   J. A. Hardon, *The Catholic Catechism* (Garden City, N.Y.: Doubleday, 1975), 90.

2   The Protestant evangelical position is found in the *Wycliff Bible Encyclopedia* (Nashville: Moody Press, 1975), 1:453–54. The devil is a personal, a superhuman, and evil created being, a fallen angel with no corporeal material form. He was the highest of all created archangels before his fall. Scripture teaches both the reality and personality of Satan. The Bible credits him with the attributes, works, and names of a personal

being. He possesses intellect, since he deceives the whole world (Rev. 12:9). He exhibits emotions, for he goes forth with great wrath (Rev. 12:12), and he does the work of a person by making war upon humanity (Rev. 12:17). To deny Satan's personality would destroy our belief in the deity of Christ. If Christ were not tempted by an external foe, his temptation was internally motivated, making him only another human in need of a Savior, the Wycliff author insists.

3 In Victor Brombert's review of F. W. J. Hemmings, *Baudelaire the Damned, New York Times* (November 14, 1982).

4 The history of the biblical doctrine of Satan has been expertly analyzed in Kittel's *Theologisches Wörterbuch zum Neuen Testament* (Stuttgart: W. Kohlhammer, 1933) in the articles "*Diabolos*" and "*Satanos*." See articles "Devil" and "Satan" in the *Interpreter's Dictionary of the Bible* (Nashville: Abingdon, 1962) and *The New Catholic Encyclopedia* (New York: McGraw-Hill, 1967–79).

5 For a rather moderate view of the Zoroastrian influence on the biblical doctrine of Satan, see William F. Albright, *From the Stone Age to Christianity* (Baltimore: John Hopkins, 1946), 275–80. A more radical opinion is found in the valuable book of Leo Jung, *Fallen Angels in Jewish, Christian and Mohammedan Literature* (New York; Ktav, 1974). Rabbi Jung sharply contrasts the Jewish Satan, an unfallen servant of Yahweh, and the fallen angelic antagonist of God which Christians borrowed from the Zoroastrians. Yet this radical separation overlooks two clearly documented facts: Christians got their doctrine from *Jewish* intertestamental sources not directly from Persia, and many Jewish religious writings from the Wisdom of Solomon and Testaments of the Twelve Patriarchs to Enoch and the Dead Sea Scrolls express opinions resembling the New Testament teachings about Satan, the fall and original sin.

6 Kittel, 2:79.

7 T. Gaster, in *Interpreter's Dictionary of the Bible,* ed. George A. Buttrick & Keith R. Crim (Nashville: Abingdon, 1976), 4:226.

8 Ibid., 4:227.

9 Herbert Haag, *Teufelsglaube* (Tübingen: Katzmann, 1974).

10 For text, see E. J. Goodspeed, *The Apostolic Fathers* (New York: Harper, 1950), 19–45; for background, see Goodspeed, *A History of Early Christian Literature* (Chicago: University of Chicago Press, 1942), 30–35, also J. B. Russell, *Satan: The Early Christian Tradition* (Ithaca, N.Y.: Cornell, 1981), 21.

11 A. Souter, *The Text and Canon of the New Testament* (London: Duckworth, 1954), 21.

12 For text, see F. X. Glimm *et al., The Apostolic Fathers* (New York:

Cima, 1947), vol. 1 of *The Fathers of the Church* series (Washington, D.C.: Catholic University Press, 1965); for background, cf. J. Quasten *Patrology* (Washington, D.C.: Catholic University Press, 1966), 1:63–76.

13   For example, A. C. McGiffert, *A History of Christian Thought* (New York: Scribner's, 1932), 1:36–44; J. L. Gonzalez, *A History of Christian Thought* (Nashville: Abingdon, 1970), 1:70–80.

14   Ignatian texts referring to Satan: Eph. 10:3, 13:1, 17:1, 19:1; Magn. 1:2; Trall. 4:2, 8:1, 11:1; Rom. 6:3, 7:1; Phila. 6:2; Smyr. 6:11, 9:1.

15   Contrast Archbishop William Temple: "Shelve the responsibility for human evil on to Satan if you will; personally I believe he exists and that a large share of that responsibility belongs to him and to subordinate evil spirits." *Nature, Man and God* (New York: AMS Press, 1979), 503.

16   Hans Küng's view is equally nontraditional. In *On Being a Christian* (Garden City, N.Y.: Doubleday, 1976), 369, he dismisses belief in the devil as mythological borrowing from ancient Babylonian religion, and he attacks conventional Satanology for trivializing the power of evil because it assumes the existence of an army of individual demonic spirits and turns evil into a purely private affair of individuals. In *Does God Exist?* (Garden City, N.Y.: Doubleday, 1980), 117, Küng calls the Vatican study paper on demonology (1975) an expression of "outdated medieval thought" which "throws away all credibility for theology and church"— as bad as the encyclical against birth control and defamatory statements about women.

However, three authoritative councils of the Church recognize the devil's existence: the Fourth Lateran Council, Trent, and Vatican I. Their conciliar definitions imply the existence of personal, nonhuman beings. Furthermore, the Church Fathers were unanimous in their agreement that the devil exists (G. J. Dyer, ed., *An American Catholic Catechism,* [New York: Seabury, 1975], 55). Michael Schmaus, *Dogma* (New York: Sheed & Ward, 1975), 2:218–29, quotes approvingly a source saying that for Holy Scripture, particularly the New Testament, wherever evil looms large in history it is a manifestation of the devil.

17   On Wingren's background, see S. Paul Schilling, *Contemporary Continental Theologians* (Nashville: Abingdon, 1966), 161–81.

18   Gustav Wingren, *The Living Word* (Philadelphia: Fortress, 1960), esp. 42, 53–54, 165–66.

19   Gustav Wingren, *Theology in Conflict* (Philadelphia: Muhlenberg Press, 1958), 23–44.

20   Helmut Thielicke, *Man in God's World* (London: James Clarke, 1967), 163–98.

21   Ibid., 11.

22 Helmut Thielicke, *The Evangelical Faith* (Grand Rapids, Mich: Eerdmans, 1982), 3:448–53.

23 In Thomas Mann, *Dr. Faustus* (New York: Knopf, 1948); and Leszek Kolakowski, *Leben trotz Geschichte* in *The Evangelical Faith* by Helmut Thielicke (Grand Rapids, Mich.: Eerdmans, 1982), 3:448–53.

24 Thielicke, *Man in God's World*, 173ff.

25 See Thielicke's sermons on the fall, *How the World Began* (Philadelphia: Fortress, 1961), 121ff.

26 Thielicke, *Man in God's World*, 180ff.

27 Reginald Garrigou-Lagrange, *The Three Ages of the Interior Life*, trans. M. Timothea Doyle (St. Louis, Mo.: Herder, 1951), 617–27.

28 St. Anthony of Egypt (250–356) and the Curé d'Ars (1786–1859) were often assaulted by the devil (see the *New Catholic Encyclopedia*, 1:594 and 14:636–37 for their biographies).

29 For my own explanations of *Divine Principle* teachings on Satan in the context of Jewish, Christian, and other religions, see relevant sections in *Unification Theology and Christian Thought* (New York: Golden Gate, 1975), *World Religions* (New York: Golden Gate, 1976), and *Unification Theology* (New York: Holy Spirit Association for the Unification of World Christianity [HSA-UWC], 1980). These can be usefully compared and contrasted with the older Protestant view of Satan and the fall in Charles Hodge, *Systematic Theology* (New York: Scribner's, 1875, reprint 1970), vol. 2, chap. 7. Fundamentalists continue to repeat that doctrine: Cf. Lewis S. Chafer (of Dallas Theological Seminary) and John F. Walvoord, *Major Bible Themes* (Grand Rapids, Mich.: Zondervan, 1974), 156–64; and Hal Lindsey, *Satan Is Alive and Well on Planet Earth* (New York: Bantam, 1974).

4 The Fall and Misogyny in Justin Martyr and Clement of Alexandria

SARAH E. PETERSEN

Introduction

A theology of the fall is often a source of misogyny because of the perception of the role of Eve as "bringing death into the world." The questions posed in this paper are whether a theology of the fall based on Genesis 3 must be misogynistic and whether it must contribute to a patriarchal or oppressive view of women. Justin Martyr and Clement of Alexandria are examined; while they are both part of the Alexandrian tradition, Justin precedes Clement and a movement in theory can be observed (e.g., from emphasis on the demonic to emphasis on free will). These authors are also interesting because important elements in their theology of the fall resonate with Unificationist thought. This discussion approaches the issue of misogyny from a perspective wherein both males and females are understood to share equally in God's power, grace, and love; and wherein salvation comes equally to the female as woman and to the male as man.

Some elements which may tend toward misogyny are the following: (1) the defining of female by function, e.g., childbearing; (2) a theology which considers Adam and Eve as the first parents of humankind, but which considers the messianic figure as male only; (3) a view which emphasizes Eve's disobedience and primary role in bringing sin into the world, but which understands the nature of Mary's obedience to be the virgin birth, an obedience which other women cannot imitate; (4) the position that the qualities of virtue and reason are generally inferior in the female, compared to the male; (5) a dualism which splits the spirit/body relationship, symbolizing the male as spirit and reason, and the female as emotion and body; (6) the view that sex is naturally or originally sinful, and

...en are the symbol of temptation; and (7) a complementary ... that de-emphasizes an earthly kingdom of Heaven, thus making the realm of the female inferior to the realm of the male.

Justin Martyr and Clement of Alexandria are both significant figures in second century Christian history. Both were of the Alexandrian school. Justin was an apologist from a faith perspective, while Clement was a philosopher and theologian. They were part of the earliest development of Christian theology, which was to appropriate the tools, arguments, and some views of the popular Greek philosophies of Platonism and Stoicism, while establishing the figure of Christ at the center of the new worldview.[1]

Justin Martyr

Justin Martyr is considered the most important apologist of the second century. Born in Hellenized Samaria around 100 A.D., he was martyred in Rome between 163 and 165 A.D. He converted to Christianity after embracing Platonism. "... [H]is philosophical approach was not unlike that of Philo and it was carried forward in the Christian school of Alexandria, especially by Clement." He taught at Ephesus and then headed a school in Rome.[2]

In his writings, Justin uses "serpent" and the devil or Satan interchangeably to describe the agent of evil in the world, and the agent of the fall. The serpent is an apostate or fallen angel. Justin states in the *Dialogue with Trypho:* "In the Septuagint it is written, 'Behold, you die like men, and fall like one of the princes,' to point out the disobedience of men, that is, of Adam and Eve, and the fall of one of the princes, namely, the serpent who fell with a great fall because he deceived Eve . . ."[3]

In the *Exhortation to the Greeks,* Justin calls the devil the enemy of humankind, cast out of heaven because of his first diabolical persecution of people.[4] In the *Dialogue,* Justin describes the temptation of Christ "by the Devil (that power which is also called Serpent and Satan) . . ."[5] For Justin, the Serpent in the garden is another name for the chief of fallen angels, Satan.

Describing Justin's conceptions of angels and demons, Erwin Goodenough finds that reference to the Palestinian Hebrew traditions regarding angels clarifies much of Justin's angelology. He probably thought of angels as having human form and made of a fiery substance which consumes nourishment (as in the stories of angels eating). Some angels are permanent, others exist for a day and then expire. Angels are messengers and helpers of God—God's footmen. There are good and bad angels—a division which occurred long ago and is now permanent.[6]

Angels, like people, have free will; and according to Justin, some angels choose the way of evil, so that they too must repent and be saved. Leslie Barnard states that Justin is following a Jewish tradition in this regard. Justin follows the earlier Jewish-Christian interpretation of Genesis 6:2–5. The Hebrew version of Genesis 6:2–5 says the sons of God were attracted to women and begot giants by them; the same phrase is translated in the Septuagint as "angels of God." There is a tradition in Greek Judaism that it was the union of angels and women which produced giants, although some rabbis of that period disagreed. Justin is the first Christian to substitute demons for giants; he states that an entire host of evil powers later multiplied from these demonic children.[7] Athenagoras and Tertullian both agreed with Justin in this interpretation of Genesis 6:2–5, although the view was later expressly rejected by Christian theologians.[8]

After the birth of the demonic children, both their angelic fathers and the sons (it is not clear that there are female demons) were called either "demons" or "evil angels" and formed an array of evil powers very real to Justin. Goodenough states:

The company of demons and fallen angels was led by an arch fiend, Satan (*Dial.* 131.2), who fell in an uniquely sinful manner. It was he who deceived Adam and Eve, and as a result of this treachery he was cursed and fell with a great overthrow (*Dial.* 124.3; 79.4). His name, said Justin, is a Hebrew compound meaning Apostate Serpent (*Dial.* 103.5; 124.5).... Satan ... was apparently one of the many angels ... given duties in the universe, but was the first and chief apostate of the group.[9]

Justin's exegesis of "Satan" is quite interesting. Barnard states that in the *Dialogue* 103:5, Justin interpreted Satan to be composed of two forms: *Sata*, in Hebrew and Syriac is "decline from religion" or "apostate" while *nas* is "serpent."[10] *Nachash* is the usual Hebrew word for serpent. Apparently, the Samaritans, among whom Justin was born and lived, omitted the guttural between two homogeneous vowels in their pronunciation (thus omitting the *ch* in *nachash*).[11] Irenaeus also followed this interpretation of the name of Satan.[12]

Justin is very concerned with the activity of demons in the world. They are active in the political sphere (influencing or being the rulers of some cities, imitating Christian practices, fomenting heresies, leading people into "sins and lusts of matter and mammon"), active as the gods of the Greeks, and responsible for the persecution of good Christians and the parody of Christian practices. Justin believed in demonic possession, although he also associated demonic possession with possession by the souls of the dead in which demons and dead souls were not distinguished. This was apparently the influence of the Hebrew tradition of demonology, as seen in Josephus and Philo, although Tatian, shortly after Justin, denied that the demons who attack people are human souls. War, adultery, and crime are all due to the influence of demons. Even the judges who persecute Christians are inspired by the devil, according to Justin. Barnard comments that Justin's account of good and evil angels is very similar to that found in the Synoptic Gospels.[13]

For Justin, men and women are like Adam and Eve in that, influenced by the demons, they choose sin, while exercising their free will. "Men were created like God, free from pain and death, provided they obeyed His precepts and were deemed worthy by Him to be called His sons, and yet, like Adam and Eve, brought death upon themselves.... each is to be judged and convicted, as were Adam and Eve."[14]

The sin of Adam and Eve put people under the influence of Satan, or the demons, but free will remains, so that sin is not a necessity. Both Barnard and Goodenough point out that Justin is close to the Hebrew tradition (Palestinian and Hellenistic) in this regard. For Justin, "There is no inherited sinfulness which has any actuality apart from the commission of acts of sin."[15] Justin states:

Man ... from the time of Adam had become subject to death and the deceit of the serpent, each man having sinned by his own fault. For God, in His desire to have the angels and men (who were endowed with the personal power of free will) do whatever He had enabled them to do, created them such that, if they chose to do things pleasing to Him, He would preserve them immortal and free from punishment, but if they preferred to do evil, He would punish each one as He pleased.[16]

Furthermore, the fall did not impair human reason, upon which free will relies for discernment: "Indeed, in the beginning when He created man, He endowed him with the power of understanding, of choosing the truth, and of doing right; consequently, before God no man has an excuse if he does evil, for all men have been created with the power to reason and to reflect."[17] Thus, people control their own power to choose the good. "Our creation was not in our own power. But this—to engage in those things that please Him and which we choose by means of the intellectual faculties He has bestowed on us—this makes our conviction and leads us to faith."[18] Both angels and people are capable of free will, repentance, and salvation. "But, since God from the very beginning created the race of angels and men with free will, they will justly pay the penalty in everlasting fire for the sins they have committed. Indeed, every creature is capable, by nature, of vice and of virtue."[19] Thus, Justin does not believe in inherited guilt or original sin, and places the blame for evil on the demons, an originally good creation by God, who freely choose to do evil and who lead people into evil.

Justin thus sees all people, male and female, as capable of good, and equally burdened by evil temptation through the demons. Unlike other authors (e.g., Philo, who blames Eve for the fall) he is more concerned with deception by the evil angels than with the gender of the deceived. Thus, his theology of the fall is not overtly misogynistic.

In Justin's discussion of the virgin birth, however, the obedience of Mary redeems the disobedience of Eve, but in an act, the virgin birth, which cannot be imitated by other women. "He (Christ) is born of the Virgin, in order that the disobedience caused by the serpent might be destroyed in the same manner in which it had originated. For Eve, an undefiled virgin, conceived the word of the serpent, and brought forth disobedience and death. But the Virgin Mary, filled with faith and joy, when the angel Gabriel announced to her the good tidings . . . answered: "Be it done unto me according to thy word . . ."[20]

Justin states that "Jesus Christ . . . was not born as the result of sexual relations . . ."[21] Mary's obedience is merely a response to God's choice of her role as child bearer, not a conscious choice between good and evil. However, fairness requires that the same criticism could be applied to Christ as a male model. Many men suffer death but only Christ's death redeems humanity. Christ is God's only son (although if coupled with preexistence, Christ chose to be born). Thus the theology of the virgin birth is not misogynistic, since neither male nor female can fully imitate the saving behavior.

These views could contribute to the oppression of women if they were coupled with cultural views which deny women education, make wives and daughters the property of husbands and fathers, associate moral virtue with the male mind (as Plato did), or add other elements of theology, as mentioned in the introduction. It must be remembered that Justin wrote as an apologist, not simply a philosopher, during a period of intense persecution by the authorities, when both males and females proved themselves equally faithful in martyrdom as well as leadership. The political power of males and females was more evenly distributed in a persecuted and charismatic community, as Ruether and McLaughlin have suggested.[22] The Christian community shocked the Hellenistic mind by having female leaders and meals in common. Justin did not make overtly misogynistic statements, and his theology of the fall could only contribute to misogyny if coupled with cultural misogyny or some theological changes.

Clement of Alexandria

Quasten states that Clement was the founder of speculative theology. Born in Athens about fifty years after Justin, Clement was of pagan parents. About 180 A.D. he became a student and a teacher at the Christian school headed by Pantaenus in Alexandria. He taught under Pantaenus, and then succeeded him as head of the school for twenty years. He fled Alexandria during the persecution under Septimus Severus, probably going to Jerusalem where he died between 211 and 215.[23]

A contemporary of Irenaeus of Lyons, like Irenaeus, Clement saw the danger of Gnostic Christianity and the possible Hellenization of the faith. Unlike Irenaeus, however, Clement did not hesitate to place the tools of philosophy in the service of faith. He promoted a harmony between faith and knowledge, asserting that the beginning of philosophy is faith.[24] Thus, Clement followed Justin's pioneering role in using philosophy for the advancement of Christianity.

In addition to the Christian Platonism which Justin and he shared, Clement's theology of the fall was developed in response to the influence of Gnosticism. He was concerned with demonstrating the goodness of the creator and of God's creation, and with emphasizing the free will of human beings in choosing good or evil. Floyd states that Clement's reflection on the problem of evil was dictated by his Gnostic opponents. Clement himself had an optimistic view of life, and evil was not the central issue of his theology.[25]

For Clement, like Justin, the serpent of the fall is Satan, the same being who tempted Christ in the desert. However, Clement's demonology alternates between allegorical interpretations of demonic activity and descriptions of Satan's realistic and, for Clement, historical activity.[26] On the one hand, Clement follows Philo's lead and the tendency of the Alexandrian school in the interpretation of the fall allegorically.

At his most allegorical, Clement expounds Genesis exactly like Philo, almost as if he had the Philonic text in front of him ... Clement says that Adam fell a victim of pleasure, for the serpent that creeps upon the belly, an earthly evil, reared to return to matter, is an allegory for pleasure. Elsewhere the serpent is the embodiment of deception (Str. IV.12:4; cf. Protr. 7:6) or wisdom of a crafty and subtle variety.[27]

However, Clement also asserts the historicity of a rebellion and fall of the angels, of Adam and Eve, of Eve's deception by the serpent, and Adam's inducement by Eve. Floyd comments that in contrast to Philo, Clement is able to espouse the merits of the allegorical system without falling prey to its inherent weakness.[28]

An issue relevant to the topic of misogyny arises in considering the influence of Philo on Clement. While Floyd states that Clement follows Philo in his interpretation of the fall, the authors note significant exceptions. Chadwick holds that Clement's debt to Philo is large but measurable and not to be exaggerated.[29] Hering, however, puzzles over an assertion by Heinisch that Clement follows Philo in the fall, since Philo traces the origin of evil directly to the woman, Eve. Hering cites Heinisch as attributing to Philo the view that the fall was engendered by the fact of the existence of woman, the very sight of whom kindles desire: "When woman was created, he greeted her while regarding her ... and this desire engendered carnal sensual pleasure which is the origin of injustice and sin."[30] Floyd also agrees that Philo blames Eve totally.[31]

Clement's original and unique view of the nature of Adam's and Eve's transgression will be mentioned later. Despite Clement's emphasis on free will, he places the initiatory action of the fall with Satan, from whose deceptive action we can only be rescued by Christ.

"Because the evil reptile with his charlatanism reduced to slavery and still mistreats people.... Also, since it is only he who deceived Eve and now leads to death other people, we have only one protector and help, the Lord."[32] Thus, although Clement, like Justin, was heavily influenced by Hebrew tradition, he does not follow Philo in blaming Eve. Even Clement's emphasis on Satan is tempered, however, by his insistence on free will in the fall, both of angels and people, and thus the goodness of God's handiwork and the role of personal reponsibility.

Floyd points out that the Alexandrian worldview legitimated a belief in spirits, angels, and demons, whose intervention explains social upheaval to the popular imagination. "[In] 2nd century Alexandria . . . virtually everyone, pagan, Jewish, Christian or Gnostic, believed in the existence of these beings and in their function as mediators, whether he called them daemons or angels or aions or simply 'spirits.'"[33] Like Justin, then, and like the world of his own time, Clement believed in angels, and in the fall of angels to become demons. Clement envisaged three ranks of angels prior to the fall: (1) seven first-born princes of angels, (2) archangels, and (3) angels. They knew God directly and all the secrets of the eternal truths. Some of them fell from this position by their own free will to inhabit the lower realms.

Floyd points out that Paul combined the lust of Genesis 6:1–4 with the disobedience of Genesis 3 and the rabbinic view of the human psychological tendency toward evil imagination. The resulting combination became the basis for all later Christian interpretations.[34] Like Justin, Clement saw a fall of the angels in Genesis 6:1–4; the interpretation of this story by I Enoch is employed, in which "watchers" are seen by Clement as "angels." "The sons of God were seized by sexual desire, slipped back to the ground from carelessness, and sank into pleasure with the daughters of men." This gave rise to duplicity, the loss of purposeful simplicity, and to demons. Clement saw this event as occurring only once.[35]

According to Clement, the evil angels inhabit the lower zones of heaven, closer to the earth. Satan, known as the Prince of Evil, [36] the devil, the serpent, the dragon, and the tyrant, is the leader of the powers of darkness. Thus, although the world is basically good, the powers of evil distract people from their eternal goal, which is to conform to the likeness of God. Thus Clement avoids Gnostic dualism.

Clement's view of the nature of the human fall seems to be unique for his time.[37] He believed in the perfectibility of Adam, and saw the fall as originating in Adam's longing for marriage and a family (not sex) before he was fully mature. Adam was immortal before the fall. Adam was the perfect image of God but was to mature from infancy into the perfect likeness of God, a goal to be achieved through the conscious and free exercise and practice of virtue, and with God's grace. Adam (and Eve) would become the true children of God, in Paul's sense of sonship (Rom. 8:15–17 or Gal. 4:5–7), only upon maturity. Adam was in a state of innocence in Eden, morally just, a rational animal with vast knowledge and a faultless intellect. Thus Adam could name the animals and Eve—a prophetic act.

Before the fall, Adam and Eve may have enjoyed sex, an appetite as natural as food and drink. The human sin was an irrational disobedience, but arose more profoundly out of the desire for a family and lineage. "The first man of our race did not bide his time, but desired the *favor of marriage* before the hour, and fell into sin by not waiting for the time of God's will." Through this act Adam achieved manhood, where maturity is seen as the ability to know good and evil, before the proper time.

The fall was thus a lapse due to weakness and immaturity. Clement does suggest that the serpent is a symbol of material or sensual desire, but does not see sex as evil, nor does he suggest that pride or a desire for intellectual knowledge motivated the fall.[38] If Clement's theology of the fall seems obscure, as researchers complain, it is due in part to his focus on God's goodness and concern to stem Gnostic dualism.[39]

Elements of a misogynistic or patriarchal perspective in Clement arise in his theory of the original creation, rather than in the fall. Although the nature and virtue of male and female are the same, Clement holds that the female sex was created specifically for pregnancy and childbirth[40] and that Eve was a helpmeet sexually fit for Adam.[41] This would define Eve's role in relation to Adam, the man, rather than in relation to God.

Although Clement saw Adam and Eve as the singular parents of humanity, he did not believe in original sin in the sense of inherited guilt. He states that guilt cannot be transmitted, for then Christ would have inherited guilt.[42] Humanity experiences the effects of the original sin: mortality, ignorance, and a tendency to act wrongly. Thus we inherit from Adam and Eve a tainted social environment conveyed in part through parental example, attitudes, and ways of thinking. But, like Adam, who was to practice virtue and become fully righteous, all people are equally capable of acquiring virtue. For Clement, only a personal act can stain the soul, although Adam's bad example of refusal to be educated by God has influenced his progeny. Quasten suggests that Clement's viewpoint was a reaction to the Gnostic dualistic view that matter is evil.[43] Thus, Clement would not encourage infant baptism, as baptism for him was the cleansing of sin committed by the person.

Clement's strongest theme is freedom of choice. In the *Stromata* he states that Adam's innate nobility lay in his freedom of choice, which he abused.[44] Through free will and the exercise of reason it is the human responsibility to live in conformity with God's plan. Clement states: "But man's duty is to cultivate a will that is in conformity and united throughout his life to God and Christ, properly directed to eternal life."[45]

Clement emphasizes the failure of reason in the fall. "With good cause was he (Adam) considered unreasonable and likened to the beasts." ". . . [H]e who sins against reason is no longer rational, but is an irrational animal wholly given up to lust, whom every sort of pleasure sits upon and drives."[46] Lust for Clement refers to excessive physical pleasure in eating, drinking, sex, clothing. One's entire way of life should be moderate and free of an overemphasis on sensual pleasure. Thus the body of the Christian should conform to the educated judgment of reason, seeking truth, and accomplishing its duty in actual deeds: a moderate way of life.[47] To avoid sin one must avoid excessive indulgence, or that which goes against nature.[48] Clement holds that both angels and people have free will. He had more hope than Justin for the eventual repentance and salvation of even Satan and his cohorts.[49]

It has been mentioned that all people, like Adam, are capable of perfect virtue in Clement's eyes, despite the tainted environment. This is true of both male and female. For Clement, virtue is the only path to true happiness. Despite Clement's functional view of women as childbearers, he gives women a virtue equal to men.

Let us recognize, too, that both men and women practice the same sort of virtue. Surely, if there is but one God for both, then there is but one Educator for both.

One Church, one virtue, one modesty, a common food, wedlock in common, breath, sight, hearing, knowledge, hope, obedience, love, all are alike [in man and woman]. They who possess life in common, grace in common, and salvation in common have also virtue in common and, therefore, education too. The Scripture says: "For in this world, they marry and are given in marriage," for this world is the only place in which the female is distinguished from the male, "but in that other world, no longer." There, the rewards of this life, lived in the holy union of wedlock, await not man or woman as such, but the human person, freed from the lust that in this life had made it either male or female.[50]

Ferguson finds this attitude highly unusual for Clement's age.

> This was an attitude not found in traditional Judaism. . . . It was not found in Greece. . . . It was not found in Rome. . . . It is authentically the spirit of Jesus, whose freedom in speaking with the woman of Samaria startled his disciples, who denied a two-fold standard of morality over the woman taken in adultery, and whose attitude to Mary and Martha speaks of a new type of relationship. . . . This partnership between men and women was part of the Christian revolution, the Christian transvaluation, and Clement is in the true tradition in offering it.[51]

Clement actively defended marriage against the Gnostic rejection of it. It was not wrong of Adam to get married; he only married prematurely. Marriage is a patriotic duty and is for the procreation of children. Although he thought that sex should be restrained and moderate in marriage, he did not infer thereby that celibacy is better. St. Paul was married; according to Clement this was a good advertisement.[52] The successful married person may attain even more virtue than the single celibate because of the additional challenges and temptations that arise in heading a family. Clement's view is unparalleled, says Quasten, and was probably connected to his anti-Gnostic polemic.[53]

It is in Clement's view of the family that one notices patriarchal restrictions regarding women. Women are created for childbearing and domesticity. While men may exercise at the gymnasium, women should get exercise serving their husband at home. Men and women should both wear simple clothing, but Clement prefers a woman to wear a veil, so as not to excite desire in either males or females. These views temper the enthusiasm of the remark on female virtue.

Clement does, however, suggest that a wife could share the dangers of travel with her husband (perhaps in missionary work). There is much material regarding women in Clement's discussion of marriage and his views on daily conduct. However, it is clear that his suggestions originate more from the culture of his day and from his theory of creation than from a theology of the fall.

Conclusion

The question of this discussion is whether a theology of the fall based on Genesis 3 must contribute to misogyny or patriarchy. Justin and Clement reflect different emphases within an important early Christian school of thought. This author must state that she has seen no evidence in either scholar that belief in the fall of Genesis 3 elicits an oppressive attitude toward women. This, of course, is not necessarily true of all of the Fathers of the Church. It can be noticed in Clement that his theology of creation can be restrictive toward women, which raises the issue of the distinction between culture and theology. However, if certain elements of Justin or Clement's theology of the fall are rearranged or omitted, significant changes regarding women could occur.

In the transition from Justin to Clement it has been seen that although the latter ignores Philo's blaming of Eve for the fall, Clement partly allegorizes the demonic, and emphasizes more than Justin the role of free will, reason, and sensual desire. The question is whether de-emphasizing the agency of Satan (by allegorizing the serpent) and promoting the activity of free will and reason may work against a positive female image in other theologians.

This may occur in two ways. First, if the serpent is allegorized, Eve's temptation of Adam is emphasized. Second, the female in Platonism is disassociated from reason and moral virtue; the view of women emphasizes emotionality and sexual capacity in childbearing. The Augustinian view that associates women with the body and emotion while placing the spiritual qualities with the male, leads to greater blame placed on the female for the fall. It should be remembered that both male and female were tempted and both responded.

The agency of the serpent must, in this light, be taken seriously. Did the female tempt the male out of an original deficiency in her quality of reason, or is another aspect of original nature more significant in this event? If the serpent is a willing, reasoning, and emotional (angelic) being, the initiative of that being relieves the apparent stupidity of the female in believing a slithering animal over God's word. Finally, if the initiator in the fall event is a (male) reasoning angel, knowledgeable of God's creative plan, reason or knowledge cannot be the motive of the fall. It can only be an aspect more powerful than reason, knowledge, or truth.

A profound understanding underlies the fall. Does God reveal to humanity through this event an aspect of Godself which is so fundamental and significant that it precedes the rational? Unificationism says this aspect of Godself is heart or love, and that the fall is the loss of the possibility of the human perfection of love (until Christ). Thus, love may transcend the question of truth; the quality more often associated with the female character may in the final analysis reflect the inner core of God's nature, the quality to which Satan gravitated.[54]

Notes

1 *The Westminster Dictionary of Church History*, ed. J. C. Brauer (London: Westminster, 1971), 211–13.

2 Leslie W. Barnard, *Justin Martyr, His Life and Thought* (Cambridge: Cambridge University Press, 1967), 6; *Westminster Dictionary of Church History*, 468–69.

3 Justin Martyr, *Dialogue with Trypho*, chap. 124, in *The Fathers of the Church. Saint Justin Martyr. The First Apology, The Second Apology, Dialogue With Trypho, Exhortation to the Greeks, Discourse to the Greeks, The Monarchy of the Rule of God*, ed. Thomas B. Falls (New York: Christian Heritage, 1949), 341.

4 Justin, *Exhortation to the Greeks*, chap. 28.

5 Justin, *Dialogue*, chap. 125.

6 Erwin R. Goodenough, *The Theology of Justin Martyr. An Investigation into the Conceptions of Early Christian Literature and Its Hellenistic and Judaistic Influence* (Amsterdam: Philo Press, 1968), 193–98.

7 Barnard, 106–7.

8 Goodenough, 193.

9 Ibid., 201.

10 Barnard, 108, f. 8.

11 Barnard cites A. L. Williams, *Dialogue with Trypho* (London, 1930), 216.

12 Barnard cites *Adv. Haer* v. 21:2; *Preaching* 16 by Irenaeus.

13 Goodenough, 202–4; Barnard, 109–10.

14 Justin, *Dialogue*, chap. 124.

15 Barnard, 115; Goodenough, 229.

16 Justin, *Dialogue*, chap. 88.

17 Justin, *First Apology*, chap. 28.

18 Ibid., chap. 10.

19 Justin, *Second Apology,* chap. 7, p. 127.

20 Justin, *Dialogue,* chap. 100.

21 Justin, *First Apology,* chap. 21.

22 *Women of Spirit: Female Leadership in the Jewish and Christian Traditions,* ed. Rosemary Ruether and Eleanor McLaughlin (New York: Simon & Schuster, 1979).

23 *Westminster Dictionary of Church History,* 211.

24 Johannes Quasten, *Patrology,* vol. 2, *The Ante-Nicene Literature After Irenaeus* (Westminster, Md.: Newman Press, 1953), 20.

25 William Gregory Floyd, *Clement of Alexandria's Treatment of the Problem of Evil* (London: Oxford University Press, 1971), xviii–xix.

26 Ibid., 72.

27 Ibid., 43–45.

28 Ibid., 44.

29 Ibid., 43 n. 1, cited from Henry Chadwick, *Early Christian Thought and the Classical Tradition* (New York: Oxford, 1966), 141f. n. 65.

30 Jean Hering, *Étude sur la Doctrine de la Chute et de la Preéxistence des Ames chez Clément D'Alexandrie* (Paris: Editions Ernest Leroux, 1923), on p. 20 cites M. Heinisch, *Der Einfluss Philos auf die älteste christliche Exegese* (Münster, 1908), 169–71, who quotes Philo, *de opif. mundi,* 151.

31 Floyd, 51, see Philo, *Opif.,* 151–52; *Virt.,* 203–5.

32 Clement of Alexandria, *Le Protreptique,* intro. and trans. Claude Mondésert (Paris: Editions du Cerf, 1941), 51–52.

33 Floyd, 62, from Dodds, *Pagan and Christian,* 38.

34 Ibid., 42.

35 Ibid., 66–67.

36 Clement, *Protr.,* 90.1.

37 For the following, see Floyd, 46–52. Cf. Clement, *Protr.,* 90.1; *Str.,* iii.94.3, iii.81.

38 Ibid., 50, also Clement, *Le Protreptique,* chap. XI, 111, 172.

39 Hering, 27.

40 *Str.,* iv.59.4.

41 *Protr.,* III.1.

42 *Str.,* iii.102.

43 Quasten, 312.

44 John Ferguson, *Clement of Alexandria* (New York: Twayne Publishers, 1974), 127, referring to *Miscellanies (Str.),* bks. 1–3, chap. 11.

45 Clement of Alexandria, *Christ the Educator, (Paedagogus)*, trans. Simon P. Wood, C.P. (New York: Fathers of the Church, 1954), 102:91.

46 Ibid., 102:90.

47 Ibid., 102:90–91.

48 Floyd, 49.

49 Ibid., 72. Clement, however, is less specific about universal salvation than Origen.

50 Clement, *Christ the Educator*, bk. 1, chaps. 4, 10, pp. 11–12.

51 Ferguson, 72.

52 Floyd, 178.

53 Quasten, 35.

54 One example of this can be found in the work of Carl Gilligan, *In A Different Voice* (Cambridge: Harvard University Press, 1982).

5 The Islamic Concept of Sin
SULAYMAN S. NYANG

Since the beginnings of human society, people have always been concerned about their relations with the spiritual and invisible world. Such concerns and fears about how the human being is viewed by the forces above have led people to develop a number of beliefs and views about sin. To the traditional African religionist, for example, personal sin is not widely accepted. What is of primary importance is ethnic and group taboos. The individual African is not told by the priestly class that people have to settle their personal accounts with the High God at the end of time. What such a traditional African learns early is that the individual lives in a vitalistic universe wherein he or she interacts with countless beings and creatures, that personal survival and safety is inextricably linked to the fortunes of the community, and that success depends on relations with fellow humans as well as the spiritual beings within the universe.[1]

The idea of sin is indeed peculiarly Abrahamic, and an African scholar probing this question can only understand it by leaving traditional African ontology and moving into the borrowed theology of the children of Abraham. Given this situation, one is then forced to differentiate the three strands of thought within the Abrahamic tradition. They are the Judaic strand, the Christian strand, and the Islamic strand. Each of these branches of the Abrahamic tree has developed over the last millennium or more into communities of beliefs that are diverse but integrated by a core of values, concepts, and feelings about their respective traditions.[2]

The Judaic tradition with its several schools of thought has evolved from the time of the Judges right through the days of the Diaspora. Today, rabbis of the Jewish community, the embodiment of such a tradition, have written voluminously about sin and the manner in which the concept relates to the life situations of modern men and women living in industrial society.³ Though there may be hermeneutical disagreements here and there, the fact remains that in Jewish thought the concept of sin plays a prominent role. Indeed, in the first chapter of the Torah we read about the Adamic fumble which later led to the expulsion of Adam and Eve, the first couple whose procreative activities started that human chain of beings stretching down the millennia right through our time.

The concept of sin has a larger place in Christianity. The very mission of Jesus is predicated on human sinfulness and the divine mission to redeem humanity by dispatching his only begotten son. Indeed, one can argue that the Adamic sin in the Garden of Eden was the prologue to the cosmic drama of human frailty and that, in Christian theological terms, the advent of Christ as Messiah and Redeemer of Adamic sin on earth was the highest point in the human drama.⁴

It is against this background of Abrahamic theology that we now proceed to the analysis of the Islamic view of sin and the Muslim efforts at dealing with its moral, spiritual, and eschatological consequences. To facilitate our analysis, this paper is divided into three major sections: a discussion of the Islamic view of sin and its relation to the purpose of the human being on earth; a discussion of sin and human society; and a discussion of sin and the divine penalties.

Sin and the Islamic Vision of the Human Being

As pointed out above, one of the critical factors that distinguishes the religions of the Semites from those of the tropical Africans or the Far Eastern Asians or some of the North and South American Indian tribes, is the greater emphasis on sin. In the Islamic tradition, this sharp focus on sin is evident in the Quranic vision of the human being. In various chapters of the holy book there are striking statements which together give a fairly accurate picture of what Islam teaches that people should and must be in order to win the favors of Allah (God).

In the creation story we learn that God's decision to create man and woman was for a specific purpose. God told the angels that though they had entertained apprehensions about human responsibility on earth, God knew what they knew not.⁵ From this divine answer numerous theological arguments about human destiny have been constructed. Some Muslim thinkers have taken it to mean that on the scale of spiritual development there is no limit to human advancement, and people may even surpass the angels.

Related to this Quranic statement is the *ayat* (sign in the holy book) which affirms that the human being was not created for sport.[6] This divine pronouncement makes it categorically clear that a person's brief sojourn on earth is for a serious mission. The Quran constantly reminds people that their road to *al-Janat* (heaven) is likely to be blocked by Satan, that all deeds on earth are to be accounted for, and that firm faith in the Supreme Being is strengthened by the purity of their thoughts and deeds.

Another teaching of the Quran, with regard to the human role in the universe, is the understanding that sinfulness corrupts the soul and turns people from the *sirat al-mustahim* (right path) to the path of Satan and his confederates. In order for people to move closer to the Islamic vision of human beings, they must live above mere life (above animal existence) and act out in daily life the teachings of the *Sharia* (Muslim law and traditions). It is only through faithful practice of the Quranic teachings that a person can become a full-fledged Muslim. And by doing so a person learns to see the more positive side of his or her being and the great rewards that await in the hereafter (*al-akhira*).

In talking about sin and the Islamic vision of human being, one can add that Islamic thought takes a totally different view of human destiny from the related Abrahamic faiths. Whereas Christians of various denominations still believe that the historical manifestation of Jesus Christ was true, and that his crucifixion was ontologically and eschatologically significant because it opened the door of salvation to human beings whose genetic links to Adam and his wife had condemned them *ab initio* to eternal damnation, the Muslim theologians make no such claims for the Prophet Muhammad. Rather, they argue that Muhammad and his prophet counterparts in history were protected from sin by Allah, and that the best thing we as individuals living in society can do for the good of our faith and our community is to follow the example of *al-Imam al-Muslimin* (the Imam of the Muslim).[7] This Islamic imperative is heeded by the Sufis who set the Holy Prophet Muhammad as the *al-Insan al-Kamil* (the Universal Man). They began their quest for *Nur Muhammadiyya* (The light of Muhammad) through vigorous vigils, prayers, and retreats (*halwa*). Such a spiritual exercise following the example of Muhammad is also known to orthodox Muslims, although their sophistication and worldly learning convinces them not to dabble in Sufism and not to confuse the Divine Message with the *bidas* (innovations) and superstitions of the common people.

From what has been said so far, it is clear that the concept of sin is crucial to Islamic ontology, Islamic metaphysics, and Islamic eschatology. When viewed ontologically from a Muslim perspective, sin becomes a unit in the human/spiritual universe. According to the Quranic version of the creation story, the rebellion of *Iblis* (the Archangel) was the first and most significant act of sin in creation.[8] It was sinful because the perpetrator committed an act of negativity towards his creator at three levels.

First of all, by refusing to bow before man as his creator willed, this favored archangel of Allah introduced into cosmic time and into the realm of human consciousness what was hitherto alien: *the concept of disobedience*. This is to say, the act of disobedience on the part of Iblis demonstrated at the angelic level what was to be later replicated at the plane of human life and activity by Adam and his wife.

Second, the defiance of Iblis, according to the Quranic story of creation, opened up a new beginning in cosmic time in the sense that Allah identified an enemy within the inner circle and then meted out the appropriate punishment. Prior to Iblis's defiance the universe was orderly and obedient to all divine orders. Viewed from this perspective, one can argue that Iblis's defiance was ontologically and eschatologically significant in that his act of rebellion set a poor example for the subsequent history of Adam and his children. Here is one of the serious ironies of cosmic and religious history. It was indeed the creation of Adam and his wife that led to the refusal of Iblis "to bow before those who are created out of dust"; yet it was the same Adam who in turn went against the divine order only to suffer the same expulsion as the archangel who had earlier refused to bow before him.

The third point to be made here about Iblis's rebellion and its implication for the Islamic concept of sin and its vision of the human being is that the downfall of Iblis from the pinnacle of angelic glory to the pits of the Seven Hells anticipated at the angelic level what was to happen on the human plane. This development linked human history to cosmic history and resulted in Allah's decision to divide up humanity into two categories, namely, people of prophecy and people of society.

The difference between these two types is the differential in divine mercy and divine grace. The former are protected from sin and for this and other reasons could transmit the divine message without falling into the web of temptations spun by Satan and his confederates. The latter, however, do not enjoy such spiritual favors and for this reason need guidance from the chosen prophets among humankind. It is indeed in this context that Muslim teachers argue that the Holy Prophet Muhammad was sent only as a *mundhir* (a warner) and a *huda* (a guide) to humanity. He was not God, and could not forgive anyone his or her sins. Even when it comes to intercession for others on the Day of Judgment, he would be able to intercede only at the pleasure of Allah. This Islamic view, I would stress here, is another affirmation of the humanity of the Prophet Muhammad and the spiritual and historical limitations of his role as Allah's chosen messenger to the children of Adam.[9]

The Islamic View of Sin and Society

To gain a better view of the various elements in society, the people of prophecy often identify persons on the basis of categorization. In the Quran, we read about the three types of people in society and the differences in spiritual levels of attainment. First of all, there is the *nafs al-amara* (self-afflicted spirit), which includes men and women whose lives resemble very much those of animals.[10] Condemned to live on the level of mere life, such humans lack the basic moral values and will to elevate themselves from the low levels of moral decadence to a higher point on the morality scale. Because of this state of affairs they become the most despicable embodiments of the satanic presence in human society. They live in sin, trade in sin, and swim in and out of sin.

Muslim theologians and exegetes, commenting on the *nafs al-amara* type, have maintained that there is need for joint efforts on the part of society and the individual to effect change in the sinner's life. The individual sinner has a responsibility to himself or herself and an obligation to society and Allah to cleanse himself or herself and to amend his or her ways. For by remaining at the bottom of the spiritual ladder, such a person actually negates the very purpose for which he or she was placed here on earth. The Quran declares that Allah has created people out of the best mold, but because of decisions to do evil, they can become the lowest of the low in creation.[11]

Society, on the other hand, has a specific role to play in the moral development of human beings. The Quran contains numerous references to the need for communal action with regard to encouraging good and eschewing evil in society. I believe the significance Islamic thought gives to communal action in human moral development is evident in the five daily communal prayers, the weekly Friday prayer, and the annual feasts of *Id al-Fitr* (which comes soon after the month of fasting) and *Id al-Kabir* (which is celebrated during the month of *Hajj* or Pilgrimage). Given the nature of Islamic communalism and the way of life that goes hand in hand with Islamic rituals, one can now argue that in Islam the individual is not only required to engage in an ongoing moral development, but also to join the rest of the community in purging sinfulness and satanism from society.

The individual who abandons such responsibilities and at the same time gives himself or herself up to the pleasures of this world is the second type of person, classified by the Quran as *nafs al-lawama* (the self-accusing spirit.)[12] Such individuals have moved up on the spiritual ladder and their actions are now governed by a sense of right and wrong. They have imbibed some ethical and moral values, and their lives are no longer dominated by the forces of sin and evil. In Islamic thought, such people can be useful to society in the sense that they can encourage other people to do good and eschew evil. Through faithful acts of worship and through responsible human relations, they help stabilize the moral order and contribute to the containment of evil on earth. Yet their bodies are not completely dominated by the spirit of total submission to Allah. Because of this state of affairs in their moral and spiritual development, such people need the moral reinforcement and encouragement of fellow believers. It is indeed under these conditions that the *Sharia* becomes a reality in human society. For without faithful practitioners, there is indeed no *Sharia* at work.

The third type of person is the *nafs al-mutmain* (the self-satisfied spirit).[13] These individuals have reached some of the highest points on the spiritual ladder. According to the Quranic verse, God is pleased with them and in return the person is also pleased with their Creator.[14] Such Muslims are the ideal type who are closest to the model set by the Holy Prophet Muhammad. Their daily lives are a mirror reflecting the human will to worship and serve Allah. Their acts of devotion and obedience to the Creator serve as an example to those who are still at the level of *nafs al-lawama* and *nafs al-amara*.

Given this analysis of the Islamic vision of the human being and the Muslim's efforts at self-purification, one can say that the

Islamic prescription is that sinfulness can and must be dealt with at both the personal and communal levels. This is to say that Islam expects individuals to straighten themselves out morally and spiritually before it is too late for them to face the sanctions of society. The stiff penalties imposed for such crimes as murder, adultery, and theft are indications of the close relationship between personal morality and public morality. It is part of the Islamic logic that a person who lives in a *Sharia*-dominated society cannot be forgiven for such heinous crimes as murder, fornication, and adultery. The main reason is that a properly socialized member of Muslim society will be so imbued with the values of his or her community that he or she would not degenerate to such evil. To kill one's neighbor or brother or sister is to demonstrate lack of faith in Allah and submission to passion and emotion. To commit adultery knowing full well that the penalty is death is to accept injustice in human relations and to fall victim to the rule of bodily pleasures.

Viewed in this light, one can conclude this section by saying that the Islamic view of sin and its relation to community life is strikingly different from early Christian and Jewish views. What one can identify as a unique feature of the Islamic tradition is *its greater emphasis on human efforts at combating and containing sin in human society*. Added to this is the Muslim's optimistic view that he or she enters this world as a free agent who, unlike his or her Christian brother or sister who believes in original sin, inherits no sin from Adam and Eve and can work for his or her salvation through faith and good works.[15]

Mention was made above of the two types of people in human society—the people of society and the people of prophecy. The former was already explained and analyzed. Let us now discuss what is meant by people of prophecy. While people of society are not prophets and do not claim to receive any prophetic mandate from above, such multitudes are afflicted by the same problems of existence as their more meditative brethren and sisters. They are also preoccupied with the quest for moral choices and the meaning of life. The Islamic tradition maintains that because of their realities people always grope for spiritual guidance. It is therefore at this juncture that the disciple meets his or her teacher and master. Meeting such a teacher lights up the fires of self-discovery in him or her. Under these conditions the disciple sees the teachings of the master as a road map that can help the person travel more securely along the highway of life.

The teacher, the Quran tells us, is only a guide, a warner, and an example to those who have eyes to see and ears to hear. The teacher is a chosen person who is assigned by Allah to carry Allah's will for a given period of time. As a prophet to the people and an example to the community, the teacher serves as the first human defense line against the encroachment of Satan and his cohorts in human society. It is because of the social dimensions of sin that persons of prophecy become important to the social, moral, and spiritual development of a society. They are so perceived because in the execution of their duties and services to the community they inspire enough men and women to reduce the effectiveness of Satan and his human agents.

Sin and the Divine Penalties

After having examined the Islamic concept of sin and its relation to human destiny as well as human community, let us now proceed to an examination of sin and the divine penalties. In the Quran such penalties are well articulated. Indeed, there are vivid reminders telling people what to do and what not to do. Muslim theologians and exegetes have combed through the Holy Book and come up with a list of sins that people must avoid committing. The most serious sin against Allah is *shirk,* that is, associating partners with Allah. Writing on the unity of Allah, the Pakistani scholar Maulana Muhammad Ali points out that "Shirk is . . . of all sins the most serious because it degrades man and renders him unfit for attaining the high position destined for him in the Divine Scheme."[16] This statement was written of Quranic verses stressing the privileged position of the human being in creation.

The various forms of *shirk* are identified in the Quran. For example, in chapter 3, verse 64, the Holy Book sums it up in these words: "That we shall worship none but Allah, and that we shall ascribe no partner unto Him, and that none of us shall take others for Lords beside Allah." This passage lists three forms, but a fourth one is mentioned separately in the Quran. This is the indiscriminate worship of anything besides Allah and, most unfortunately, the blind following of one's own desires.[17]

Going hand in hand with faith in Allah is the belief in the hereafter. A person who does not believe in the hereafter is most likely to abdicate his or her responsibility to self, to community, and to Allah. If one's faith in Allah is strong and one's belief in the hereafter affects one's attitude toward life, one would be more particular about doing good and eschewing evil. No matter how secret things may be for that person, he or she would always know that worldly deeds are to be accounted for and the Quranic references to the Day of Judgment would always reverberate in the mental firmaments of his or her soul.

Given these conditions and bearing in mind that human life here below is short, one can say that Allah has given each living human being a chance to work for his or her salvation. In the Islamic tradition, human destiny is linked to one's fidelity to the *Sharia* which governs one's community, and to the record one builds for oneself while travelling along the highway of life. Indeed, the good Muslim is one who maintains proper and correct relations with other humans, his or her community and the Creator. This triangular relationship is the bedrock on which each person builds a spiritual mansion. Otherwise, he or she would fail just like the man in the biblical story who constructed his house on sand and then lost it to the flood.

In conclusion, one can say that the Islamic concept of sin is one variant of the rich Abrahamic tradition of ethics and eschatology. To the Muslim, sin is that act which embodies satanic and human defiance of the divine will. As we have seen, there is the abiding belief among devout Muslims that humankind can deal successfully both with Satan and his human confederates. This, however, can be achieved only when there is a firmly established pattern of cooperation between the individual believer and the community. Of course, this means that under Islamic law politics and morality cannot be separated, and the liberal notion of separating individual private morality from public morality poses a threat to the good of society. Muslims believe that in the moral economy no invisible hand *à la* Adam Smith exists; rather, the moral order can be maintained only through a visible agency called the *Sharia*. It is their view that individual people working together as members of society can help advance the cause of good and limit the domain of evil.

Notes

1   See my "An African Cosmology," *UNESCO Courier,* Feb. 1982.
2   For views on Islamic, Christian, and Jewish belief systems, see James

Kritzeck, *Sons of Abraham: Jews, Christians and Moslems* (Baltimore: Helicon, 1965); Abraham I. Katz, *Judaism and the Koran* (New York: A. S. Barnes, 1954); Seyyed Hossein Nasr, *An Introduction to Islamic Cosmologies* (Boulder, Colo.: Shambhala, 1978).

3   For some views of modern Jewish thought on sin, see Solo W. Baron et al. *Great Ages and Ideas of the Jewish People* (New York: Modern Library, 1956); Bernard J. Bamberger, *The Story of Judaism* (New York: Schocken, 1957).

4   The role of Christ in history is explored in the following works: C. T. McIntire, *God, History and Historians* (New York: Oxford University Press, 1978); M. C. D'Arcy, *The Meaning and Matter of History: A Christian View* (New York: Noon Press, 1959).

5   Cf. *The Holy Quran,* trans. Yusuf Ali (Beirut: Dar Al Arabia, 1968), 2:30–34; 35–39; 7:11–25; 15:31–44; 17:61–65; 18:50; 20:116–23; 37:71–85.

6   *The Holy Quran,* 21:16–17.

7   For the passages on the sinlessness of prophets, see *The Holy Quran,* 2:151; 21:25–27; 66:6. For a Muslim scholar's analysis of this fact, see Maulana Muhammad Ali, *The Religion of Islam* (Cairo, Egypt: National Publications and Printing House, n.d.), 233ff.

8   For details on Iblis's rebellion, see the following passages of *The Holy Quran:* 2:34; 7:11–18; 15:31–44; 17:61–65; 18:50; 22:116–23; 38:71–85.

9   For discussion on the humanity of the Holy Prophet Muhammad, see Ameer Ali, *The Spirit of Islam* (London: Methuen, 1965).

10   *The Holy Quran,* 12:53.

11   For the Quranic verse on the human being as the creature fashioned out of the mold, see 95:4.

12   *The Holy Quran,* 75:2.

13   Ibid., 89:27–30.

14   Ibid.

15   This view is generally identified with the Asharite School which is currently dominant among Sunni Muslims. There were, however, other schools such as the Mutazilla and the Qadarites.

16   Maulana Muhammad Ali, 146.

17   *The Holy Quran,* 25:43.

6 Some Reflections on the Unification Account of the Fall

JONATHAN WELLS

Introduction

Compared with most modern Christian theologies, Unification theology is distinctive not only for its interpretation of, but also its emphasis on, the fall of Adam and Eve. This interpretation and emphasis are of more than theoretical interest, since the Unification doctrine of the fall determines its doctrine of restoration, which in turn has profound and far-reaching consequences for the actual lifestyle of Unification Church members.

Although the fall is discussed in a variety of Unification Church publications, for the purpose of this seminar I take *Divine Principle* as the standard text, since it is the most widely used and the most thorough treatment. *Divine Principle* is based on *Wol-li Kang-ron,* which was written by Hyo Won Eu based on the teachings of Sun Myung Moon. Those teachings, according to *Divine Principle,* are in turn based on "revelation from God" and on Sun Myung Moon's spiritual experiences "with many saints in Paradise and with Jesus."[1]

This paper is intended to serve as a prolegomenon to a larger discussion of the fall. First comes a summary of the Unification version of the fall story. Then follows a discussion of the question of "monogenism" (i.e., whether human history began with only two individuals). Following that, various aspects of the Unification account are compared with some more traditional Christian versions of the fall. Because of limited time and space, no attempt will be made to cover all of the topics which could be included in a prolegomenon to discussions of the fall; for example, neither the relationship between the Unification account and scripture nor many of the philosophical issues relevant to theodicy will be dealt with.

A Summary of the Unification Account of the Fall

According to Unification theology, God created the world in order to generate joy. Since maximum joy is generated by a relationship of love between a "subject" (initiator) and an "object" (responder) in which the "object" reflects the perfect character of the "subject," human beings were created in God's image (which is both masculine and feminine). The closest analogy for the ideal relationship between God and human beings is the relationship between parent and child. Accordingly, *Divine Principle* refers to God primarily as our heavenly Parent.

Divine Principle describes God's hope for the creation in terms of our fulfillment of "three great blessings" (cf. Gen. 1:26–28). The first blessing is to "be fruitful" in the sense of complete physical and spiritual maturity and a perfect relationship with God. A perfected individual ". . . feels all that God feels, as if God's feelings were his [or her] own. Consequently, he [or she] cannot do anything which would cause God grief. This means that such a man [or woman] could never fall."[2] In Unification terminology, such a perfected individual would be under the "direct dominion" of God's love.

The second blessing is to "multiply" after reaching individual perfection, by marrying and giving birth to sinless "children of goodness." The expansion of this God-centered family would lead to societies in which people ". . . would not perform any act which would hurt their neighbors, because the whole society would experience the same feeling toward those in trouble as God would feel in His grief over them."[3] Such societies would function effectively and harmoniously, just like healthy bodies.

The third blessing is to "have dominion over the creation." After fulfilling the first two blessings, human beings could establish a God-centered relationship with the rest of creation. Through highly developed science, technological achievement, and economic development, they would establish an extremely pleasant social environment on earth. It is important for this environment to be a product of human effort, because to be children of God, human beings must "inherit God's creatorship and participate in His work of creation."[4]

The fulfillment of the three great blessings would result in God's ideal world, "the kingdom of heaven," both in the physical world and the spirit world. Such a fulfillment would bring joy to God as well as to the entire human family.[5] However, if human beings are to be true children of God, and not merely emanational extensions of the Godhead or preprogrammed robots, they must have free will. Only through the proper exercise of this free will, through the fulfillment of a human "portion of responsibility," can human beings achieve the three great blessings. Individual perfection, harmonious societies, and the inheritance of God's creatorship are contingent upon the successful completion of a "growth period" in human development, during which God's dominion is only "indirect." A human being ". . . reaches perfection only . . . by going through the period of indirect dominion, fulfilling his [or her] own portion of responsibility, and inheriting God's creatorship."[6]

In order to help the first two human beings, Adam and Eve, through the growth period without depriving them of their freedom and responsibility, God gave them a commandment (expressed symbolically in Genesis as a commandment not to eat the fruit of the tree of knowledge of good and evil). According to Unification theology, the commandment was God's advice to his growing children, warning them not to misdirect their love by entering into a premature or improper sexual relationship. If they had succeeded in reaching perfection by directing their love faithfully toward God, the commandment would no longer have been necessary. Adam and Eve could then have become husband and wife under the direct dominion of God's love.[7]

Why did God create Adam and Eve so that their immature love was strong enough to be a potential problem? *Divine Principle* offers two answers to this question. First, God could not trust Adam and Eve to exercise a dominion of love over the entire creation unless they first demonstrated their trustworthiness by fulfilling their own portion of responsibility. In other words, they first had to establish dominion over *themselves*. Second, God wanted them ultimately to relate to God freely because of love rather than necessity. Love had to be the strongest force in the universe, so that God could dwell with humankind eternally in an indissoluble relationship of love. If God had made the force of love weaker, then Adam and Eve might have been in no danger of falling; but they would never have been capable of the deep and freely chosen relationship that God hoped to have with them.[8]

Before God created Adam and Eve as God's children, God created the angels to be servants and messengers. The angels were to minister to Adam and Eve as they grew to maturity, after which Adam and Eve were to assume dominion over the angels as well as the rest of the creation. When God created Adam and Eve, God's love for the angels did not diminish; but since Adam and Eve were God's children, God loved them more than the angels, who were servants. Lucifer, the archangel, felt the disparity between God's love for him and God's love for Adam and Eve and became envious. Unification theology emphasizes that envy, in itself, is not evil, since it can motivate a person to seek constructive self-improvement. The envy which Lucifer felt was the manifestation of a natural desire for God's love, and was therefore a by-product of the original nature of creation. Motivated by this desire, Lucifer was strongly attracted to Adam and Eve, who were in a position to share God's love with him.[9]

Since Lucifer had been God's servant for eons, and had even participated in God's creation of the world, he had much more knowledge than Adam and Eve. Eve was attracted by Lucifer's knowledge, and as Lucifer and Eve had more give-and-take, two things happened: Lucifer's envy was increasingly directed toward Adam, since he knew that Adam was destined to be Eve's husband and therefore to be closer to Eve than he could be; and the relationship between Lucifer and Eve grew into love, developing an erotic character which eventually went past the point forbidden by God's commandment. At that point, Lucifer and Eve fell by having a *spiritual* but nevertheless real and substantial sexual relationship with each other (the "spiritual fall").[10]

Despite the spiritual fall, all was not lost. If Adam had persevered in growing to perfection through the responsible use of his free will, Eve could soon have been restored to God through perfected Adam, and the consequences of the spiritual fall would have been nullified. However, the reciprocal give-and-take between Adam and Eve gradually led to the same erotic attraction that had precipitated the spiritual fall. As the relationship between Adam and Eve deepened, the power of love drew them closer. Adam also ignored the commandment, and they had an illicit sexual relationship (the "physical fall").[11]

Lucifer was supposed to be the servant of God and of God's children. When Eve yielded to him and Adam to her, the natural order was inverted, and Lucifer (who thereby became "Satan") acquired the dominion that should have been God's. According to Unification theology, this satanic dominion is the most important consequence of the fall. Since it separated Adam and Eve from God, who is the source of spiritual life, they "died" spiritually just as God warned them they would. Though they continued to live physically, their spirits were dead to God. Furthermore, since the fall consisted of fornication, mankind inherited Satan's spiritual lineage, becoming "Satan's children" in a spiritual sense (though *physically* all human beings are descendants of Adam and Eve).[12] This is why Jesus said that fallen people are of their "father the devil" (John 8:44). In Herbert Richardson's words, the human race is "turned into Satan's family."[13] Since people cannot alter their own ancestry, they "cannot eradicate the original sin, however hard they try, by themselves."[14]

Yet despite the original sin, fallen people retain vestiges of their original nature, which was created by God. As a result, fallen individuals suffer from an internal contradiction between good and evil impulses. People with this contradictory nature find themselves in a "midway position" where they can "deal with either God or Satan." In other words, Satan's dominion over fallen people is not absolute; instead, it is at least partly contingent upon their own free choices. Although fallen people are handicapped by their fallen nature, they are still capable of morally responsible decisions. Unification theology thus distinguishes between "original sin," which places mankind in a midway position between God and Satan, and subsequent sins, which result from individual instances of the misuse of free will.[15]

Because of their relationship to Satan, fallen people inherit "four aspects of fallen nature" which have their origin in Lucifer's behavior during the fall. The first aspect is the "failure to take God's standpoint." Lucifer was supposed to love Adam as God loved Adam, and help him to fulfill God's ideal; but instead, he satisfied his own desire at Adam's expense. The second aspect of fallen nature is "leaving proper position." Lucifer deserted his position as servant of Adam and Eve. The third aspect is "reversal of dominion." Lucifer was supposed to be under the dominion of Adam and Eve, who in turn were supposed to be under the dominion of God; but Lucifer usurped God's position and assumed dominion over Adam and Eve. The fourth aspect of fallen nature is the "multiplication of sin." The evil give-and-take between Eve and Satan spread to Adam, adding the physical fall to the spiritual fall. Therefore, fallen nature is manifested as selfishness, irresponsibility, arrogance, and a desire to involve others in unrighteous behavior.[16]

Another consequence of the fall is that people failed to establish proper dominion over the creation. The progress of science and technology has been unnecessarily delayed for thousands of years;

and because of the delay, excessively hard physical labor has lowered the quality of life for most human beings. In addition, epidemic diseases and natural disasters have caused much needless suffering and millions of premature deaths.[17] Thus the creation, instead of serving primarily as an opportunity for the blessing of creative dominion, has become for many a curse of physical suffering—the source of so-called "natural evil" which complicates all attempts at theodicy.

Unification theology repeatedly emphasizes that the fall and its consequences were not part of God's original plan for creation. The fall introduced contradiction and struggle, distorted sexuality and disrupted families, crime and wars, needless physical suffering, and premature death—none of which were intended by God. Worst of all, the fall separated human beings from their source of life, truth, and love; and it deprived God of His children, causing God profound grief. According to *Divine Principle,* God "feels the sorrows and pains of His fallen children," and wants to save them.[18] The emphasis is on God's suffering and compassion, rather than God's wrath (there is no eternal damnation in Unification theology). As a loving Parent, God takes ultimate responsibility for the fall, though "responsibility" is not the same as "blame": "The human fall is, of course, the result of man's own error. However, God, too, is responsible for the result, as the Creator. If God had not created man, the fall would not have occurred. Therefore, God has felt compelled to restore the result of man's error to its original status before the fall."[19]

Monogenism

Educated people nowadays often react to serious discussions about the fall of Adam and Eve with disbelief and amusement. Hasn't evolutionary biology forever laid to rest the notion that the human species began with one original pair in a state of paradisiacal bliss? Isn't the only alternative an anti-scientific "creationism" which attempts to salvage an anachronistic literal interpretation of Genesis?

Actually, the issues are neither as clear-cut nor as settled as these rhetorical questions seem to indicate. To begin with, the notion of paradise is separable from the question of an original pair. Augustine described the Garden of Eden in fabulous terms as a place where Adam and Eve suffered no want, no hunger or thirst, no disease or accident, no disharmony, no passion, and no moral struggle. If they had not fallen, they would never have experienced death.[20] Such a description is incompatible with the present state of our scientific and historical knowledge. However, in the Unification account, the situation of Adam and Eve before the fall is described only in terms of innocence and immaturity, not in terms of perfection and paradise; so Unification theology is not affected by this incompatibility. On the other hand, since the essence of the fall for Augustine is a spontaneous act of the will which *preceded* the overt act of eating the fruit[21] and which could just as easily have occurred in all of the members of a larger population, it could be argued that monogenism is not essential to the Augustinian account of the fall.[22] However, the Unification account relies heavily on a specific and complex series of events involving three specific individuals (Adam, Eve, and Lucifer); so monogenism is indispensable for Unification theology.

From the theological standpoint, theories about the origin of the human species have customarily been divided into two categories: "monogenist" and "polygenist." Monogenism can take at least two forms: (1) all human beings are descended from an original pair or (2) all human beings come from Adam, including Eve (who is made from Adam's rib). Karl Rahner argues that the second form is as theologically unnecessary as it is biologically implausible; and for the purpose of the present discussion, "monogenism" is used only in the former sense.[23] Polygenism can likewise take at least two forms: (1) the human species began its existence as a population comprising more than two individuals or (2) the human *races* arose separately and independently from different prehuman ancestors. The second view has in the past been repeatedly used to justify racial discrimination; but the scientific support for it is minimal, and years ago it ceased to be widely held among scientists.[24] So, for the purpose of the present discussion, "polygenism" is used only in the former sense. The issue, then, is whether the human species began with only two individuals or with a larger population.

To begin with, it can be noted that the available fossil evidence does not settle the issue one way or the other, since there is too little of it and since there is no consensus in the scientific interpretation of it. A recent textbook which surveys the fossil evidence concludes that ". . . there is a lack of unanimity among scholars of primate evolution. . . . Not only is there disagreement as to the classification of various forms, there is also disagreement as to the total evolutionary scheme itself."[25]

It is not fossil evidence, but a theory of the origin of species ("speciation"), which provides the rationale for belief in polygenism. Darwin assumed that the evolutionary change within a species (which can be observed in nature and which can even be artificially produced or regulated) eventually leads, given enough time, to the emergence of new species. Since *intra*-species evolution occurs only within a population, this suggests that *inter*-species evolution also requires an entire population (i.e., polygenism). However, although Darwin's assumption is plausible, it must be considered an uncorroborated hypothesis rather than an established scientific law. No one has ever observed the emergence of a new species by this process, nor is there any scientific consensus as to how it might lead to speciation. The closest thing to a scientific consensus concerning speciation is that it probably takes so long (e.g., thousands of years) that it is virtually unobservable. So, it appears that belief in polygenism rests on a hypothesis about speciation which is not only uncorroborated but also virtually uncorroboratable, and about which there is widespread disagreement concerning its specific mechanism.

Challenging a belief in polygenism is *not* equivalent to challenging evolution per se. I am not suggesting that we should return to the old belief that species are fixed and eternal; I am not doubting geological estimates for the age of the earth; I am not questioning the validity of the pattern of evolution which has been inferred from the fossil record; and I am not attempting to slip in a precarious "God of the gaps." Nor do I suppose that the foregoing analysis disproves polygenism. I am merely pointing out that polygenism is one of the more questionable aspects of evolution, and that the case against monogenism is considerably weaker than many people may think. Monogenism does not conflict with science, but only with a particular unsubstantiated hypothesis about the mechanism of speciation.

If scientific or historical research were eventually to disprove monogenism, it seems to me that the Unification account of the fall would have to be abandoned or radically reinterpreted. In the absence of such disproof, the claim that the human species began with one male and one female may be unscientific evidence; but it is not unscientific in the sense of being in conflict with evidence or with well-corroborated scientific theories.

Unification and Some Traditional Christian Views

Augustine's glorious account of paradise before the fall (referred to above) has given rise to the popular misconception that he considered Adam and Eve to be fully perfect before they fell. Some modern critics, pointing out that such perfection would have rendered the fall impossible, have incorrectly charged Augustine with inconsistency on this issue. But Augustine did not claim that Adam and Eve were fully perfect: only if they had persevered in their obedience to the commandment would they have attained a state of perfection which included wisdom, immortal spiritual bodies, and the inability to sin (*non posse peccare*).[26] Irenaeus conceived of the pre-fallen state as one of physical and spiritual immaturity: Adam and Eve were "innocent and childlike," and "had no understanding of the procreation of children, for it was necessary that they should first come to adult age."[27] Thus, the Unification view that Adam and Eve had to grow to perfection by the responsible exercise of their free will, and that they fell during this growth process, is similar to traditional Christian views, especially that of Irenaeus.

The Unification view that the fall involved fornication between Eve and Lucifer, though untraditional, has some points of contact with the Christian tradition. The Genesis account itself is replete with sexual imagery; and Ricoeur points out that there is an "indissoluble complicity" between sexuality and sin "from time immemorial," though he considers the sexual aspect of the fall subordinate to the disruption of "filial dependence" on God.[28] Francis Clark notes that early Christians were used to the notion of "carnal commerce between angelic spirits and women." However, Clark continues, the notion that the fall of Adam and Eve involved such an act of improper love, though "not indeed unheard of in the long history of Christian thought," nevertheless "sharply contrasts with the accepted Christian theology of the past 1500 years."[29] Both Irenaeus and Augustine considered sexual passion a *consequence* of the fall rather than an ingredient in it, since both of them interpreted the fall as the literal eating of an actual fruit. However, both of them failed to explain why the eating of a fruit should lead to concupiscence manifested as *lust* rather than *gluttony*. Kierkegaard objected to these traditional views (which attributed the fall primarily to pride or selfishness), since they said nothing about "the significance of the sexual." Kierkegaard preferred to describe the fall as a transition from innocent sensuousness to explicit sexuality under the influence of the anxiety provoked by the possibility of sinning.[30] In its association of the fall with sexuality, the Unification view is closer to Kierkegaard's than to Augustine's or Irenaeus's. However, sexuality itself is not evil in the Unification view, but is part of God's original plan for an ideal world. Only the *misuse* of sexual love is evil.

Notes

1   *Wol-li Kang-ron* (Seoul, Korea: Segye Kidokyo Tongil Shillyong Hyophwe, 1966); *Divine Principle* (New York: Holy Spirit Association for the Unification of World Christianity [HSA-UWC], 1973; 16.

2   *Divine Principle*, 43.

3   Ibid., 43–44, 101–102.

4   Ibid., 37–38, 44, 55, 59, 77, 82, 97, 100–102, 128.

5   Ibid., 41–46.

6   Ibid., 55–56.

7   Ibid., 80–83.

8   Ibid., 91–97.

9   Ibid., 76–90.

10   Ibid., 76–79.

11   Ibid., 79–80.

12   Ibid., 83–84, 167–70.

13   Herbert Richardson, "A Lecture to Students at the Unification Theological Seminary in Barrytown, New York," in *A Time for Consideration: A Scholarly Appraisal of the Unification Church*, ed. M. Darrol Bryant and Herbert Richardson (New York: Edwin Mellen, 1978), 311.

14   *Divine Principle*, 83–91.

15   Ibid., 2, 91–95, 221–23, 239.

16   Ibid., 90–91.

17   Ibid., 127–29.

18   Ibid., 99–103.

19   Ibid., 104.

20   Augustine, *The City of God*, XIV:24, 26.

21 Ibid., XI:11, 13. See also Augustine, *On Free Choice of the Will,* III:25.

22 Karl Rahner, *Theological Investigations,* trans. David Bourke (London: Darton, Longman & Todd, 1974), 11:253, 261.

23 Ibid.

24 John C. Greene, *The Death of Adam* (Ames, Iowa: Iowa State University Press, 1959), 327.

25 Frank E. Poirier, *Fossil Evidence: The Human Evolutionary Journey,* 2d ed. (St. Louis, Mo.: C. V. Mosby, 1977), 298.

26 Augustine, *The City of God,* XIII:20, 23, 24; XXII:30. See also *The Enchiridion,* XXVIII; and *On Free Choice of the Will,* III:22, 24.

27 Irenaeus, *Against Heresies,* III:22.4. See also *Proof of the Apostolic Preaching,* XIV.

28 Paul Ricoeur, *The Symbolism of Evil,* trans. Emerson Buchanan (Boston: Beacon, 1967), 28, 246–49, 255.

29 Francis Clark, "The Fall of Man in *Divine Principle,*" in *Ten Theologians Respond to the Unification Church,* ed. Herbert Richardson (New York: Unification Theological Seminary, 1981), 149–52.

30 Soren Kierkegaard, *The Concept of Dread,* trans. Walter Lowrie (Princeton: Princeton University Press, 1957), 29, 39, 42–72, 82.

7 The Fall in *Divine Principle*
DURWOOD FOSTER

One of the most salient theological elements in *Divine Principle* is the doctrine of the fall—that is, of what originally went wrong with and still essentially despoils the world.[1] In what follows I propose to examine this doctrine in comparison with traditional and current mainstream Christian teachings, providing for assessment of the coherence and value of the specific Unification contribution at this pivotal thematic point.

The fall has classically symbolized the fact that, in every moment of their present existence, human beings both individually and corporately find themselves already overtaken by guilty deviance from what ought to be. This deviance, since it is a *fait accompli,* can only be referred antecedently to an original derangement that precedes and thereby universally determines the present human world. On the other hand, as guilty deviance it has simultaneously the character of a continuous mode of being in which all responsibly participate. A fundamental tension thus inheres in the symbol between primordial facticity, which alone would be fate, and contemporaneous complicity, which alone would be sin simply as such. Original sin gains its peculiarity as a notion by dialectically fusing this fate and this guilt, reciprocally qualifying each by the other.

Wherever the original derangement is placed in the scheme of being and/or history, it is logically necessary to posit as antecedent to it an unfallen creation. Here we note that *Divine Principle* emphatically agrees with historic Judaism and Christianity in affirming the omnipotence of the all-wise God and therewith the primordial goodness of creation as expressed in Genesis 1:31: "And God saw everything he had made and, lo, it was very good." This complex of ideas, combined with a deep sense of something wrong with the world, both requires and is required by a strong doctrine of the fall. No such doctrine is needed if evil is either negligible or is consistent with the fundamental nature of things—that is to say, is necessary. A doctrine of the fall, therefore, is a statement that evil is seriously real and yet unnecessary, which is also to say: susceptible of ultimate rectification and removal. It is in this way that original sin is not really a pessimistic doctrine, but in the last analysis forms a chord with eschatological hope—which has been a dominant force in Unificationism.

Because modern thought finds no place for primeval unfallenness as a segment of real history, much contemporary theology has wanted to think of creation as originally falling away from ideal possibility rather than from actual goodness. But possibilities, to be responsibly actualized, must inhere in an actual subject or subjects. On the other hand, original goodness cannot be construed—despite traditional portrayals of unfallen Adam and Eve as paragons of virtue—as exclusively actual. If original humanity were already perfect, with no unresolved possibilities, it could not fall. Therefore, the unfallen state of original goodness must in fact be conceived—whether in empirical history or in a kind of prehistory—as a *mixture* of actuality and possibility. It is a merit of the view put forward in *Divine Principle* that this is recognized: the fall of Eve and Adam occurs in their "growth period"; they are posited as actual but inchoate subjects of decision, not yet fully realized. This agrees with what is known of human evolution. Original perfection must be read as original perfectibility. For as Schleiermacher emphasizes, the actual creation of humankind becomes perfect only in Christ,[2] and therein of course only at an *individual* point—a view which *Divine Principle* incorporates in projecting further states of familial perfection and world dominion. It is of a piece with Schleiermacher's insight to hold with Ritschl that all sin is conditioned by ignorance and thus forgivable and finally rectifiable: with the sole exception of the "sin against the Holy Ghost."[3] This latter is the completely mature sin, the final state of "hardening," where no more unresolved possibility remains. It comes only, if at all, at the end of history and posits the figure of the Antichrist as its prime subject. Broadly, *Divine Principle*'s purview is in agreement. It leaves open whether an ultimate condemnation—particularly that of Satan, who then would be in the position of the Antichrist—must in fact occur.

In accord with the foregoing it is plausible to envisage the fall as continuously occurring throughout history, in the tense of the Greek imperfect—a happening already fully initiated but not terminated. With the possible exception of the very beginning, original sin is in this sense assignable to every moment of human life and yet *confinable* to no moment or series of moments. This registers the pervasive complicity in the guilt whereby "sin is in each the work of all and in all the work of each" (Schleiermacher), [4] the *sinful* aspect being the willful acquiescence wherein each individual recapitulates the paradigm of Genesis 3, the *original* aspect being each individual's radical dependence, retrospectively and prospectively, upon the social nexus of moral worth and guilt. For progeny make their ancestry guilty no less than the other way around. *Divine Principle,* for its part, evinces a strong sense not only of the interconnection of moral liability but also of the continual incursion into history's course of fresh human default (e.g., Abraham's failure to cut the doves [Gen. 15:10–13]).[5] Thus the original lapses, not only of Eve and Adam, but also of Cain, of Moses, of John the Baptist—and surely, in more piddling measure, of all the rest of us (except those who bear the office of Christ)—extend and compound the common condition of fallenness characterizing our human mutuality.

While it is imperative not to forget that a restorative force with which we may cooperate is also at work, nevertheless, the human race emerges on this view as a mass of perdition. In this mass, comprising the biological as well as psychic, social, legal, and spiritual plenum of humanity, the poles of individuation and participation *both* retain categorical integrity, so that it is as wrong to think of the individual as discretely and exclusively responsible for anything as it is to think of him or her as unresponsibly subsumed into the generality per se. Individual and collective guilt are both valid, just as each of us is subject to both freedom and destiny. Historically, the dialectic here has been expressed in the debate between "creationism" and "traducianism," maintaining respectively the origin of the individual *de novo* and his/her devolvement as an extension of ancestry. No adequate view of the human situation can dispense with the relative truth of either of these poles. In this connection, while not losing the sense of ancestral and corporate liability, *Divine Principle* accents well the individual "portion of responsibility."

A problem in the conception of original sin is how to understand its transmission and pervasive inherence in the human plenum without annulling its moral character or flying in the face of contemporary knowledge. In current theology this problem is by no means solved—partially because of the question whether the human species can be reasonably construed as originating through a single common ancestry. The Catholic Church has, at least until recently, insisted upon monogenesis, whereas modern Protestant theologians have wanted to find some way of divesting the strictly bio-anthropological issue of theological significance. *Divine Principle* is of course *prima facie* committed to monogenesis, and it is an open question—one strategically crucial for future development—how open Unificationism may be, at this point as well as *überhaupt,* to demythologizing reinterpretation. Towards the overarching issue, *Divine Principle*'s attitude appears to vary—prompting the question (which, presumably, will one day be more fully unpacked than it has been so far) of the *unity* of the text. That is to say, sometimes *Divine Principle* seems to evince an unbroken literalism that could have emerged as well before as after the eighteenth century, the account of the fall being a prime example of this. On the other hand, sometimes a more sophisticated hermeneutic asserts itself and it is suggested that exegesis must "satisfy the intellect of modern men," as in the account of the Resurrection.[6] In papers prepared for this colloquy, it will be of particular interest to experience how Unificationists are prepared to wrestle with the literalism in *Divine Principle*'s envisagement of the fall. The struggle that faces them at this point is, of course, one in which all modern theology is embroiled.

If a polygenetic origin of *homo sapiens* should be acknowledged as possible or probable, Unificationism would still presumably want to assert, along with traditional Christian theology, the unity of humankind in original sin. For, as things presently stand, the envisagement of and the recipe for salvation are largely framed and grounded in the diagnosis symbolized by the fall. It could be questioned, though, whether this need imply a uniformity of chronological antecedence, such as common ancestors. Would it not be conceivable to ground a prescription for human unification upon, for example, the clear and present danger of nuclear annihilation? The appeal of such Unification projects as the International Conference on the Unity of the Sciences and that of the Assembly of the World's Religions would seem to lie in a sense of common peril as well as common promise for the enhancement of human life. Mutual human fulfillment can be well represented by the symbol of God's kingdom. Would not the cogency of its positive lure, as well as the palpable impediments (such as racism, sexism, and the oppression of the poor) which do or may thwart it, remain what they are regardless of whether humanity has evolved from one or several sources? The fall would still express the mutual complicity—viewed now as a continuous all-inclusive happening—

in which merging and coalescing humanity stands against the judgment and grace of God's approaching kingdom.

Whether or not a single ancestry of human life is posited, there is the pluralism of cultures which has become an obsession in recent theology. Christian thinkers are now attempting to deal with this pluralism more adequately than in the past, and the Unification movement also appears sensible of the need to incorporate, in a complete envisagement of the human story, the histories now missing from *Divine Principle* (e.g., Africa). In such a conspectus it goes without saying that the great non-Christian religions must have a place. Each of these has its own view of the primal human problem, along with its own mythic rendition(s) of how this originates. Is it not probable that each, for its own matrix, throws some light on the fall or what corresponds thereto—if not on the absolutely primordial lapse of an Eve and Adam common to all, yet on determinative paradigmatic events in the shaping of this or that culture? Surely the complete reality of the fall is the compound of all the various cultural tributaries of human evil when these stand finally over against the kingdom—or, as Kierkegaard says, the Christ (who embodies the kingdom).[7] It would be surprising if the myths residual to these tributaries had nothing to contribute to the overall understanding of evil. Thus what a theologian like John Cobb today learns from the Buddhist construal of the human problem bodes well to make his Christian harmatology more universal.[8] And while *Divine Principle*'s account of the fall is one salient rendition among others, the meta-institutional dynamism of Unificationism, drawing in dialogically many intercultural insights, provides encouraging opportunities for widening and deepening the diagnosis of the human plight. In this connection it would be interesting to trace in the ongoing interpretive rescensions of *Divine Principle*—the Level 4 and Level 5 formats as well as the systematic thematizations of Young Oon Kim, Jonathan Wells, and others—to what extent an influence of dialogical interaction may be discernible; but such an inquiry is beyond the scope of the present paper.

Another problem in the conception of original sin is its mode of transmission or of structural efficacy, that is to say, the dynamics by which the effect of the fall is exerted throughout the human plenum. Elements of understanding employed by historic Christianity—and also by *Divine Principle*—to deal with this problem include: imputed guilt, active infection through genetic continuity, and volitional bondage to Satan. Modern theology has partly interpreted, partly supplemented these notions—and also widely abandoned them—through insights into socio-economic alienation stemming from Marx, and into depth-psychological distortion described by Freud and Jung. Let us parse briefly each of the mentioned elements.

Imputed guilt, which has often been attacked as an absurd and immoral notion—which it would be if the human individual were a totally detached unit of responsibility—is illuminated by the deep-seated mutual complicity of classes, generations, races, and sexes in exploitative constructs of the economic and political as well as ideological milieu which molds, subserves, and expresses individual identity. We *are* in other words our heredity and our interpersonal connectivity. We today *are*—as traducians maintain—an expression of the germ tissue, and so far as Jung is right, the psychic archetypology of those proto-humans who genocidally eliminated their competitors (the "missing links") during the fore-dawn of history—not to mention what has happened since.[9] We also *are* the socially defined roles we have taken on, the commonly determined language that mediates even our inmost self-consciousness, and (both as recipients and agents) the subjective side of the exploitative oppression built into our political and economic systems. Thus the guilt of original sin imputable to the whole of humanity is not a matter of irrational arbitrariness. "Therefore," as *Divine Principle* says, "in order to be restored through indemnity, man must reverse his fallen nature endowed at the creation, by practicing God's will. . . . Man himself must set up the due condition of indemnity by fulfilling his own portion of reponsibility."[10] This notion of the "consoling" of God by humanity is functionally parallel—and in some ways connotatively superior—to St. Anselm's "satisfaction" of divine honor, which has played a central role in tradition (along with its distorted variant, "penal substitution").[11] Anselm admonished that one who failed to see the guilt and atonement at stake here had "not yet considered the gravity of sin."[12] So far as a great deal of modern theology has lost the meaning of this historic theme, *Divine Principle* may be seen as offering a wholesome restatement of the seriousness of our common culpability. Unification theology might well make use of Marxian and Freudian insights in this connection. But insofar as the culpability can only be measured finally by our collective violation and unfulfillment of divine will (the overarching ground and purpose of creation), *Divine Principle*'s salient God-centeredness figures to remain a conspicuous asset.

While imputed guilt expresses what is owed to the original and essential telos of humanity as grounded in God, the perduring actuality of original sin has classically been represented as a systemic contagion within the human plenum which unavoidably infects every individual (requiring the Christ, if he is to be exempted from the general condition, to be born of an immaculately conceived virgin). With respect to the conceptual imagery available for such representation, an intrinsic tension exists between notions that stress the distortion of natures, and hence haplessness of will, and notions that register the acquiescing participation of will required for responsibility. Insofar as both poles (fate and act) are fused in the peculiar notionality of original sin, *Divine Principle* is notable for its interweaving of them. It espouses the bold image of "evil blood and flesh" deriving from Eve's contamination by intercourse with Satan (which she passed on to Adam by becoming "one body" with him).[13] "Until the present era," we read, "not a single man has known the root of sin" as thus disclosed.[14] Intriguing questions about the emphasis upon transmission through a polluted "blood lineage"[15] are (a) how literally this may once have been taken in the beginnings of the Unification movement—in correlation, for example, with the rumored ritual of *pikarume* ("blood cleansing"),[16] and (b) what degrees of deliteralization have since ensued—so that today the engrafting within a purifying messianic "bloodstream" is conceived spiritually but not literally—except possibly for Reverend Moon's very own progeny.[17] Development in the latter direction would reinforce the pole of volitionality, or moral act, in the overall representation of original sin. In any event, it is not to be left out of the account that already in *Divine Principle* the "elements" Eve received from Satan and passed on to Adam are said to be a "sense of fear" stemming from a "guilty conscience" and "wisdom."[18] Making no reference whatever to blood or genetic tissue, this particular pericope in *Divine Principle* bolsters strongly the moral-spiritual dimensionality of the fall. Guilty fear induced by dawning insight into humanity's true end is a graphic portrayal of the consciousness that reports itself in the symbolization of original sin. But how does *Divine Principle* intend the seemingly literalistic imagery of the contaminated bloodstream—for which modern genetics raises formidable problems—to correlate with the psychological-spiritual description of the "inherited elements"? This is one of the points at which further inquiry into the unity of the text is indicated.

The motif of volitional bondage to Satan is naturally not wholly separable from either the actual infection of sin or imputed guilt; in a sense it combines their thrusts, embodying as it does both fateful enslavement to sin as a standing condition and volitional conformity therewith as guilt. Satan is the willful deviation from creational purpose so far as this deviation can or must be conceived as extra-humanly centered and grounded. If with Whitehead we think of every actual occasion as involving a prehension primitively analogous to will, one in which (as quantum theory suggests) an initial contingency inheres, it is not implausible to symbolize whatever disparity marks off the whole concourse of creation from God's purpose as satanic will. The realm subtended by this disparity is the kingdom of Satan, which, though it ontologically lives from, also opposes the kingdom of God. In some ways, of course, the collectivity of perversities opposing God's will is not centered—and is thus better described as "legion."[19] But in other respects, as in a cancer, the Nazi state, or an exploitative economic system, evil is organically unified—is, as Tillich says, a "structure of destruction";[20] and the more this is the case, the more apt the symbol of Satan becomes. Such a symbol has been useful in thematizing original sin for two main reasons: to express the transcendental coherence of the general disposition to sin, and to supplement the explanation of how this disposition first arises. Since, in Kierkegaard's phrase, "sin posits itself," in depicting its occurrence in Eve and Adam a *prius* is suggested. Of course, in Satan too the self-positing recurs, since it belongs to the nature of sin that it cannot be causally derived. The effort to ground even Satan's fall *ab initio* leads in *Divine Principle*—exactly as in Karl Barth—to construing it as a "by-product of the original nature of creation, like the shadow of a thing produced by the light."[21] However, this is a denaturing of sin, which *qua* sin can have no logical justification. To refer its mystery antecedently to Satan is plausible, since human decisionality arises—no doubt at first inchoately—from the entire nexus of the pre- and extra-human. But the mystery must be preserved there, if sin is sin, and the concomitant responsibility of humankind be maintained. In *Divine Principle,* if not the former, at least the latter is clearly intended.

For biblical monotheism it is axiomatic that Satan, like humankind, be construed as originally or essentially good. It would be plausible, as also in the human case, if the fall of Satan (or Lucifer—*Divine Principle*'s name for Satan's original goodness) should occur in his (or her) "growth period," that is, within cosmic maturation or development. There is some suggestion to this effect in *Divine Principle*, in that the archangel, created to serve humanity, never (yet) exercises that function, but deviates into iniquity, as it were, on the way to it. This makes more sense than a Satan perfect from the beginning in maturity and function. It allows more intelligibly for what *Divine Principle* at one point envisages as the final surrender of Satan and hence his conceivable restoration as Lucifer, servant of God and humanity.[22] Thus, the recalcitrant forces of universal process would be brought back again from their medial diremption into an ultimate reconciliation—the *apokatastasis* foreseen by Origen.[23] Contrariwise, the final apocalyptic would possibly be the eternal fall of Satan, the resolute choice (coterminous with ultimate human hardening) to be damned by God. Neither *Divine Principle* nor Christian tradition generally wants this to transpire, though both confront here an eschatological dilemma of freedom against love.

In *Divine Principle* the magnitude of Satan seems to vacillate, as it does also in historic Christianity. Distinct strands in Christian theology have estimated Satan very incongruently, and many modern theologians have dispensed with the symbol altogether. At the same time, nowadays occult and even popular cinematic images of Satan project him or her more powerfully than God. In *Divine Principle* it is hard to understand why a being created to serve humanity would be invested with the range of potentialities imputed to Lucifer, such as jealousy and wrongful love. Even more inexplicable is the power Satan acquires, power—and cleverness—which so far in history seem almost to outdo God's. Given the openendedness of history, does *Divine Principle*'s outsized projection of Satan's resiliency permit reasonable hope in divine victory? Traditional Christianity has believed Satan was in principle decisively conquered—and the fall likewise in principle (that is, in beginning and power) overcome—in the Cross and Resurrection of Christ. *Divine Principle*, on the other hand, sees the Cross as a satanic victory. As is perhaps par for the course theologically, the grimness of its fall may well be too much for anyone who does not grasp the credibility of its hope.

In Christian history, the conception of Satan's dominance over the fallen world has ever and again resulted in a crass dichotomy between the satanic community and the redeemed community of God. This dichotomy was, however, significantly qualified in many theologians by the imputation of "prevenient grace" as a factor considerably alleviating the ruin of original sin and providing a foundation for moral distinctions in the world at large.[24] In contemporary theology, the widespread revulsion against exclusivistic triumphalism has strengthened the affirmation of the non-Christian and the indictment of the professedly Christian world almost to the extent of annulling any difference between these. Unificationism, for its part, seems to evince at least two opinions. On the basis of *Divine Principle*, it posits—in much of its praxis—a very sharp dichotomy between God's side and Satan's, between the Abel and the Cain position, between the unified family of the blessed and the unblessed. On the other hand, also on the basis of elements of *Divine Principle*, it sees Heavenly Providence at work throughout history, the Abel and Cain positions as easily interchangeable, the victory of Satan in would-be servants of God (like John the Baptist) and potential allies for the preparation of the kingdom in a wide spectrum of friends regardless of doctrine. A tension thus exists between, let us say, the recruitment centers on the one hand and the International Cultural Foundation/New ERA and the International Religious Foundation events on the other. How this tension will resolve itself is not yet apparent. So far the interior commitment seems to energize wholesomely the exoteric outreach and dialogue, though the theoretical reasons for this remain obscure.

In thematizing the fall, historic Christianity has envisaged its principal modes as unbelief, pride, and concupiscence. The so-called "seven deadly sins" and other analyses have further spelled out the morphology of sinfulness; and while individual theologians have leaned one way or another in emphasis, a wholistic balance has usually been struck in portraying the existentiality of sin. For its part, Unificationism has created the impression of concentrating very narrowly in its understanding of the fall upon illicit sexuality or adultery. It is important to see clearly here that it is not sexuality per se, which in its rightful exercise in the God-centered family is exalted, but premature and iniquitous sexuality which is indicted as the cardinal sin. Even so, it would be an egregious foreshortening of the fall to concentrate exclusively on sexuality as the locus of sin. Actually, *Divine Principle* does not do this consistently or for the most part. The sins it describes throughout the course of history are certainly not only, and frequently not mainly, sexual sins. But more crucially, original sin, especially in the case of Lucifer/Satan, is portrayed first of all as prideful jealousy and lust for power. As dominated by Satan, this mode of sinfulness and its attendant guilt become our own, compounding with the concupiscent lust that also was Satan's and becomes our own. Thus, *Divine Principle*, cumulatively and in the large, is more wholistic and adequate in describing the mode of the fall than it frequently is held to be. This greater wholism does not detract from but should reinforce the significance of the special thematization of sexuality—which realistically resonates with Freudian and other contemporary insights. For stripped of the wider context (of insight into unbelief, unlove, pride, and envy), the sexual concentration tends to become legalistic and repressive. The arrangement of *Divine Principle*'s presentation strikes an outsider as perhaps at fault here. A more adequate synthesis seems needed of the various sections expounding the fall. Pending that, an interconnective interpretation of the separated themes, relating them to current socio-economic and depth-psychological thought, would hold great interest. To such interpretations, one trusts, the Nassau colloquy will contribute.

Notes

1 *Divine Principle*, 5th ed. (New York: Holy Spirit Association for the Unification of World Christianity [HSA-UWC], 1977).

2 Friedrich Schleiermacher, *The Christian Faith,* ed. H. R. Mackintosh and J. S. Stewart (Edinburgh: T & T Clark, 1928), 256, 411, *passim.*

3 Albrecht Ritschl, *The Christian Doctrine of Justification and Reconciliation; The Positive Development of the Doctrine,* ed. H. R. Mackintosh and A. B. Macauley (Edinburgh: T & T Clark, 1900), 375, 383, *passim.* The "sin against the Holy Spirit" is referred to in Mark 3:29.

4 Schleiermacher, 288.

5 Cf. *Divine Principle*, 268ff.

6 Ibid., 165. We read that the biblical prophecy of resurrection in its literal form "cannot satisfy the intellect of modern men," which calls for a non-literal exegesis.

7 Soren Kierkegaard, *Concluding Unscientific Postscript,* trans. D. F. Swenson and Walter Lowrie (Princeton: Princeton University Press, 1944), 516–18.

8   John B. Cobb, Jr., *Christ in a Pluralistic Age* (Philadelphia: Westminster, 1975).

9   Cf. Carl Sagan, *The Dragons of Eden* (New York: Random House, 1977), for an intriguing overview of the prehistoric genocide that accompanied the emergence of *homo sapiens* as dominant species.

10   *Divine Principle*, 226–27.

11   Anselm's classic theory is set forth in his *Cur Deus Homo*. This is available in *St. Anselm,* trans. S. N. Deane (LaSalle, Ill.: Open Court, 1945), 171f. Connotatively, the notion of "satisfying the divine honor" has been associated with the medieval knight's attainment of satisfaction through apology or a tantamount humiliation of the offender. Here the principal consideration is in any case analogically the vindication of something positive in God, which the so-called penal substitutionary theory obscures by focusing on the imposition of a specified punishment. However, *Divine Principle*'s notion of the "consoling" of God accords more fully with the primacy of the divine parental love which is foremost for biblical faith.

12   Anselm, 228. Deane's rendering is "not as yet estimated the great burden of sin."

13   *Divine Principle*, 74, 80.

14   Ibid., 88.

15   Ibid.

16   For an objective scholarly reference to the allegation regarding *pikarume,* cf. D. W. Bromley and A. D. Shupe, Jr., *Moonies in America* (Beverly Hills: Sage, 1979), 48–49. *Pikarume* itself apparently refers specifically to sexual intercourse. That such a ritual was ever part of the movement is strenuously denied by Unificationists.

17   It seems intriguingly to be the case that, along with the spiritual-symbolic engrafting accorded to the generality of the Unification membership, there is still imputed to Reverend Moon's own family a special sanctity of privilege and procedure. For example, the marriage of the children of Moon and Hak Ja Han has not followed the pattern of Unification marriage generally. Whether this will also be the case with the children of the blessed couples in general remains to be seen.

18   *Divine Principle*, 79.

19   Cf. Mark 5:9; Luke 8:30.

20   Tillich develops this theme in *Das Dämonische,* in vol. 6 of *Gesammelte Werke* (Stuttgart: Evangelisches Verlagswerk, 1963), cf. esp. 44–46.

21   *Divine Principle*, 90. Cf. Karl Barth *Church Dogmatics,* III, 3 (Edinburgh: T & T Clark, 1961), esp. 351ff.

22 On the surrender of Satan, cf. *Divine Principle*, 236–37.

23 Cf. Origen, *De Principiis,* available in *The Ante-Nicene Fathers* (Grand Rapids, Mich.: Eerdmans, 1951), 4:260–61, 275.

24 A notable example of such employment of the notion of prevenient grace is found in the theology of John Wesley. Cf. the exposition of this point in Colin Williams, *John Wesley's Theology Today* (Nashville: Abingdon, 1960), 39–46.

8 The Unification Doctrine of the Fall and the Problem of Evil
GENE G. JAMES

One of the reasons most often given for disbelief in God is the problem of evil. Yet, paradoxically, one of the reasons most frequently mentioned for believing in God is that this helps one explain evil and suffering. Attitudes toward evil and suffering are thus at the very heart of religious belief or disbelief and every system of thought grounded in religious faith must eventually formulate a doctrine of evil and suffering if it is to be taken seriously as a theology. Although the doctrine of the fall plays a central role in Unification thought, it has not up to this time addressed itself to the problem of evil in a systematic manner. One indication of this is the small number of references in Unification thought to the classic treatment of suffering in the Christian tradition, the book of Job. The fact that Unification thought has not dealt with the problem of evil does not imply that it is incapable of doing so. To the contrary, I believe that implicit in its teachings is a systematic and novel solution. My objectives in this article are to first state and then evaluate the Unification solution to the problem of evil.

The problem of evil can be stated very simply. If God is both all-powerful and totally benevolent, how can there be any evil at all? The problem may also be stated in the form of a dilemma. If God is all-powerful, then God is able to prevent evil. If God is totally benevolent, then God wants to prevent evil. But there is evil. Therefore God is either not all-powerful or not totally benevolent.

Attempts to solve the problem of evil are called theodicies. They are explanations intended to "justify the way of God to people." Some people argue that such an attempt is presumptuous and sinful. Instead of seeking to justify the ways of God to people we should be concerned with ridding ourselves of sin. Such a response is not open to anyone who accepts the *Divine Principle*, because its central goal is to explain God's nature and God's hope for humanity. Furthermore, as John Hick points out, it is the word "justify" in the description of theodicies which seems to generate the response that theodicy is an illegitimate enterprise. "Suppose we use instead the more neutral term 'understand.' Is it impious to try to understand God's dealings with humanity? Surely, if theology is permissible at all, it would be arbitrary to disallow discussion of the topics that come under the rubric of theodicy: creation, the relation of human suffering to the will of God, sin and the fall of man, redemption, heaven and hell."[1] *Divine Principle* is a theodicy because it deals with precisely these topics.

Another objection to theodicy is that it deals with a purely intellectual problem. One should spend one's time trying to do something about evil and suffering, it is said, not just talking about them. The genuinely religious life is not one of theorizing, it is one of committed action. This response is also not open to someone who believes in *Divine Principle*. Two of its central teachings are that there is no conflict between reason and faith and that practice must be guided by theory. One can best deal with evil and suffering if one understands why God allows them to occur.

Some people have attempted to avoid the problem of evil by maintaining that evil and suffering are illusions. However, this position cannot be taken by anyone who accepts the Christian scriptures. "In these writings there is no attempt to evade the clear verdict of human experience that evil is dark, menacingly ugly, heart-rending, crushing. And the climax of this biblical history of evil was the execution of Jesus of Nazareth."[2] Unificationists not only accept the reality of evil and suffering, they believe in both the objective existence of Satan and the suffering of God.

There is a long tradition which stems from Augustine that claims that although we experience evil it is not anything positive, but is only the absence of good. It is pointed out that for anything to have certain qualities it must lack others. Evil is then said to be only the absence of perfection. Blindness, for example, is evil. But it is not something existing in its own right; it is merely the absence of sight. Everything that exists is good because it was created by God. The problem with this kind of view is that pain and suffering do not seem to be merely the absence of pleasure. Nor are cruelty and hatred simply the absence of love or kindness. Evil, therefore, has positive existence; it is not just the absence of good. Unificationists would apparently not deny this since they believe in the demonic as an active force in history.

Unificationists hold both that Satan is genuinely evil and that everything created by God was good. Does this mean then that they are duelists? There are many passages in Unification literature in which history seems to be conceived of as a struggle between two eternal, equally powerful beings. However, closer reading reveals that Satan's existence is dependent on God. *Divine Principle* is quite explicit regarding this:

> A question we must resolve ... is whether the serpent existed before the time of the creation.... If this serpent was a being in existence before creation with a purpose contrary to that of God, the struggle between good and evil ... would be inevitable and eternal. God's providence of restoration would be disproven. We cannot avoid the conclusion, therefore, that the spiritual being, likened to a serpent, was a being originally created for the purpose of goodness who later fell and was degraded to become Satan.[3]

Unificationists are aware that "since the Age of Reason, more and more Christians have attempted to describe original sin and the fallen nature of mankind without reference to the work of a personal demonic power."[4] They nevertheless think that if one's faith is to be grounded in the New Testament, then one must believe that "Satan is not simply a poetic name for the impersonal fact of evil. We rather encounter him as a person, a conscious power with a will, purpose and the ability to make his influence felt."[5]

Satan was created to serve human beings but became jealous when he learned that God intended to give people earthly dominion. Although God did not love Satan less after the creation of man and woman, Satan believed that God did. Satan also became passionately attracted to Eve. Motivated by both a desire to lower human beings in God's esteem and his attraction for Eve, Satan succeeded in seducing her. Eve then realized she had been intended for Adam, developed a guilty conscience and became fearful of God. She therefore "seduced Adam in the hope that she might rid herself of the fear derived from the fall and stand before God by becoming ... one body with Adam who was meant to be her spouse."[6] Satan's temptation of Eve and her subsequent actions totally disrupted God's plans for creation. Furthermore, Satan is still active, tempting people, and working to undermine God's purpose.

Why was Satan successful in seducing Eve? To understand the

Unification answer to this question one must examine both what they say about Satan's methods and their view of human nature. One of Satan's essential characteristics, says Young Oon Kim, is that he is a deceiver. "The devil never says, 'I will teach you how to sin.' Instead, he says to a person, 'I'll show you something interesting, pleasurable or enriching.'"[7] "He exploits an innate tendency of human nature: our openness to temptation."[8] His foothold, Kim states, is "Myself, my ambitions, pride, passions and egocentricity. The devil lodges inside the heart because of a person's self-love." However, in sinning "we are not simply slaves of an alien master, but willing subjects. By loving ourselves, we deliver ourselves over to satanic bondage. The responsibility is our own." Even though the responsibility is our own "we soon discover that we are in the grip of a hostile power which is so strong that we cannot break its hold on us." It is because we are unable to free ourselves by our own efforts that we must look to God for help in obtaining salvation.

If God is both all-powerful and totally benevolent, why did He allow the fall, which brought suffering to people and disrupted God's plans for creation? "This," says Young Oon Kim, "has been one of the thorniest problems for theologians." Unification theology, she goes on to state, "suggests that this problem of theodicy must be treated in terms of four factors: human freedom, the power of love, the immaturity of Adam and Eve at the time of the fall, and man's intrinsic dignity as lord of creation."[9] To understand the role these four factors play in Unification theodicy we must first understand how Unificationists conceive God and his purpose for creation.[10]

God is conceived in Unification thought as "the creator of all things. He is absolute reality eternally self-existent . . ."[11] However, God is not just an impersonal metaphysical absolute. God is a personal God, a loving father. The most essential attribute of God according to Unificationists is "heart." Heart is defined as "the impulse that seeks joy through loving someone or something. It is not the same as emotion . . . Heart manifests itself in love, which is not merely a sentimental emotion or a romantic longing—but a purposeful activity which serves, benefits and invigorates someone or something."[12] Since heart is purposeful activity which seeks to benefit another, God created the universe in order to experience joy by sharing God's love. However, love is not complete unless it is reciprocated. Thus God created humans to have a personal relationship with God. "[M]an was created to be God's partner. God wanted to direct His infinite love toward mankind and to receive their full response."[13]

It follows from this way of conceiving God's nature and God's purpose in creating the universe that, "if God loves mankind then God must benefit as much from the relationship as we do. . . . God longs for the ultimate satisfaction of being accepted as a partner."[14] It follows also that God can experience disappointment and grief. God suffers every time people sin, every time people fail in their mission. God especially felt great sorrow when Adam and Eve fell and when Jesus was crucified.

Since Unificationists conceive of God as a loving, suffering God, they totally reject the position that either the fall or the crucifixion could have been predestined by God. Jesus' mission was not to atone for human sins by dying on the cross. "If God had sent His only-begotten Son to be punished and killed in place of sinful man, He is not at all the fatherly God Jesus believed in."[15] Neither the fall nor the crucifixion were part of God's plan; to the contrary, they both frustrated the divine hope for creation.

This brings us back to the question: If God is all-powerful and a loving God, why does God allow events to occur which frustrate God's purpose? If God experiences grief and suffering, does this mean that God is impotent to prevent events which are counter to God's own will? Unless Unification theodicy can provide plausible answers to these questions, it should be considered inadequate.

The first of the four factors Professor Kim mentions as relevant to answering these questions is human freedom. Because God desired that His own love be freely returned, God created man and woman with free will. "If we lack free will, we become mere robots, puppets controlled from outside. To believe that is to turn Christianity into fatalism. . . . Hence, it is important to affirm man's liberty as well as God's sovereignty."[16] Indeed, according to Unification theology, God not only created man and woman with free will, God created them to be a *partner in creation*. "The characteristic possessed by all human beings which most nearly resembles God, and which most distinctly sets them apart from the rest of the creation, is *creativity*."[17] This is what Unificationists mean in speaking of humans as the lords of creation, another of the factors mentioned by Kim.

Human freedom and creativity not only apply to the external universe, they extend to human character. People are responsible for what they make of themselves: "Adam was created to be lord of creation.... To be fully qualified for that position, he had to rely on his own powers of judgment in perfecting his heart according to God's image. God waits until man learns how to govern himself before He lets him govern the whole world. In this way God wants man to share in His creative work."[18]

Because the person plays a role in the formation of his or her character he or she is not mature at creation but must go through a growth period. "[I]n order for any creature to be perfected, it must grow to maturity through the three orderly stages of 'formation', 'growth' and 'perfection'."[19] People are not an exception to the rest of creation in undergoing a growth period. "The universe did not suddenly come into being without a lapse of time, but it took considerable time for the generation of the universe to take place."[20] The description of creation given in the Bible, "is in accord with the evolutionary sequence ... known to modern scientists."[21] Humans are unique, however, in that as lords of creation they share in perfecting themselves. Since man or woman is a free creative being, his or her "perfection is ... not a static condition but a dynamic one.... To be perfect is ... to realize one's true being as a child of God.... Perfection refers to simplicity of intention and purity of affection."[22]

Unificationists stress immaturity and lack of perfection in explaining Adam's and Eve's fall: "Why did the first human ancestors fall? They fell during their growth period, while they were still immature. If man had fallen after he had become a perfect embodiment of goodness, the goodness itself would be imperfect. Accordingly, we would have to reach the conclusion that God, the absolute subject of goodness, is also imperfect."[23]

Adam and Eve were imperfect because their love was misdirected. They should have centered their lives on God and carried out God's plans. Eve, for instance, knew that she should obey God's commands but her attraction for Satan was too strong. She also engaged in an act of misdirected or unprincipled love in seducing Adam. "A man and a woman should experience full union of love ... only after their individual love for God has become unconditional."[24] It is not freedom which leads to sin, then, but incorrect desire. "Despite the fact that freedom allowed Eve to respond to the angel, leading her to the ... fall, it was by no means freedom but the power of non-principled love that made her overstep the line ..."[25]

Why then did God not prevent the fall? *Divine Principle* answers that to have done so would have been to interfere with man's and woman's freedom, to rob them of their creativity and deny their responsibility. Had God done this, God would have been going counter to God's own purpose in creating humans in the first place. "God . . . would be ignoring the principle of creation, in which He exalts man as the dominator of all things by giving him a creative nature."[26]

At this point we encounter a seeming paradox in Unification thought. On the one hand we are told that God is omniscient; on the other that God has been repeatedly disappointed by the failure of central figures in history. *Divine Principle* also states that God is omnipotent. Yet we are informed that God's purpose can be carried out only if man and woman assume part of the responsibility for creation. How can God be both omniscient and not omniscient, omnipotent and not omnipotent?

The Unification answer to the puzzle regarding God's omnipotence is that there is a sense in which God is omnipotent and a sense in which God is not. God is omnipotent in the sense that God can bring about any logically possible state of affairs. For example, after the fall, "God could have created a new Adam and Eve if He had wished . . ."[27] God could have created them without free will so that they would have instinctively loved and obeyed God. In that case they would not have been subject to temptation and would never have acted selfishly. However, because they would lack free will, it would make no sense to praise or blame them for their actions and they could in no way be said to be responsible for their own characters. Such creatures would not be human beings. They would be, as Professor Kim states, robots or puppets.[28]

If God's purpose was to create beings with free will, then for God to have created a new Adam and Eve not subject to temptation would have been to act in such a way that God's previous actions "would have become meaningless; He would have . . . contradicted His own principles."[29] As a rational being, God is bound by God's own purposes. God does not act in ways counter to the goals God wishes to achieve. God does not act in an arbitrary fashion, but is a God of principle. This means that man and woman can rely on the same laws always being at work in nature and history.

If God is a God of principle, then there is a sense in which:

d is not omnipotent. His power is far greater than man's but it is limited by His own nature and His cosmic laws. God is not free to violate His essential relatedness because that is part of His very being. Also, man was created in such a way that he can restrict God's purpose. Our responsiveness can determine the effectiveness of God's acts in history.... Man's response to the divine initiative can either frustrate or bring to fruition the intent of God.[30]

The most radical implication which seems to follow from the Unification view is that, in creating humans, God deliberately created beings whose actions God cannot predict. If this is true, then God is not totally omniscient. "His omniscience, like his omnipotence, has to be qualified by man's free will. God does not know everything that will happen because even though He wills some result it cannot take place if we do not cooperate."[31] The suggestion is that if the human being is genuinely free, then not even God who made him or her can know exactly how he or she will behave. God is omniscient in the sense that "He knows all possibilities. Nothing we may do ever surprises Him."[32] But God does not know which possibility we will choose in a given situation.

If God is dependent on the human being to realize God's purpose in creation, but cannot predict how the person will act in a given situation, then there is an element of contingency in the universe. Things may not work out as God hopes. Unificationists, of course, have faith that God's purposes will be realized. They believe that "God's will can be hindered for a time when we do not act responsibly. However, we can be certain that God will ultimately triumph."[33] Because God is eternal, no matter how many times people fail, God will continue to challenge them. God's resolve to realize the purpose of creation never slackens.

Since God is dependent on people but never ceases to challenge them, it follows that "the aim and direction of history are absolute and decided ... but the concrete developmental process of history is shortened or extended depending on whether the providential people leading it perform their duties perfectly ..."[34] Seen this way, "history is not fully deterministic nor completely indeterministic. That is, the goal of history is predetermined while the process ... is not."

If, in the ultimate analysis, the human being is responsible for what goes on in history, then it is the human being and not God who is responsible for evil. People are, of course, constantly tempted by the devil, but if they succumb it is because of their failure to resist. They cannot blame their failure on any other being.

This does not mean that they do not need help in overcoming temptation. But, they must seek it. Persons cannot find salvation unless they first seek it. "Man himself must set up the conditions which enable God to realize His purpose for creation."[35] If a person turns away from God, failing to fulfill his or her portion of responsibility, the result is tragic for both the person and God. Man and woman and God suffer.

There is no way, from the standpoint of Unification theology, to deny the reality of evil, since it can even affect God. However, evil is in no way willed by God. In creating people with free will, God created the possibility of evil, but evil can only be actualized through human actions. Because God is all-powerful, God could have created other worlds, but God could not create a world in which there is free will without there being the possibility of evil. This can be considered a limitation of God's power only if one interprets "omnipotence" to mean power to act contrary to one's own purposes. Since God is totally benevolent, this would be for God to act in an evil fashion. But because God's most essential characteristic is heart, we can be certain that God would never do this. God is a God of principle.[36] God's omnipotence is limited by God's benevolence. This is not an external limitation, but one that is self-imposed and grounded in divine omnipotence. Even though there is evil in the world, God is nevertheless both omnipotent and totally benevolent.

Unification theology seems both consistent and plausible. However, as Unificationists are well aware, to formulate an adequate theodicy is perhaps the most difficult of all theological tasks. In the remainder of this article I shall therefore consider some objections which might be raised against Unification theodicy.

Many people would no doubt object to the frankly anthropomorphic and personal character of the Unification God. The Unification reply to this is quite simple. Although there may be problems in conceiving of God in personal terms, persons are the highest beings with which we are acquainted. "When we describe God as a person we are admitting that He is like the best we can imagine."[37]

An even larger number of people are likely to take exception to the Unification belief that Adam and Eve were actual persons and that Satan has external existence. *Divine Principle* states that creation took place in a manner consistent with the evolutionary sequence discovered by modern scientists. Modern science, however, rejects the notion of a first human pair. Would anything essential to the Unification position be given up if Adam and Eve were interpreted as symbolic figures? Since the temptations Adam and Eve felt are universal human experiences, I do not see that anything would be lost from their theodicy. However, interpreting Adam and Eve as symbolic figures would, I suspect, require significant changes in their doctrine of redemption.

A number of theologians would argue that assuming Satan to have external existence increases, rather than decreases, the problem of arriving at an adequate theodicy. John Hick may be taken as representative of these theologians. He writes:

The puzzles attending human imperfection, free will, and sin are reiterated, but not further illumined, by transferring them to a superhuman plane. Indeed, the only effect of such a transference is to throw the discussion into metaphysical regions in relation to which the already sufficient difficulties of knowing whether we are talking sense or nonsense are compounded to a point that is, literally, beyond all reason.[38]

Could Satan be interpreted symbolically without anything crucial to Unification theodicy being sacrificed? Since the role of Satan is only that of a tempter, and in the final analysis it is the human being who is responsible for sin, nothing essential would seem to be lost. If Satan sinned without there being an external tempter there is no reason to postulate one to explain human sin. This does not mean that one would have to abandon the idea of the demonic. To the extent that one's character is molded by external evil influences, one may still be "in the grip of a hostile power," and need outside help to break free. Once again, however, this might cause problems in other areas of Unification theology, especially in its philosophy of history.

Most philosophers today would quarrel with the conception of freedom which seems to underlie Unification theodicy. They would argue that freedom and predictability are not incompatible and that if God created human beings, then there is nothing that God could not know about them.[39]

Frederick Sontag has objected to the Unification concept of God on the grounds that God seems unduly limited and lacking in imagination:

It is as if God elected one plan and has no choice but to keep trying until he can make the original plan work.... He used a formula in creating man, and now he must labor through creation until he can find a way to induce men to live up to it. The whole history of Providence is the story of God trying again and again to make the formula work. He controlled creation with full power in his initial act, but paradoxically, he now seems bound by his own hard work.[40]

A sufficient answer to this objection seems to have already been stated. God, as conceived by Unification theology, is not "bound by his own hard work"; God is bound by divine benevolence, a desire to create free beings, and a concern for them once God has created them.

Sontag draws attention to another problematic feature of Unification theodicy. "Do we live in the only possible order God might have created," he asks, "or could He have created an order more conducive to our success than the one in which we live? The *Divine Principle* skips over these issues and seems to assume we live in the only order God could have ordained and that it is the best one."[41] There are at least two problems here. Unificationists seem to assume without argument that a world in which there is maximum freedom is the best world God could have created. This makes freedom more valuable than either human well-being or following God's will. This may be true, but it needs defense. The second problem concerns the occurrence of natural evils such as disease and the suffering of animals.

If this is the best world God could have created, why is there disease and pain which does not seem in any way merited by those who suffer it? Unificationists believe that suffering came into the world as a result of the fall. Man and woman were intended to be masters of creation, using intelligence and creativity to share in the control of the universe. But because of sin, the human being "fell to the status of a barbarian with a spiritual sensibility as dull as that of the animals. Thus, he lost the external domination over creation."[42] The suggestion is that suffering comes about because people have failed to master creation as they should have. Just as fire may benefit or harm people, depending on their knowledge and use of it, bacteria could benefit people rather than cause disease if people only understood and controlled them. This has not occurred, because people have spent their time pursuing egoistic goals, trying to dominate one another rather than nature. People must, therefore, rid themselves of sin before they can master creation and enjoy a life free of pain. "God waits until man learns how to govern himself before He lets him govern the whole world."[43] According to Unificationists, then, although the child who suffers from cancer did not do anything to merit pain, his or her plight is nevertheless due to man and woman, not God. People collectively bring pain on themselves. Given the initial assumptions of Unification theodicy, this is a plausible doctrine. If one finds it implausible, he or she will have to quarrel with those initial assumptions.

But why do animals suffer? Since they do not have free will there is no way that they can be said to have even collectively brought it on themselves. Sang Hun Lee maintains that animals suffer because people failed to care for them as they were supposed to. "If man had not fallen, but instead had realized the Purpose of Creation, he would have dominated all things with love, preventing needless struggles among animals."[44] Thus, if people perfect themselves and assume their role as lords of creation, "the disharmony of things and even the phenomenon of the 'stronger preying upon the weaker' will disappear."[45] This leaves an important question unanswered. If God is both omnipotent and benevolent, couldn't God have prevented the suffering of innocent animals? I find no answer to this question in Unification literature.

A final objection to Unification theodicy is that because people have free will one should not be nearly so confident as Unificationists are that God's kingdom on earth will eventually be established. In the final analysis this is no doubt a matter of faith. However, it is relevant to note that their hope for universal redemption rests partially on the belief that sin is merely misdirected or non-principled love. One can therefore hope that this will some day be redirected toward God. What if sin is rooted more deeply in human nature? Suppose that at least some people have a love of cruelty for its own sake. There would then be no need to look outside people for the demonic. There would also be far less hope for human redemption.

Notes

1 John Hick, *Evil and the God of Love*, rev. ed. (New York: Harper & Row, 1978), 7.

2 Ibid., 243.

3   *Divine Principle*, 5th ed. (New York: Holy Spirit Association for the Unification of World Christianity [HSA-UWC], 1977), 70. Although *Divine Principle* refers to the Archangel as Lucifer before his fall to emphasize his original goodness, and Satan thereafter to draw attention to his fallen nature, in the interest of stylistic economy, I have referred to him as Satan throughout the present article.

4   Young Oon Kim, *Unification Theology* (New York: HSA-UWC, 1980), 107.

5   Ibid., 108.

6   *Divine Principle*, 80.

7   Kim, 109.

8   Ibid., 108.

9   Ibid., 119.

10   This account is not intended as a complete exposition of the Unification conception of God.

11   *Divine Principle*, 27.

12   Chung Hwan Kwak, "God and Creation in Unification Theology," in *God: The Contemporary Discussion*, ed. Frederick Sontag and M. Darrol Bryant (New York: Unification Theological Seminary, 1982), 87–88.

13   Kim, 61.

14   Ibid., 62.

15   Ibid., 164.

16   Ibid., 119

17   Kwak, 88.

18   Kim, 121–22.

19   *Divine Principle*, 53.

20   Ibid., 52.

21   Ibid., 51. It should be noted, however, that Sang Hun Lee denies this in *Explaining Unification Thought* (New York: Unification Thought Institute, 1981), 61.

22   Kim, 71.

23   *Divine Principle*, 54.

24   Kim, 121.

25   *Divine Principle*, 94.

26   Ibid., 96.

27   Lee, *Explaining Unification Thought*, 223.

28   This is argued by Ninian Smart in "Omnipotence, Evil and Supermen," *Philosophy* 36 (1961): 188–95.

29   Lee, *Explaining Unification Thought,* 223.

30   Kim, 67.

31   Ibid.

32   Ibid.

33   Ibid.

34   Sang Hun Lee, *Unification Thought* (New York: Unification Thought Institute, 1973), 260.

35   Kim, 231.

36   This phrase is borrowed from Frederick Sontag, "The God of Principle: A Critical Analysis," in *Ten Theologians Respond to the Unification Church,* ed. Herbert Richardson (New York: Unification Theological Seminary, 1981).

37   Kim, 66.

38   Hick, 13.

39   See, for example, Anthony Flew, "Divine Omnipotence and Human Freedom," in *New Essays in Philosophical Theology,* ed. A. Flew and A. MacIntyre (New York: Macmillan, 1955).

40   Sontag, 120–21.

41   Ibid., 119.

42   *Divine Principle,* 128.

43   Kim, 122. Unificationists believe that this is beginning to occur in our era. Professor Kim, for instance, writes that "with the astounding scientific and technological advances of our century, man is at last able to exercise effective control over nature. God's third promise to Adam is coming true." Ibid., 224.

44   Lee, *Explaining Unification Thought,* 44.

45   Lee, *Unification Thought,* 159.

9 A Good Thing Spoiled: Reflections on the Personal and Social Dimensions of Sinfulness

J. DEOTIS ROBERTS

Studies of human history confirm the prolonged history of humankind. Through this extensive stretch of time, humans have expressed in their behavior what biblical theology describes as fallenness from a more exalted ethical and spiritual status. Human sinfulness defies temporal and spatial barriers. "All have sinned" is a universal assertion which is well documented in the record of the human sojourn on earth.

We are, I believe, on safe ground in launching our discussion with this consideration firmly established. All the current discussions on "evolutionism" vs. "creationism" notwithstanding, we maintain this assertion. Whether humans evolved from lower forms of life over eons of time or whether they were created by divine fiat does not turn us from the pursuit of this point. The biblical description of the fall reflects the realism of human sinfulness well supported by the testimony of history. It is with this fact of human sinfulness in view that we move forward in our discussion.

Our subject needs a bit of unpacking. By a "good thing spoiled" we mean to describe what we view as a lapse in the human condition. Humans were created for a close relation to God, the Holy One. Through sinfulness, humans are separated from that exalted estate. Beings capable of ascending angelic heights can and often do descend into diabolical depths. In our reflections, we wish to consider both the personal and social dimensions of human sinfulness. The consequence of sin is triadic: reaching into all relations with God, the self, and other humans. By association, sin's consequence is also cosmic, having a corruptive effect upon all creation. This latter consideration will not receive treatment here. It requires thorough treatment in its own right and cannot be handled within the limits of this discussion.

The Nature of the Fall and Original Sin

Perhaps no scholar in the English speaking world during the modern period excelled F. R. Tennant in the treatment of the fall and original sin. During his Cambridge years the relation between science and theology was much discussed. He developed his thought from the insights of Darwin and Spencer. Samuel Alexander was in the same stream. Henri Bergson and others on the Continent espoused similar ideas, and Whitehead too was indebted to the same sources. Informed by the theory of evolution, Tennant brilliantly brought all his knowledge of theology, philosophy, and natural science to bear upon the discussion of human sinfulness. As a result, his contribution to our theme is considerable.

Tennant, like most British theologians, mastered the classical background. He was at home in biblical, historical, and philosophical theology. He discussed sin from these perspectives and argued with the great theologians of Christian history. He also brought the discussion home to the modern period. His grasp of evolutionary thought put him in touch with natural science, psychology, and the humanistic and artistic development of the Renaissance and beyond. With respect for the time-honored doctrine of original sin, Tennant reconceived it in more acceptable terms for the modern period. I am personally deeply indebted to him for his insights.

Sinfulness is not genetic. There are no sinners in the cradle. Therefore, a baby dying before the dawn of personal consciousness does not need to be cleansed in the waters of baptism in order to avoid hell. Humans are not born as sinners. There is no automatic transmission of sins throughout history. Humans are born into a sinful environment and only thus are they subject to the behavior of the sinful. From the dawn of personal consciousness humans are set in the context of an environment which is saturated with sin. It is thus that we are "born in sin and shaped in iniquity."

Before stating more completely the nature of sinfulness, it will be well to say something about human nature and its remaking.

Human life is often taken with impunity; it would appear to be insignificant. But the Christian faith against its biblical background views human life as the ultimate divine creation. Human beings are God's creative masterpiece. Humans are, as Augustine states, beings which God made for a closeness with the divine. Humans are "exalted" in the mind of God and have a significant place in the providence of the Maker of Heaven and Earth.

Humans may be described from different angles of vision in physical, ethical, intellectual, or spiritual terms. All of these are partial views of human nature. The Christian understanding of humanity as the *imago Dei* is holistic. Human life is precious because humans are in a unique sense "like God." Humans are a reflection of God's glory. This refers, at present, mainly to human possibility. It does not refer to what humans actually are. It rather points to what humans have been and may be. The possibility of greatness is still inherent in human beings. But because of our fallen condition, there has to be a "restoration" before the "marred image" can be restored to its exalted original status. Human nature, described as being a "little less than God" (Ps. 8:4–5) must be re-created or re-made. Human nature is "a good thing spoiled."

Sin has separated humans from God. There remains, however, the possibility that this estrangement may be overcome. The reclaiming of human nature is vividly described in chapter 15 of Luke's Gospel where the Lost Son is reunited with a loving father. Humans are estranged from God just as the son of that story was lost in the far country.

But just as the son was restored by the father's love, God the divine parent receives humans unto a new divine relationship through redeeming love. For those who have no earthly father to whom they can relate positively, God may image to them a mother or even a grandmother who demonstrates to them the best embodiment of love. What is implied in the parable is that this is how God loves us. Love unites humans with God not as strangers (those who have never met), but as those who were estranged who are reunited. God and humans belong together. Humans who are separated from the divine source of life are restless and unfulfilled.

It is true that we are mortal creatures and that we are children of nature. This, however, is not the whole story, for we are at the same time children of God. We are to affirm the goodness of creation. Creation itself comes from the hands of a good God. But physical satisfaction is not the true purpose of human life. A loving fellowship with God is the final end of human life. Blessedness for humans is manifest only in a close and saving fellowship with God, the author of life and the parent of our spirits.

Personal Sin and Salvation

Humans are not as they ought to be. Human nature as we know it falls short of its potential. Sin has to do with moral evil, but it also has to do with a broken relationship with God. Wrong conduct is an indication that something has gone wrong within. Sins of the flesh indicate sins of the spirit.

Humans are endowed with the ability to think and to exercise freedom of choice. We are given "the knowledge of good and evil." Humans have perverted all these gifts. We have said *yes* to self and *no* to God. In doing this, we have cut ourselves off from the source of life. We have sown the seeds of misery and unhappiness through our disobedience to the divine purpose for human life.

Human freedom is real. We actually make choices, and when we make them, we are accountable. We understand sin against the background of this assertion, for we are to understand sinfulness in a manner which supports human dignity as well as divine glory. If sin is inherited, the infant is *not free* not to sin. It follows that the choice of sinning or not sinning is not open to the infant. Free will and personal guilt are related, as are freedom and moral responsibility. To bear the weight of guilt and responsibility, humans must be free to choose between good and evil, right and wrong, truth and error.

We are not only free, we also have the ability to think. We are beings that are endowed with the power to reason. Aristotle's assertion that humans are "rational animals" has much truth in it. Humans do have reasoning ability. This is basic to our awareness of right and wrong, truth and falsehood. This "knowledge of good and evil" undergirded by freedom of choice is the basis for guilt and responsibility in reference to human sinfulness.

Humans are sinful by choice. Human nature is a good thing spoiled. Each person is Adam or Eve. In the presence of freedom and the knowledge of good and evil, we have chosen evil over good. We have chosen the sinful way, though a better way is both known and possible. Knowledge and freedom are available to do *better,* but we prefer to do *worse.* Sin is self-centeredness—it is willful disobedience.

Personal salvation is to be seen against this background. Human nature fallen from its original creation is to be re-created. This restoration has a human part. Repentance and faith are prerequisites for divine grace and forgiveness. Divine grace is God's unmerited favor toward human redemption. We will not discuss here the theological point as to whether this divine grace is prevenient, enabling, or cooperating. The divine part is the manifestation of divine grace, however appropriated. Fallen human nature requires "re-making" or "re-creating" if the *imago Dei* which is corrupted by sin is to be once again brought into a saving relationship with God.

Social Sin and Salvation

In preparation for a brief discussion concerning social sin and salvation, we need to say a word about the relation of sin to selfishness. Self-centeredness is perhaps a better way of stating the meaning here. We cannot estimate the terrible blight of sin upon social relations without understanding what it does to the self.

We are persons in relation to other persons. Sin as self-centeredness (selfishness) accounts for an inherent conflictual posture for persons in community. Human life in its sinful state is prone to self-glory or the idolatry of self. Sinful humanity is centered in self rather than God. This preoccupation with self leads to a brokenness in the relationship to other selves who are equally self-centered.

The sociology of sin is often overlooked in the understanding of sin as personal. Another way to state the case is to assert that sin is only a broken vertical relationship between God and the individual. The limited view of sin as individual does not account for sinful social structures. Without some awareness of the cumulative and collective dimension of sin in the social environment, we cannot comprehend the radical nature of sin as moral evil. Reinhold Neibuhr as well as Martin Luther King plumbed the depths of "immoral society." Unless we are willing to grapple with the structural nature of sin in the social order, we will never be able to break its tremendous power over communities.

We struggle consciously against the fallen "Adam within." We may even sense the conflicts between ourselves and those intimately associated with us. It is most difficult to analyze and grapple with "principalities and powers" and to deal effectively with the stranglehold which evil has over collectivities of individuals. What does it really mean "to be born in sin and shaped in iniquity"? I understand this to refer to the awesome power of evil as it is spread over masses of human beings. In this context, otherwise honest and gentle people are swept up in the throes of a violent mob. Good people who are followers of evil persons with a lot of charisma are engulfed by the floodtide of sin and evil. Only recently in liberation and political theologies have we begun to make a powerful witness in thought and faith against this dimension of sin.

Only thus may we really break the power of sin. We must have a profound understanding of this almost unlimited horizontal reach of sin and evil if we are to overcome its reign in the world.

To tackle sin on this grand cosmic scale is not to ignore the blight which sin brings to the individual life. It is rather to relate this to a realistic context. It is to come to the understanding that social transformation is essential to personal redemption. One clearly sees that God's grace requires involvement beyond one's personal well-being. The healing word of God becomes the liberating word. We are laborers with God for the eradication of the powerful reality of sin which militates not only against a proper relation with God, but corrupts the entire social, economic, and political environment so that all humanity and the whole creation long for redemption. Against this background the Cross has its meaning and the Resurrection its power.

10 The Cracked Mirror: Liberal Protestant Understandings of the Myth of the Fall
PAUL MOJZES

Purposes

The purpose of this paper is to point out how liberal Protestant theology dealt with the biblical story of the fall and to point out some of the interpretations which were forwarded by liberal theologians as they aimed to relate the biblical story to reality. Additionally, the writer's own interpretations will be presented. Finally, it will be pointed out briefly how the liberal Protestant theological understanding of the fall may be used in dialogue by such Protestant theological liberals with Marxists and then with Unification theologians. It should be stressed that this paper is intended to be a broad overview of issues rather than a carefully documented study of various theologian's views.

The Liberal Protestant Theological Posture

The liberal theological movement in Protestantism arose indigenously within Evangelical Protestantism in the nineteenth century. It attempted to liberate Christianity from dogmatic adherence to creeds and traditional theological interpretations and to offer a greater autonomy to the rational and moral elements in Christianity in its encounter with contemporary intellectual and social movements. It tried to rediscover the essentials of faith. In order to do that, many liberals felt constrained to remove outdated beliefs (i.e., beliefs which the individual theologians felt were out of line with the best scholarly and creative thinking of that time). Most liberal theologians felt that such a rediscovered Christian message needed to be expressed in contemporary terminology so as to be readily understood by contemporary people. In this attempt, many abandoned certain traditional formulations of their religion and invented new terms to express what were felt to be the abiding truths found in the traditional religion.

It must be clearly pointed out that liberal theologians never agreed on specific content, postulates, or affirmations. Theological liberalism was and remains today a method of approach. This approach consists in the willingness to apply all critical methods of investigation to all religious claims, no matter where this may lead, and in the use of reason as the final arbiter between conflicting faith claims. That experience, proposition, or hypothesis is tentatively the most truthful which passes the test of coherence; that hypothesis is best which answers the largest number of questions in a plausible manner. Hence, to dismiss one liberal theologian's views or the consensus of liberal theologians of a certain period does not invalidate liberal theology in general, unless one is to find fault with the method itself.

Two theological approaches of immediate relevance to this paper, higher biblical criticism and historical theology, brought about the onset of Protestant theological liberalism. Higher biblical criticism undertook to scrutinize the Bible by means of those scholarly methods which were being used to study and understand other ancient writings and traditions. This revolutionized biblical studies. Historical theology subjected theology to investigation and discovered that much of it was culturally conditioned. This, too, radically affected the understanding of Christian doctrines. In both instances it was the aim of liberal theology to preserve the basic tenets of the Christian faith. It sought to uncover the essentials of faith and separate them from the layers of nonessential and perhaps distorting formulations which have accrued over the ages. Liberal Protestantism was and remains a search not to abandon Christianity but to correlate it to the insights of the modern world and express this faith in a language suited to the concrete circumstances. It is believed that the core meaning of the Old and the New Testament, particularly the teachings of Jesus, have much which is relevant today. Relevancy became a central motto, along with belief in the existence of an abiding message which can be stated intelligently and convincingly.

As stated above, the central thrust to Protestant liberalism came from Christianity in the Evangelical tradition. Additionally, however, one can also discern the influence of the Enlightenment, Humanism, Transcendentalism, Darwinism, Positivistic Naturalism, the growth of secular political democracy and capitalism, the new interest in history, social and natural science, and to a very small degree even Marxism. Those liberals who espoused the "Social Gospel" were sympathetic to certain forms of socialism, but it should be noted that while almost all Social Gospellers were theological liberals, most theological liberals were not Social Gospellers. If anything, most liberals were definite contributors to individualism, and explored primarily the implications of the Gospel for the individual.

It might be said that Protestant liberals tended to accept the evolutionary theory of human development, which did not start with the premise that the human species developed from an original human pair, Adam and Eve, but rather held *homo sapiens* to have developed gradually in many regions of the world out of lower species. Since many did not think there was an Adam and Eve, many likewise thought of Jesus not as the New Adam or a perfect human being, but rather as a great watershed in history who had boundless faith in the infinite value of human beings. If there is no belief in a perfect human being then there can be no literal fall from such perfection, nor can there be a restoration to perfection. Many liberals did believe that humanity was evolving toward perfection, toward an ideal society, though many would have preferred the term "perfectibility" of the human being.[1] Original sin was either rejected or at least reinterpreted along less mechanistic lines than were prevalent in much of popular evangelical theology.

Interpretations of the Fall

The notion of the fall now needs to be explicated from a variety of perspectives found in liberal theology.

Most theological liberals believe in progress, some even in inevitable progress. In that respect they shared the notion widely held by modern people that evolutionary development takes place from lower to higher forms of life, and from lower to higher social constellations. Such progress was perceived even in religion, theology, and morality, where less developed forms gave way to better, higher notions and practices. It is not surprising that many liberal theologians found the doctrine of the fall an anachronism: it was "out of sync" with their understanding of how the universe operates, of how both nature and history work. The doctrine of the fall was consequently de-emphasized, reinterpreted, or by some totally neglected, since continuity rather than discontinuity was one of the main principles of liberal theology.

Some of the ideas which liberal theologians proposed were not altogether new. At the very time when the orthodox Christian view of the fall and of original sin was being formulated by St. Augustine, Caelestius (ca. 412), in opposition to Augustine, denied the universal consequences of Adam's sin and taught that newly-borns were perfectly innocent, hence the purpose of baptism was not for the forgiveness of sins of infants.[2] Caelestius was excommunicated!

Rationalists and Romanticists of the nineteenth century considered human beings basically good and unspoiled and vehemently rejected the notion of original sin.[3] The thinkers of the Enlightenment were not unaware of moral evil but considered absurd the idea that it would be passed from one or two persons to all their descendants.[4] To them much of modern civilization was decadent, but this decadence was the result of later artificiality, i.e., a gradual departure from the original good. They sought, in other words, answers to the origin of moral evil apart from the biblical story of the fall. As Paul Tillich pointed out, the Enlightenment thinkers carried out a strong attack on the notion of the fall, not only because they considered it too literalistic and the source of much superstition, but also because it was in "conflict with belief in the progressive improvement of the human situation on earth."[5] This humanistic view which pervaded most of liberal theology reigned until Reinhold Neibuhr showed some of its weaknesses, though Tillich's conviction was that this mood is still very much alive.

As might be expected from the earlier statement that liberal Protestant theologians generally do not agree with one another in content, they certainly did not agree in regard to the fall or to original sin. Some based their insights on the traditional orthodox Christian concepts; others were more greatly impressed by the Rationalistic, Enlightenment, and Transcendentalist denials of the traditional views.

Friedrich Schleiermacher, who is undoubtedly the father of modern Protestant theology, especially of modern liberal Protestant theology, dealt with the issue in his book, *The Christian Faith*. According to Claude Welch, Schleiermacher did not consider original sin as a past event, but a condition typical of the entire human race, which was there from the very beginning, but continues to be present in every person and in all societies. It is the human incapacity to be good, which calls for God's redemption and love prior to our ability to perform any personal moral act. For Schleiermacher, the central theme in this respect was that sinfulness is both timeless and common—a universal human condition.[6] On the other hand, he maintained that this original sin coexists with original perfection.[7]

Hegel considered the fall as a fall into history, namely into human self-alienation. He perceived, like Schleiermacher, the ambiguity of human nature being both good and evil.[8] By nature, humans are defective images of God, according to Hegel. The biblical story of the loss of innocence is symbolic of the evil which comes through disharmony when the individual, in order to come into being as an individual, separates himself or herself from the universal. Alienation is the price of being oneself.

Another nineteenth century thinker, Horace Bushnell (1802–1876), attempted to place himself between the "total depravity" of human beings and "the essential goodness" of people. He started out by stating that the Orthodox Christian claim is correct, that "every child is truly born into a world of sin and in bondage to sin."[9] But he maintained that traditional theology did not understand this concept correctly and therefore the Unitarians were forced to attack it as immoral—an attack rather justified in Bushnell's view. Sin (as well as virtue) is the product of "organic courses," by which Bushnell wanted to say that the character, feelings, principles, and the spirit of our ancestors, especially parents, are both voluntarily and involuntarily repeated by the new generation. As he stated vividly in *Discourses on Christian Nurture* (1847), for each new person "the odor of the house will always be in his garments, and the internal difficulties with which he has to struggle, will spring of the family seeds planted in his nature."[10] Claude Welch noted that Bushnell, like most Protestant liberals, did not ascribe the fall to metaphysical, but to social, psychological, and historical factors. Sin cannot be transferred because we can be responsible only for our own actions, yet, since we live in society we become corruptors of each other. In order to be virtuous one cannot simply follow one's natural inclinations; to the contrary, it seems to be an uphill struggle.

When one looks at the writings of many twentieth century liberal Protestant theologians, one tends to find little explicit treatment of the fall and of original sin, though a good deal of discussion does take place about various forms of evil, including sin. Walter Rauschenbusch, the father of the "Social Gospel," however, very emphatically believed in the biological and even more in the social transmission of evil (e.g., in the form of harmful personal influence and in corrupt institutional and social structures).[11]

According to George Buttrick, the common person knows that the biblical story of the fall is somehow right because personal experience shows that the world is in some way out of joint, that "things have somehow gone wrong." "Our planet appears to have run off the track."[12] According to Buttrick, pride blinds people "to the fact that to be human is to be free yet dependent—on God."[13] He believed that the book of Genesis does not explain why this is the case, but that it affirms a truth which many humanistic optimists failed to confront, namely, that evil is a part of the human predicament. The unwillingness to face up to this in itself leads to further evil, as has been demonstrated by recent historical humanistic movements (e.g., Nazism and Marxism) which brought about great cataclysms. Buttrick affirmed with the Bible that there is a fatal flaw in nature and in history as well as in each individual human being, that all these are evil, and that we human beings can neither adequately understand it nor effectively control it.[14] In his *God, Man, and Evil*, Buttrick, however, failed to actively use the concepts fall or original sin. The notion of historical sin, to which he devoted a chapter, comes closest to original sin.

Henry P. Van Dusen's *The Vindication of Liberal Theology* likewise eschews a positive appreciation of the fall or original sin. He points out that liberal theology, sometimes at its own peril, identified too closely with the modern principle of continuity; nevertheless, he found that liberal theology did tend to avoid some of the pitfalls into which its very critics have fallen. Thus he felt that despite a great deal of current discussions about the fall and original sin by post-liberals, the general moral practices of society have drastically deteriorated, and that some people use the fall to "justify carefree practice of specific sinfulness."[15] But misuse of a concept is obviously no solid argument against its validity. Van Dusen's primary objection against it is that neither the fall nor total depravity is to be found explicitly or implicitly in the teachings of Jesus. For him this is of crucial importance, since he saw the genius of liberal theology in its return to the only true center of Christian theology, namely, God's incarnation in Jesus Christ.[16]

My former professor of systematic theology at Boston University School of Theology, L. Harold DeWolf, has been considered by many as an able exponent of liberal theology in the second half of the twentieth century. Since I share many of his views, I shall present them at somewhat greater length. According to DeWolf, the sinfulness of human beings is not one of the most important affirmations concerning human beings; central, rather, is the affirmation that we are created by God.[17] Sin itself shows that we are in a relationship with God, although it is a sign of having become estranged in our relationship with God. The notion that the sin of one man and one woman can make all subsequent generations sinful in the eyes of God must be categorically rejected, according to DeWolf, as being inconsistent with the goodness of God. He labeled it as both irrational and blasphemous.[18] Sin does beget sin, but the actual nature of a "first" sin is unknown to us. While certain liberals maintained that babies are born good or at least morally neutral, most liberals, in DeWolf's opinion, agree that some sort of transmission of sinfulness does take place. But liberals refuse to agree that babies are born guilty and condemned by God. While babies are born morally neutral, none will make their actual moral choices uninfluenced. All somehow miss the target of doing what is right in a consistent manner.[19] "By the time he is able to make any kind of meaningful decisions he will have become deeply involved in a world full of fear, hostility, selfishness, and guilt. In many ways these conditions will have made their mark on him and he will continue to live his life amid the tensions, temptations, and ambiguities which they bring to bear upon him."[20]

When sin—"this dire evolution of self-discovery as a free person into unrestrained egoistic struggle for advantage"—begins, cannot be stated.[21] Sin is a condition which gives rise to moral evil rather than merely the concrete acts of wrongdoing; but human finiteness and one's natural, organic inclinations which are given by God cannot be regarded as sin.

In DeWolf's opinion, the Bible does not reduce all sin to a single source. That is, it was not a single, specific act of Adam or Eve which caused the fall. That would be an oversimplification. Rather, both traditional and contemporary theology have given a whole series of interpretations of sin, each of which has more or less merit in our attempt to understand what has twisted humans away from being unmarred in God's image.

Thus basic sin may be one or more of the following:

(1) Acting contrary to acknowledged standards, or violating one's own norms or those standards of right which do not depend on one's own judgment.

(2) Rebellion or disobedience to God; acting against the primary obligation to do the will of God, or acting as if we were divine; the pretension of being what we are not.

(3) Willful pride; the usage of one's own ideas, desires, and volition as supreme.

(4) Claiming to have wisdom which we in fact do not have when we foolishly turn away from God.

(5) Idolatry or the worship of false gods; a turning away from God to lesser concerns.

(6) Lust or concupiscence; the use of human sexuality for mere self-satisfaction and the rendering of the partner into a sex object.

(7) Alienation, the blaming of others, egotism, greed, self-glorification, and cruelty may be other sources of sin.[22]

While the traditional theologians tended to emphasize sensual or misplaced love, irrationality, and idolatry as causes of the fall, the liberal Protestant theologians tend to emphasize denial of love, hypocritical pretense, greed, folly, the bond of habit, and the continuation of childhood egotism into adulthood as basic sin, with the understanding, of course, that no single interpretation of sin is universally applicable. One's basic sin may not be another's basic sin.

According to DeWolf the fall symbolizes the following truths:

(1) All are in debt to God and need grace; none can repay God.

(2) All people suffer temptations to sin and are unable to resist them, often the result of sins of the previous generations.

(3) It is not easy to fulfill our responsibility; to do what comes naturally usually means to drift downward into irresponsibility.

(4) Empirically we know that all people are actually sinful, even those whom we consider superbly good.

(5) The need to repent not only for our conscious sin but also for unconsciously performed wrongdoings.

(6) The need to repent for sins of others with whom we are identified (e.g., to ask forgiveness of others for immoral acts of our nations even when we disagree with those very policies).

(7) Our actions do not take place in a vacuum but in a system of habits, ideas, and motives which give rise to wrong choices.²³

Personal Interpretation of the Fall

In recent years biblical scholars and scholars of history, phenomenology, and comparative religions have shed better insight into the nature of myth. No longer are we hesitant to label a biblical story a myth, afraid that somehow it might imply that the story is unreal or untrue.

Armed with this new understanding of humans as mythmakers in order to express some abiding, profound levels of human experience not adequately expressible in non-mythic terms, we can now approach the myth of the fall and say that Adam is every man and Eve is every woman and the fall is an archetypal story. Each person, destined by God to be fulfilled and whole, is instead broken, sick, and in need of healing and restoration to wholeness. Neither as individuals nor as communities do we fulfill our potentials and our destinies. Many problems are due to circumstances which emerged prior to the individual's birth or the communal beginning, which we neither desire nor can eliminate. Often it causes as intense a suffering as do our own sinful actions—personal or societal.

The notion that such archetypal sin affects our lives is not to be confused with the notion that somehow, mechanically, the sin of an ancestor, even a symbolic ancestor, is passed down, and unless a supernatural action is performed by a messiah or some other this-worldly or other-worldly figure, we are condemned. Sin is not hereditary. Yet it is compatible with being human. It is so well domesticated that I foresee no liberation from it as long as we are human. To be human means to live with the ambiguity of being a "cracked mirror" or a distorted image, rather than a perfect reflection of God. We can aim to improve the image, but it will not be perfect, i.e., sinless. (Note that there is no immaculate conception or anything else immaculate in Protestant liberalism!) Only painful *perfectibility* laced with progress and regress, with victories and defeats, is possible. But a deliberate choice to emphasize human goodness, rather than sinfulness, is made as a recognition of God's creative implanting of the divine "spark" in human beings. The original and essential humanity is not sinful!

Many of the above mentioned views, especially those of DeWolf, are compatible with this writer's views. The concepts of the fall and of original sin are aspects of my understanding of human nature. The experience of twentieth century horrors—and this author's personal witnessing of segments of the Holocaust, as well as the bestial conflicts of his native Yugoslavia caught up in the conflagration of World War II, and the post-war revolutionary convulsions—prevent any cheap optimism about human nature. Neoorthodox theology served as a corrective to the sometimes too easy euphoria of the increasing progress of the human species. In the twentieth century, people have perpetuated some of the most unspeakable horrors, often exceeding the cruelties of previous centuries. Therefore, experience agrees with the assessment of Scripture and the central core of the Judeo-Christian tradition, regarding the grandeur and misery of human beings. In us is a spark of divinity; we are in the image of God. But the mirror which we are does not reflect God's image well. It is "cracked" and it distorts the image of goodness.[24] Here contemporary Protestant liberalism seems to be closer to the classical Roman Catholic position on human nature than it is to the Reformation notion of the utter corruption of human beings.

Implications for Dialogue with Marxists

The reason for choosing to reflect upon this particular interface in this paper is strictly personal; I have devoted many years to fostering the Christian-Marxist dialogue. The topic itself, to my knowledge, has never been the subject matter of a concrete dialogue. But discussion often comes around to the questions of "human nature." A liberal Protestant theologian could most usefully offer some of the above mentioned insights to his or her Marxist partner as a much needed counterbalance to what appears to this author as a sometimes naive optimism about the inevitability of progress and a concomitant belief that by radically altering certain social structural relationships one may practically eliminate evil. Marxism has not adequately reflected on the persistent and radical nature of evil, including sin, but tended to gloss over these problems with assurances of a happy future. It would be a great service by liberal Protestants, specifically because of their reputation of not being preoccupied with the evil side of humanity, were they to seriously challenge Marxists to reinvestigate their notion of human beings and their treatment of sin and evil. Just what might come out of such a dialogue is impossible to predict, though it is certain that the outcome would depend on which concrete Marxists were to be in dialogue with which concrete liberal Protestants. Marxists who tend to emphasize social problems could learn something about the pervasiveness of sin in individual lives and how to cope with it; liberal Protestants may gain useful insights from Marxist understandings of evil social structures and how to change them.

Implications for Dialogue with Unificationists

The liberal Protestants are likely to challenge what appears to them as biblical literalism in the Unificationist approach to the fall on the one hand, as well as an interpretation which does not seem on the other hand to be warranted either by the biblical narrative or by the Christian tradition. The liberal Protestant is also likely to be dissatisfied with the designation of the basic sin as immature love, and with the sexual nature of Eve's and later Adam's fall. It is also evident that there is a discrepancy between the Unificationists' insistence on a literally real Satan and the view of most liberal Protestants that the awful reality of evil does not require such an hypothesis, even though Satan may be seen as a symbol for the reality of that evil which has not been generated by humans. These anticipations were confirmed by the actual dialogue in the seminar in Nassau of the New Ecumenical Research Association.

That the areas of agreement would be more significant than the differences was not anticipated by the author. This author perceived a positive feature in the Unificationist mythology of the fall in the insight that the misplaced love of God's children away from the Parent would lead to a too narrow human mutual infatuation. The price of relating to one another without including God in the relationship results in alienation from God and from each other. This, indeed, is still the case today, even among religious people. Instead of accepting the common responsibility for the human mess and joining forces to do something about reconciling those who are estranged, we continue to indict one another for our wrong theologies and for our inadequate actions. Thus we perpetuate the fall through today.

The actual dialogue brought to light additional areas of positive interaction. It was evident that both Unificationists and liberal Protestants underscored the central place of love. It was obvious that, unlike many other literalists, the Unificationists affirm love as more important than the question of the origin of sin. The common motivation for both liberal Protestants and Unificationists is to overcome alienation by becoming reconciled through divine love.

Another area of agreement was that God created good humans and that evil is clearly subsidiary to goodness. This divine and human goodness is perceived both as fundamental and as ultimately victorious. Sin is everything that opposes the full advent of God's reign. God's will can be frustrated by the misuse of human freedom, but not forever. Both liberal Protestants and Unificationists share the common assurance that God's purpose for humanity will gain ultimate ascendancy.

Notes

1   Kenneth Scott Latourette, *A History of Christianity* (New York: Harper & Brothers, 1953), 1419–20.

2   Adolph Harnack, *Outlines of the History of Dogma* (Boston: Beacon, 1959), 366.

3   Claude Welch, *Protestant Thought in the Nineteenth Century,* vol. 1, 1799–1870 (New Haven: Yale University Press, 1972), 34.

4   Ibid., 40.

5   Paul Tillich, *A Complete History of Christian Thought,* ed. Carl Braaten (New York: Harper & Row, 1968), v, 47.

6   Welch, 82.

7   It is not our aim to present here how he reconciled this paradox.

8   Welch, 102.

9   Ibid., 264.

10   Ibid., 264 n. 11

11   L. Harold DeWolf, *The Case for Theology in Liberal Perspective* (Philadelphia: Westminster, 1959), 118.

12   George A. Buttrick, *God, Pain and Evil* (New York: Abingdon, 1966), 42.

13   Ibid., 43.

14   Ibid.

15   Henry P. Van Dusen, *The Vindication of Liberal Theology* (New York: Scribner's, 1963), 82.

16   Ibid., 147–48.

17   DeWolf, *Theology in Liberal Perspective*, 115.

18   L. Harold DeWolf, *A Theology of the Living Church*, rev. ed. (New York: Harper & Brothers, 1960), 198.

19   Dewolf, *Theology in Liberal Perspective*, 118.

20   Ibid., 119.

21   Dewolf, *Theology of the Living Church*, 196.

22   Ibid., 180–89.

23   Ibid., 198–200.

24   It is not the intention of the author to stretch this analogy beyond the discussion of sin and construe an image of humans that only passively reflects God. Human beings are active, creative, developing, struggling creatures—features which are not adequately recognized in this limited metaphor.

11 The Response to Suffering
THOMAS WALSH

. . . it is in the response to suffering that many and perhaps all men, individually and in their groups define themselves, take on character, and develop their ethos.
   H. RICHARD NIEBUHR, *The Responsible Self*

The rational need for a theodicy of suffering and dying has had extremely strong effects.
   MAX WEBER, "The Social Psychology of the World Religions"

Introduction

This essay takes up the doctrine of the fall in a rather indirect way. The central focus will be on the problem of suffering, or more specifically the "suffering of God" image as it may operate to inform and shape the moral orientation of an agent and/or moral community. My basic thesis suggests that such a thematization or way of imaging God is a significant advance over other theodicean options, especially theocentric dualism.

Theocentric dualism, as I shall define it, images God as impassible power. Furthermore the relationship between God and human is characterized by an ethical incommensurability. That is, the human moral orientation has virtually no bearing on the ways of divine governance. Theocentric dualism, I shall argue, tends to give rise to two unsatisfactory moral orientations. The first, accented in the "Weber thesis," is prudentialism or mere anthropocentrism. The other is a tendency toward passivity, as evidenced in H. Richard Niebuhr's symbolization of responsibility.

My objective is to engage in a kind of ethical analysis of the meaning and moral implications of a particular guiding image of God: namely, one of God suffering as the result of the fall and sin. In articulating the features of this image and in suggesting the way in which it shapes an ethos, I shall attempt to illustrate the way in which it avoids the errors of both prudentialism and passivity. My referent for understanding the significance of the suffering of God is the Unification movement. Those predecessors who shape my approach to the topic are Max Weber and H. Richard Niebuhr. To Weber's insight into the sociology of theodicy and to Niebuhr's constructive "response to suffering" I am indebted throughout.

First, previewing the argument relying on Weber will underscore the social relevance of theodicy as a response to suffering. I will attempt to show, following an insightful remark of Gregory Baum, that "theodicy is implicit in action."[1] Furthermore, and continuing in a Weberian key, I shall present the flaws of a moral orientation based in theocentric dualism. Second, I will move to an analysis of the Unification ethos, informed by an image of the suffering of God. The focus shall be on the way in which such an image transforms and nuances the notion of responsibility, as compared with the way in which this same notion is employed and thematized by Weber and Niebuhr. The argument will be made that the Unification perspective avoids the prudentialism of Weberian ethics and the passivity of Niebuhrian ethics. This image of God and the image of the moral agent that it suggests hold promise for an ethical perspective of theocentric liberation of nature, humanity, and God.

Max Weber's Sociology of Theodicy

This section shall serve as prolegomenon to the subsequent section by accomplishing several tasks. First of all, and most simply, it is an attempt to illustrate the way in which theodicy, as response to suffering, is implicit in action. At the same time it will underscore, as Weber has done so well, the social relevance of theodicy. Finally it will follow the "Weber thesis" insofar as it lights the path, albeit by way of unintended consequence, from theocentric dualism to prudentialism. Throughout the section, I do not wish to profess the "truth" of the Weber thesis, only (true to the Weberian method) its heuristic value.

It is an axiom that human beings seek meaning and adequate, if not good, reasons for doing whatever it is that they do. Suffering, being a surd in the way of meaning, is a universal problematic that theodicy attempts to solve. If we define action, according to Weber, as "human behavior when and to the extent that the agent or agents see it as subjectively meaningful,"[2] then it follows that action entails or implies meaning. Furthermore, action implies theodicy, and we may say that *theodicy has social relevance*; this is the core point of the Weber thesis.

For Weber, ideas are correlative to the "ideal interests" of agents. An ideal interest is an interest in making sense of the world. As a "material interest" seeks to eliminate the problem of scarcity, and the suffering that accompanies scarcity, an ideal interest has as its project the elimination of unintelligibility and meaninglessness. Interests, both material and ideal, are related to a fundamental soteriological drive. Ideas, and particularly theodicies, are constructed in order to constitute a world in which one can act. The greatest hindrance to the task of constructing a realm of intelligibility lies in the experience of unwilled suffering, a discrepancy which violates our common sense vision of an ought world. There is tension between the experience of the "is" and the experience of the "ought." Weber says, "The metaphysical need responded to the awareness of existing and unbridgeable tensions, and through theodicy it tried to find a common meaning in spite of it all."[3] Theodicy attempts to constitute a realm of meaning "in spite of it all"; it attempts to give an account for the "it all," giving a "response to suffering," an account of the fall.

Talcott Parsons has pointed out that Weber's sociology of religion is primarily concerned with "the relations between religious ideas and commitments and other aspects of human conduct."[4] It is more accurate to state that Weber's focus is on the interplay among primary human interests, "world images" (largely understood in terms of theodicy), and action. In a now classic passage from "The Social Psychology of the World Religions," Weber states:

Not ideas, but material and ideal interests, directly govern man's conduct. Yet very frequently the "world images" that have been created by "ideas" have, like switchmen, determined the tracks along which action has been pushed by the dynamic of interest. "From what" and "for what" one wished to be redeemed and, let us not forget, "could be" redeemed, depend upon one's image of the world.[5]

For Weber, the primary repositories of "world images" are religions. And central to these world images is an account or rationale that answers to the problem of suffering. As such, at the very heart of religion is a soteriological project that answers to human interests, both material and ideal, and which seeks to construct an intelligible and compelling image of the world. Weber says: "This problem—the experience of the irrationality of the world—has been the driving force of all religious evolution."[6] In this sense religion seeks to undermine irrationality by providing some adequate and compelling account of the problem of suffering and injustice. In fact, religion, rationalization, and theodicy are each dimensions of the same historical process. Religion is a form of rationality that according to Weber disenchants the world, eliminating the world image of magic. Friedrich Tenbruck argues that

> Weber's important discovery . . . lay in the knowledge that rationalization in all its historical fragility was born from the compulsion of an inherent logic, which was situated in the irresistible drive towards the rationalization of religious ideas. Therefore, the process of rationalization is at heart an historico-religious process of disenchantment, and the stages and moments in the history of rationalization derive their unity from the process of disenchantment.[7]

What Weber termed *Entzauberung,* translated here as disenchantment (often translated as demagification), is the result of an "irresistible drive," or as Weber stated it, a "metaphysical need" for greater rationality "in spite of it all." Religion thus answers to this metaphysical need, which is evoked by suffering, with theodicy. Tenbruck says, "The rational compulsion, to which religions have to accede, derives from the need to possess a rational answer to the problem of theodicy."[8]

According to Weber the two most formidable theodicean proposals are to be found in the doctrine of *karma* and in the Calvinist doctrine of the *deus absconditus* with its theory of predestination. Weber argued that the Calvinist image of God provided the basis for the transformation of Western civilization. It was Calvinism that asserted the existence of "an unimaginably great ethical chasm between the transcendental God and the human being."[9] Human moral action was utterly incommensurable with divine wisdom, and hence no behavior on the part of human beings had any bearing on the divine election. Instead of fatalism, the expected outcome, this image gave birth to a most extreme version of "inner-worldly asceticism." That is, the anxiety evoked in the believer by the *decretum horribile* demanded at least some psychological *certitudo salutis.* This assurance came through the achievement of success in one's calling; success came through the rational mastery of one's social and economic circumstances.

The type of rationality appropriate to the task of world mastery and capitalism Weber refers to as *Zweckrationalität,* an instrumental or bureaucratic form of rationality; it is formal, legalistic, and impersonal. Such rationality frees one from any magical or enchanted view of reality. It follows from the dualistic nature of the theodicy (separation of God and world) that the world becomes objectifiable and disenchanted. In time, however, the theological dimension of theodicy came to be less and less relevant, while the rational mastery of the world via bureaucratic organization gained ascendancy. Wolfgang Schluchter offers a cogent analysis of this Weberian scenario:

After dualistic theocentrism radicalized itself through ascetic Protestantism and thus legitimated the rationalism of world mastery, pure intellectualism was then free to make its own worldview absolute. It became the proponent of the worldview diametrically opposed to that of religion. Ascetic Protestantism had championed the rationalism of world mastery "in the name of God"; scientific rationalism now propagated it "in the name of man." Anthropocentrism takes the place of theocentrism, anthropodicy that of theodicy.[10]

The Weber thesis is really Weber's attempt to solve the puzzle of the emergence of the distinctiveness of modern, Western capitalist civilization. This distinctiveness, he argues, derives from the inner logic of dualistic theocentrism itself. The "iron cage" of modernity is an unintended consequence of this theodicy. As I view it, the problem with the Calvinist solution to the problem of suffering is its separation of the realm of morality (i.e., human responsibility), from the realm of soteriology (i.e., divine responsibility). As such, two general options emerge: either a thoroughgoing theocentrism that leaves redemption as God's concern, or a thoroughgoing anthropocentrism that dispenses with the need for God.

It seems clear that, for many in our age, anthropodicy takes precedence over theodicy; for many the theodicy of Christian thought has been superseded by the anthropodicy of either science or Marxism. The "response to suffering" that Marxism provides has a compelling quality that has attracted millions. Peter Berger has said:

The social theodicy of Christianity (that is, its legitimation of the inequities of society) has been collapsing along with the over-all plausibility of the Christian theodicy—a point, incidentally, which has been seen much more clearly by the antagonists of Christianity than by

Christians themselves. If the Christian explanation of the world no longer holds, then the Christian legitimation of social order cannot be maintained very long either.[11]

If the Weber thesis is at all illustrative of the problematic of modernity, and I for one am convinced it is, then the human response to the inadequacy of dualistic theocentrism, be it intentional or unintentional, seems to lead to a prudential anthropocentrism. This prudential anthropocentrism is being played out most forcefully in the Marxist anthropodicy.

Marxist anthropodicy, however, which locates the fall or source of suffering in unregenerate social institutions, seeks only to replace a capitalist prudentialism with a socialist version. Both liberal individualism and Marxist socialism are anthropocentric, and as such neither seems to be compatible with a world image that is fundamentally theocentric. For Weber, Marxism was as much a species of *Zweckrationalität* as was the "Protestant ethic." Both attempt to eliminate suffering through bureaucratic rationality, and each constructs an iron cage of its own.

The Suffering of God and the Ethic of Responsibility

In the preceding section, I employed Weberian insights in an attempt to establish a framework for the following ethical analysis. The Weberian perspective, it is hoped, helps to illustrate the social relevance of theodicy, as response to suffering, and the problem of theocentric dualism. Regarding this latter point I affirmed the Weber thesis insofar as it links theocentric dualism with anthropocentrism and prudentialism. The present section now turns to focus on the moral import of an image of the suffering of God. I wish, first of all, to describe the way in which this image, existing potentially in the doctrine of creation and actualized in the doctrine of the fall, figures in the Unification worldview. Second, I wish to explore its implications as they apply to the formation of a Unification ethos. Particular attention will be paid to the way in which an ethic of responsibility is understood, arguing that the Unification notion of responsibility avoids certain weaknesses that characterize both Weberian and Niebuhrian versions of an ethic of responsibility.

In the official texts of the Unification movement, *Divine Principle* and *Outline of the Principle: Level 4,* one finds relatively little explicit thematization of God's suffering. This is in stark contrast to the authority which the image itself carries within the ethos of the movement. For example, in the chapter on "The Fall" in *Outline of the Principle: Level 4* there is hardly any mention of the consequences of the fall insofar as it impacts on God's own heart. At one point it is stated that "Adam and Eve forsook God their true father . . ."[12] On the other hand, in a speech by the movement's founder, author of the *Divine Principle,* one reads that "The Fall was the pinnacle of the suffering of God."[13] In reality it is in the speeches of the founder, Reverend Moon, and in the discourse of the members that one discovers the centrality of this image. Two passages will be quoted, one from Reverend Moon and the other from Dr. Young Oon Kim, to illustrate the weight which this motif carries. Reverend Moon stated in a "Parents' Day" speech in 1978: "God is love; God has tears and compassion. God is sensitive and feels sadness; God feels deep compassion as well. More than anyone else, God also needs a companion. The one who is most powerful in the universe is lonely too, and needs a companion. . . . *Man's fall is hurting God most because love is utmost and supreme in His life as well as ours."* (Emphasis mine)[14]

And Dr. Kim, in a chapter of her *Unification Theology* entitled "The Effects of the Fall," says: "Nevertheless, the worst result of the Fall is its effect upon God. His purpose of creation became frustrated. As a consequence of the Fall, God was virtually deprived of his sovereignty over creation. He lost His hold over the human heart. If God is the God of heart, His heart must have been broken by the seduction of Adam and Eve."[15]

In the *Divine Principle* there is indeed an articulation of the basis for any subsequent thematization of the suffering of God. This basis is found in the chapter on the "Principle of Creation," for here it is that the features of God's heart are described. Quoting from *Level 4*:

"The most essential aspect of God is Heart. Heart is the impulse to love an object and is the fountain and motivator of love. It is the nature of Heart to seek an object to love. This nature of Heart is God's motive for making the Creation. That is, God, whose essence is Heart, feels joy when he can love an object that he created. If there is no object, God cannot satisfy his impulse to express care and love, which springs limitlessly from within himself. God made the Creation to be the object which he could love.[16]

Having established the theological basis for God's capacity for suffering, the anthropological basis is explained. Again from *Level 4*: "Man cannot think that God will take responsibility for man's perfection; man will realize his perfection only when he fulfills his own responsibility, even though that responsibility is very small when compared with God's responsibility. Man fell because he failed to obey God's commandment."[17]

In essence one may correctly infer from the *Divine Principle* that God has constituted the human world in such a way as not to guarantee the requital of God's love and will. As such Reverend Moon can logically say, "Unless man becomes perfect, God remains a God of failure, not a God of success."[18] And, furthermore, "When Adam and Eve rebelled against God they indeed broke his heart."[19] The fall narrative, then, according to Unificationism, gives account not only of a human moral failure, but also of the transformation of God, from a God of joy and anticipation, to a God of unwilled suffering.

Before addressing the major implications of this image for the moral orientation of Unificationism, a word is perhaps in order as to why, after the event of Jesus' death and resurrection, the image of God's suffering could remain valid. According to *Divine Principle* God remains a suffering God even after the Cross. The atonement is yet unfinished. This is so, Unificationists argue, because Jesus could have accomplished so much more had he been received, followed, and loved, rather than crucified. *Level 4* states: "Death on the cross was not the mission God had originally intended for Jesus, his Son. Rather, it became God's painful secondary dispensation necessitated by the faithlessness of the people of Israel. What would have happened if all the people of Israel had believed in Jesus and had welcomed him, loved him, and united with him? Most certainly complete salvation would have been realized."[20]

It is necessary to introduce this point here in order to clarify the continuing authority of an image of the suffering of God after the event of Jesus' crucifixion. People remain in sin, and God an unfinished God.

If the fall transformed God into an unfinished or "failed" God of sorrow, and if, furthermore, the crucifixion of Jesus was another setback to the project of God, how does this inform and shape the Unification ethos, particularly its moral orientation? In order to illuminate this ethos I shall employ an image of the moral agent that has been suggested, albeit with very different meanings, by both Max Weber and H. Richard Niebuhr—namely, the image of the moral agent as a *responsible self*.

Weber, in "Politics as a Vocation," typifies two models of moral agency: an ethic of ultimate ends and an ethic of responsibility. The first is a Kantian-like ethic of "purity of intention," and the second a prudential ethic of "responsibility for consequences." Weber's espousal of the latter is grounded in his analysis of incommensurability between moral intention and empirical consequences. Simply put, the ethic of absolute ends does not take responsibility for the world: "The believer in an ethic of ultimate ends feels 'responsible' only for seeing to it that the flame of pure intentions is not quelched."[21] Furthermore, ". . . there is an abysmal contrast between conduct that follows the maxim of the ethic of ultimate ends—that is, in religious terms, "The Christian does rightly and leaves the results with the Lord"—and conduct that follows the maxim of the ethic of responsibility, in which case one has to give an account of the foreseeable results of one's action."[22]

The incommensurable relationship between intentions and consequences renders the ethic of intention inadequate. One could say that the ethic of ultimate ends fails to take the doctrine of original sin seriously enough, whereas for Weber, "a man who believes in an ethic of responsibility takes account of precisely the average deficiencies of people."[23]

Weber's ethic of responsibility is similar to Reinhold Niebuhr's estimate of the ethic of Jesus as "an impossible ethical ideal"; that is, the conditions of modernity rendered such an ethic, if not irrelevant, then perhaps irresponsible. Ethics, therefore, must be evaluated not according to high-mindedness, but in accordance with the achievement of certain modest aims and in accordance with a constant monitoring of consequences that follow for the implementation of means toward the end. Wolfgang Schluchter states: "In the end he [Weber] preferred the ethic of responsibility to the ethic of conviction under the conditions of disenchantment, for it alone permits conscious world mastery. The ethic of responsibility is not forced into world flight, like the ethic of conviction, but it also is not compelled to world-adjustment."[24]

Ultimately the image of responsibility that Weber employs in constructing an ethic for a disenchanted age is one of sheer prudentialism. It is utterly anthropocentric, and both post-Christian and post-Marxist. For Weber, the Christian ethic and the Marxist ethic are both versions of an ethic of ultimate ends, their ethics being governed by a high ideal that fails to appreciate the "inconvenient facts" that appear in the form of unintended consequences. Responsibility then entails a subordination of values to facts; moral decision-making requires that one abstract from particular loyalties in order that one remain open to an analysis of facts and consequences. In a disenchanted world an ethic cannot be based on an overriding value orientation. For Weber, the war among the many gods of modernity is an irresolvable one. Since there exists no way to verify or falsify a god or value commitment, a moral orientation cannot be grounded in either. Polytheism and pluralism make any particularistic ethic of conviction inappropriate.

Weber viewed the fate of our age as inevitably polytheistic, with consensus arising only in the realm of instrumental rationality. The god of Calvin could no longer sustain the eroding processs of disenchantment. Weberian ethics is constructed as a kind of liberalism that seeks to protect the individual from the encroaching bureaucratization of all life spheres. In effect, I would suggest that Weber's value orientation is one that espouses liberal individualism. In Weberian ethics one takes responsibility to protect individualism from the force of bureaucratization.

H. Richard Niebuhr's ethic of responsibility differs significantly from Weber's. Most importantly, Niebuhr seeks to respond constructively to the problem of polytheism by articulating a theocentric ethic. Furthermore, in his image of the responsible agent, he attempts to provide a theory of agency that avoids the prudentialism of traditional teleological ethics and the legalism of traditional deontological perspectives. Niebuhr's "responsible self" is modeled after George Herbert Mead's social theory of the self. He accents the "fundamentally social character of selfhood."[25] Niebuhr says: "The idea or pattern of responsibility, then, may summarily and abstractly be defined as the idea of an agent's action as response to an action upon him in accordance with his interpretation of the latter action and with his expectation of response to his response; and all of this in a continuing community of agents."[26]

But while Niebuhr underscores the theme of responsibility, it seems in the final analysis to be a decidedly passive version of responsibility. This comes through not only in his philosophical anthropology, which like Mead's own social psychology emphasizes too much the social conditioning of the self, but even more clearly in his view of the God-human relationship. This latter relationship is, taking its cue from Schleiermacher, one of "absolute dependence." Niebuhr says: "The action by which I am, is not one by which I was thrown into existence at some past time to maintain myself thereafter by my own power. It is the action whereby I am now, so that it seems truer to say that I am being lived than that I live. I live but do not have the power to live. And further, I may die at any moment but I am powerless to die."[27]

Niebuhr's image of response is in reality a response to this experience of absolute dependence, that is, whether to respond in faith as trust or in a defensive distrust. Niebuhr focuses purely on this fundamental orientation toward being. As such, his version of responsibility remains passive. He eliminates the problem of prudentialism, but only at a severe cost. Soteriology becomes for Niebuhr "the liberty to interpret in trust all that happens" as action upon us by "God the friend."[28] The fall seems to be equivalent to a fundamental distrust.

A response to suffering whose primary image is one of the suffering of God, transforms and nuances the notion of responsibility in significant ways. This transformation of the self-image of the agent as a responsible self is grounded in the experience of "absolute interdependence." The transformation itself involves both a radicalization of a view of the responsibility of the agent, ruling out the passivity that Niebuhr's position suggests, and a radicalization of the soteriological vision that avoids prudentialism.

Niebuhr, while he has articulated a philosophical anthropology that stresses sociality as well as theocentrism, still remains tied to a form of theocentric dualism. That is, there is little or no thematization of an anticipated response of God to human action. Humans are related to God in a mode of "absolute dependence." The fundamental moral act or response of the agent is one of either trust or distrust. Niebuhr eschews anthropocentrism and prudentialism, but his perspective suffers from its tendency toward inaction. As Lonnie Kliever has stated, ". . . there is no mistaking that a certain air of patient waiting, hopeful endurance and even willing suffering pervades Niebuhr's thought."[29]

If, on the other hand, one accents the interdependence of God and human being, and if one images God as suffering due to the fall and irresponsibility of humanity, then the moral orientation takes on a distinctly more radical nature. The notion of responsibility is decidedly transformed from one of trust to active effort to eliminate divine suffering. At the same time the notion of salvation is broadened to include not only nature and the universal human community, but God as well, or indeed primarily. Furthermore, the redemption of nature and humanity is not merely "for man," but more essentially for God. And, it is important to note, not merely for the luxury of God's glory but for the necessity of God's fulfillment. The elimination of suffering (i.e., liberation) is then viewed not anthropocentrically but theocentrically. Liberation is a theocentric cause, and it is loyalty to this cause which characterizes responsibility.

I do not believe this view to be discordant with Niebuhr's theocentrism; it does, however, accent dimensions of his perspective which he fails to fully exploit. For example, his relational theory of value stops short of thematizing an interdependence or mutuality between God and creation; also, his thematization of radical faith as loyalty to the cause of God fails to take an activist or liberation turn. By underscoring the suffering of God, one moves human responsibility into a new dimension—for the unredeemed quality of the world and humanity cause suffering to God. It is possible then to thematize God's own redemption in a way that is related by interdependence to human redemption. God and humanity then have a common cause, a common soteriological interest. In this way theocentrism does not entail dualism or, as Weber suggests, "an unimaginably great ethical chasm between the transcendental God and the human being . . ." The project of the kingdom of God is rather viewed as a common project of co-responsibility. Evidencing this point a Unificationist may say: "Without you God cannot achieve his goal."[30]

Any thoroughgoing theocentrism that accents God's power and impassibility tends to slip either into a kind of passivity, as I have argued Niebuhr does, or into a dualism that begets prudentialism, as does the Weber thesis. In the opening discussion I underscored Weber's insight into the social relevance of theodicy, for theodicy, as a response to suffering, is implicit in action. At the heart of this Weber thesis is a theory of the relationship between theodicean world image and ethos or moral orientation. In this essay I have attempted to unpack certain of the ethical implications of an image of the suffering of God. I have argued that such an image avoids both passivity and prudentialism in its conceptualization of responsibility. If God suffers due to human fallenness, the redemption is not merely for human beings, nor can it be effected by grace alone.

This perspective, in accenting the way in which human beings function for God, serves to correct the tendency to view God merely in terms of God's functioning for humanity. This latter functionalist view of God is at the heart of utilitarian and prudential religion. God comes to be viewed as a means to some human end, and loved or worshipped for that reason. This is anthropocentrism employing theocentrism as a means. If God suffers, however, one may view anthropocentrism as a means to God's end.

If God suffers, sin must be viewed not merely as the violation of law or as a departure from self-realization, but as that which, most importantly, causes suffering to God. This greatly increases the estimate of the seriousness of sin, as well as the nature of human responsibility. But while God's suffering illuminates the seriousness of sin and the serious toll taken by the fall, the emphasis is less on the effects of the fall on human beings, such as utter depravity; instead, the locus of concern shifts to the suffering of God effected by the fall. Moral obligation then entails an attempt to eliminate that suffering. Hence, one may introduce the notion of liberation at a theocentric level. The liberation of creation and all the various liberations of humanity figure as parts in the primary liberation of God. The theocentric perspective serves to prevent the narrowing down of liberation projects for the unifying focus; and that, for the sake of which all else is to be liberated, is primarily the elimination of God's suffering. As such, this image allows for a liberation moral orientation, and even requires a liberation orientation, but at a theocentric level. Given the universal and global nature of the experience of suffering and of a corresponding need for liberation, this thematization of God's suffering may have global relevance.

Notes

1   Gregory Baum, *Religion and Alienation: A Theological Reading of Sociology* (New York: Paulist Press, 1975), 255.

2   Max Weber, "The Nature of Social Action," in W. G. Runciman's *Weber* (Cambridge: Cambridge University Press, 1978), 7.

3   Max Weber, "Religious Rejections of the World and Their Directions," in *From Max Weber*, ed. Hans Gerth and C. Wright Mills (New York: Oxford University Press, 1981), 358.

4   Talcott Parsons, "Introduction" to Max Weber's *The Sociology of Religion* (Boston: Beacon, 1964), xx.

5 Max Weber, "The Social Psychology of the World Religions," in *From Max Weber,* 280.

6 Max Weber, "Politics as a Vocation," in *From Max Weber,* 123.

7 Friedrich H. Tenbruck, "The Problem of Thematic Unity in the Works of Max Weber," *British Journal of Sociology* 31, no. 3 (September 1980): 326.

8 Ibid., 334.

9 Max Weber, *The Sociology of Religion* (Boston: Beacon, 1964), 142.

10 Wolfgang Schluchter, "The Paradox of Rationality," in *Max Weber's Vision of History,* ed. Guenther Roth and Wolfgang Schluchter (Berkeley, Calif.: University of California Press, 1979), 50.

11 Peter Berger, *The Sacred Canopy* (New York: Anchor Books, 1967), 79.

12 [Chung Hwan Kwak], *Outline of the Principle: Level 4* (New York: Holy Spirit Association for the Unification of World Christianity [HSA-UWC], 1980), 44.

13 Sun Myung Moon, "The Pinnacle of Suffering," 22 May 1977.

14 Sun Myung Moon, "Parents' Day," 8 April 1978.

15 Young Oon Kim, *Unification Theology* (New York: HSA-UWC, 1980), 124.

16 *Outline of the Principle,* 22.

17 Ibid., 29–30.

18 Sun Myung Moon, "Happy Unification Church Members," 22 May 1977.

19 Sun Myung Moon, "The Dignity of God and Man," 1 April 1977.

20 *Outline of the Principle,* 59.

21 Max Weber, "Politics as a Vocation," in *From Max Weber,* 121.

22 Ibid., 120.

23 Ibid., 121.

24 Schluchter, 56.

25 H. Richard Niebuhr, *The Responsible Self* (New York: Harper & Row, 1978), 71.

26 Ibid., 65.

27 Ibid., 114.

28 Ibid., 143.

29 Lonnie Kliever, *H. Richard Niebuhr* (Waco, Texas: Word Books, 1977), 172.

30 Sun Myung Moon, "Yesterdays and Todays," 30 April 1978.

12 Original Sin and Human Value
LLOYD EBY

Today many people, especially people of education and culture, fear religion and religious values. This is as it should be. There are ignoble reasons for secularism and antireligiousness, but there are also noble ones. Both the history of religion and its manifestations and any observation of religious affairs in our present world demonstrate how much misery and chaos are brought about by religion. Anyone who wants to assert the value and virtue of religion, religiosity, or religious beliefs or dogmas must show that somehow—despite all the evidence to the contrary—these things contribute to and enhance human life and well-being. This is not something that is easy to do.

In addition to the public forms of misery brought about by religion (wars, class and racial antagonisms, social disruption, and so on) there are even more insidious personal and internal ones. Anyone who has grown up in a closed religious tradition and who has chafed at the results knows just how much internal suffering that religion caused and how much effort was expended in the struggle to escape from it. (In my own case the religion was Mennonitism, but any of the numerous varieties of Protestantism, Roman Catholicism, Judaism, or Islam would do just as well.) Anyone who passed through these struggles also knows that the effort is never entirely successful and that the scars are ineradicable. A great deal of popular literature deals with this topic; examples are the drama, *Sister Mary Ignatius Explains It All for You,* dealing with Catholicism, and Chaim Potok's novel, *The Chosen,* dealing with Judaism.

The charges against religion and religious pronouncements have been correct so often that many people have concluded that religion is inherently objectionable. They conclude that it is not just particular examples of religion that lead to problems, but that religion itself must be rejected because there is some defect or taint that inheres in religion as such. This conclusion, strictly speaking, does not follow from the evidence of defects in religion, and in addition, these claims that religion is inherently noxious ignore the evidence that can be given for the good effects of religion. But, in light of the evidence against religion, no claim that something is supported by religious tradition or by dogma is sufficient to argue for its general acceptability. We would do better to conclude that if something is a religious dogma, or is part of a generally accepted religious tradition, then that is *prima facie* evidence against it. There must be evidence other than religious tradition or dogma to support any valid claim.

All the charges against religion, both public and private, condense into the claim that religion diminishes or compromises human value or well-being. The question of human value and well-being leads to the question of just what human beings are, what their nature is, and what values must be promoted in order to enhance their welfare.

The topic of this seminar is original sin. I am concerned with the question of whether a view that human beings have an inherent flaw (what we might call an *ontological* flaw) contributes to or detracts from human well-being, and whether an adequate philosophical anthropology should make a claim similar to the one that religious views of human beings have made when they have claimed that humans are "fallen" or subject to "original sin." One conclusion we can reach immediately as a result of the discussion above is that we cannot assert this as a religious, theological, or traditional dogma or doctrine. If there is no warrant for this claim of humans having original sin apart from some religious claim, then we should reject it. We must therefore investigate what it is to be human, or what is philosophical anthropology.

The question or problem of an accurate and adequate view of human beings and of human nature and value is, in my view, the central problem of both philosophy and theology. The criterion of decision between competing philosophical or theological systems, claims or statements consists in the differences they would make for human nature and well-being. In other words, the criterion of decision is the anthropological implications of each view. This criterion, however, is by no means simple or easy to apply. Any philosophical or theological view will almost certainly influence or modify the anthropology that is brought as a (probably tacit) presupposition in examining it. The relationship between theology or philosophy and anthropology is one of give-and-take; each influences and modifies the other. Nevertheless, I believe that there is an underlying (probably tacit) anthropology by which we can evaluate philosophical or theological pronouncements, pending modification of that tacit anthropology by the philosophical or theological pronouncements in question. The relationship between these is similar to what has been called elsewhere a "virtuous circle" (as distinguished from a vicious circle.)[1] For example, any view that purports to justify the slaughter of large numbers of innocents is almost certainly unacceptable, unless an extremely compelling case can be made for it, and even then the argument justifying this sticks in one's mouth when the actual result of the sacrifice is observed. To put it differently, the result of human life, practice, and well-being has a compelling character that belies a great deal of sophistry in theological and philosophical argumentation. (This is the reason, incidentally, why those of us who abandon or reject an overwhelming religious tradition into which we were born do so; we leave in order to live—we see what the religion does to us and to others and find the result unacceptable, no matter how compelling the theological or religious necessity for the tradition seems to be.)

The problem of an adequate anthropology has been neglected by all modern nontheological philosophers, at least in my opinion. No contemporary philosopher of whom I am aware has said anything on this topic other than half-truths, unexamined assumptions, or more or less simple minded falsities. There are many examples of widely-admired and influential works that ultimately fail because of an inadequate anthropology.[2] This lack of an adequate anthropology vitiates most of contemporary philosophy.

Since philosophers have failed so badly in providing an adequate anthropology, perhaps we should turn to the theologians. One modern theologian who has discussed this question is Reinhold Niebuhr, in *The Nature and Destiny of Man*.[3] For my purposes here, I am most interested in what Niebuhr has to say about the anthropological question. He argues persuasively that both idealism and naturalism, in whatever varieties these have taken, lead to untoward consequences.

In regard to the Western emphasis on the individual, my thesis . . . was that individual selfhood is expressed in the self's capacity for self-transcendence and not in its rational capacity for conceptual and analytic procedures. Thus a consistent idealism and a consistent naturalism both obscure the dimension of selfhood, the former by equating the self with universal reason (as in Plato and Hegel) and the latter by reducing the self to an unfree nature not capable of viewing itself and the world from a position transcending the flow of events, causes and sequences.[4]

Part One of Niebuhr's book presents an elaborate discussion of this theme. He shows that a view of human beings in which persons are a combination of a natural and a spiritual being (i.e., the Christian view) is much superior to either the naturalist or the spiritualist view. Both of those views eventually lead to the suppression of human individuality: idealism by forgetting people's relations to nature and identifying them "prematurely and unqualifiedly, with the divine and eternal"; and naturalism by obscuring human uniqueness, tending to identify people with "blood and soil" or with socioeconomic processes. In each of these cases, no matter how much they may differ internally in their views, the ultimate result is the dehumanization of humanity.[5]

Modern culture, Niebuhr asserts, has been a battleground of these two opposing views of human nature.[6] Each view contains an implicit or explicit criticism of the other, and the criticisms are correct. Idealist criticisms of naturalism are correct in asserting the role of the rational and spiritual in human life and affairs, but naturalist criticisms of idealism are also correct in claiming that idealism neglects the connection of humans with nature and neglects the limits of rationality in human affairs. The result of this conflict has been a triumph of confusion in modern philosophical anthropology.

Modern anthropology, according to Niebuhr, contains three kinds of difficulties. First, there are the inner contradictions, spoken about above, between idealistic and naturalistic rationalists, and between rationalists of whatever type and vitalists and romanticists. Second, the modern human being has a certainty about his or her individuality which his or her own history belies. The Renaissance conception of individuality relied on a (tacit) religious basis. Because the modern human being has given up this religious basis, he or she has no grounds on which to resist either a cultural dissipation of the individualism of the Renaissance and of eighteenth-century liberalism, or the dissipation of bourgeois libertarian idealism as it has succumbed to fascist or Marxist collectivism. And third, the modern human being has an essentially easy conscience because he or she has an optimistic treatment of the problem of evil. The

Christian view that the human being is sinful at the center of his or her personality is universally rejected. The mechanistic rationalist and the Rousseauistic romantic both agree that people are essentially good, and claim that all one has to do is "rise from the chaos of nature to the harmony of mind or to descend from the chaos of spirit to the harmony of nature in order to be saved. The very fact that the strategies of redemption are in such complete contradiction to each other proves how far modern man is from solving the problem of evil." Another expression of this easy conscience is the near-universal belief in progress, which is a "secularized version of biblical apocalypse and of the Hebraic sense of a meaningful history, in contrast to the meaningless history of the Greeks."[7]

There are pessimistic views of the human being in modern thought, to be sure. Examples are Hobbes, Nietzsche, and Freud. Yet there is no uneasy conscience in those views. Egoism and will to power are regarded as normal and normative. But the fateful consequences of these views for contemporary life are apparent everywhere.[8]

Niebuhr offers a careful and detailed analysis of all of Western thought in support of his conclusion. For my purposes here, I will accept his claims as correct, and attempt to examine the consequences for my concern about anthropology and original sin. I do not accept what Niebuhr has to say about the nature and characteristics of original sin (assuming that I understand him correctly on those points), because I think that his view is mistaken in some important ways, but I do think that what he says about modern philosophical views of the human being is correct.

One immediate result of Niebuhr's analysis of Western philosophy is that the fatal flaw in philosophical criticisms of religion is exposed; the philosophical views are at least as confused and unacceptable as the religious ones they criticize. This does not show that the religious view in question, or religious views in general, are acceptable. But it does show that the widespread philosophically-based prejudice against religion is suspect because it relies on philosophical views which are even more problematic than the religious views which are being criticized. This holds for any philosophical view that has been undermined by Niebuhr's criticism, unless one can show that Niebuhr's criticism is mistaken, or unless one can show that the philosophical view in question has not been encompassed in Niebuhr's analysis. But I do not know of any current philosophical view that is not included, at least implicitly, in

Niebuhr's critique. If this is correct, then religion is on at least as good footing as philosophy, and *prima facie* on a better one, because Niebuhr shows that a more adequate anthropology comes from religion than from Western philosophy.

It may be too much to speak of "facts" of human life and existence, since one person's fact is another person's theory or hypothesis. But we can, I believe, speak of universal "experiences," of things about human life and existence that are so widespread and so clearly experienced by everyone everywhere that any adequate account of human life must include them. I do not yet know all the items that should appear on such a list, but I am convinced that the following items, at least, should be included: (1) Human beings are at the same time both natural and spiritual beings. By "natural" I mean sensuous, bodily, physical and animal; and by "spiritual" I mean thinking, self-transcending, rational, having hopes and fears, having a "mental"—as opposed to merely physical—history, having the possibility of relating with other "spiritual" entities (if there are any). (2) Human beings are creatures; they are not the ultimate origin of themselves. They are "lower than the gods." (3) Human beings are situated in history, both individually and as a group or species. The personal history of each individual includes birth, childhood, adolescence, maturation, all the cycles of living, and finally death. The history of the group or species includes the history of families, tribes, races, nations, and so on. (4) Human beings are either males or females; they have gender and gender differences. This point is controversial and will not be pursued here, but I am convinced that, in Aristotelian terminology, gender is more of an essential than an accidental property. (5) There is a flaw or malaise at the core of human existence.

The last claim, the claim that human beings have some innate flaw or ontological deficiency, is the central problem of this discussion. It is probably also the most controversial item on the list above. If it is assured only as a religious dogma, that is not sufficient reason to accept it. The claim of an inherent human flaw is certainly rejected by all, or almost all, of modern philosophy; the exception might be certain forms of existentialism, but even those views would equivocate on this claim to some degree or other. But, as shown above, the fact that philosophical views reject some claim is not sufficient to show that the claim is false, especially since the philosophical views handle the problem of philosophical anthropology so poorly. Marxists do accept the view that there is a human malaise or difficulty, but trace it to economic and social difficulties (class structures), and expect the malaise to disappear once the offensive structures are removed (once the socialist revolution succeeds). In particular, the Marxists, along with the rest of modern secular philosophy, reject the view that the malaise has its roots in human ontology—in the nature of human beings.

The particular question I am concerned with here is whether asserting an underlying human flaw—asserting that human beings exist under the cloud of what religion has called original sin—enhances or detracts from human value. I wish to claim that, paradoxical as it may seem, asserting the view that human beings are ontologically flawed—i.e., asserting that original sin is a fact—does enhance rather than detract from human value and well-being.

We might ask what results from rejecting the view that humans are essentially flawed—from rejecting original sin. One supposed result might be that we rid ourselves of "adolescent fears" or "primitive guilt" and that we become "free people." But this flies in the face of universal experience. The fears that arise from the human malaise, that accompany being human, extend well past adolescence. In fact they worsen, at least in some ways, as we age and near the end of our lives. Also, guilt is not just the plight of primitive people; indeed, the educated and cultured have at least as much guilt as the uneducated and uncultured (although the mode differs and what one is guilty about may differ). Finally, despite protestations to the contrary, we are not free (at least in any ultimate sense) no matter how much we may "progress." The most progressive or advanced people are still subject to fits of selfishness, of causing pain for others, and of ugliness. So, we can conclude this point by saying that denial of original sin flies in the face of observable facts.

An even more important consequence of the denial of original sin is what we might call the social consequence. If we reject the view that humans are ontologically flawed, this will lead us to suppose that difficulties arise solely because of bad education or bad environments or bad economic or social situations. Now, these are all causes of human difficulties, and are to be corrected to whatever extent is possible. But the view that these are the cause of all human evils leads to social, racial, economic, and cultural hubris. The final result of such hubris is racism, sexism, cultural and economic imperialism, and so on. We have seen so many examples of this in our century that there is no need to belabor the point. A belief in an inherent flaw in all human beings prevents our attributing some observed evil to some inadequate cause, and prevents our thinking it can be cured by some inadequate means. Evil is not confined to any class or structure. If it were so confined, then it would detract from human well-being to claim otherwise. But since it is not confined to any class or structure, it detracts equally from human well-being to claim that evil comes from class or social or economic causes. To be sure, social and economic structures often embody and perpetuate evil, and even increase it. But the fundamental problem cannot be solved by changing these things. Those who deny this are perpetuating a philosophical and moral sophistry. This sophistry (which is, unfortunately, very prevalent) diminishes human value and well-being far more than the assertion of the existence of original sin.

The Marxist approach to the problem of the human malaise is the most prevalent example of the bad social consequences of the denial of original sin. No Marxist restructuring of social and economic affairs has ever succeeded in eliminating evil; it has not even eliminated the social and economic evils it is supposed to solve. In fact, Marxist states have always been even more evil than the states they have replaced. (Marxists resist this claim, but must rely on moral and philosophical sophistry to do so.) In particular, the bureaucracy and military in Marxist states have been even more repressive and pain-causing than the bureaucracy and military that they have replaced. Protestations by Marxists that this comes about (if they are willing to admit it at all) because of the betrayal of Marxist principles, or because of the necessary resistance to counter-revolutionary forces from without or within are unconvincing. Why does this always happen? What is it about those principles that leads to more or less automatic betrayal? Why is it that officials in Marxist states (or in any Marxist group) exhibit the worst traits of the officials in non-Marxist states or groups? I submit that it is because Marxism has mislocated the problem of the human malaise, misunderstood that it is a problem not of class or economic situation but of the human heart, and given a false prescription for its solution—a prescription that by its nature exacerbates the ill. So it is correct to say, I believe, that Marxism provides the worst and most important example of cultural, racial, economic, political, and moral imperialism in the world today. Again, this claim is strenuously resisted by Marxists and apologists for Marxism and socialism (those are *not* the same, despite what some pro- and anti-Marxists claim), but it is nevertheless accurate, given a disinterested examination of the realities.

The facts of the human malaise are not read the same way by everyone. I am claiming that these "facts" point to an ontological problem in human beings. Others draw different conclusions. The main nonreligious alternative to Marxism today is bourgeois liberalism of various kinds (I will leave vague just what bourgeois liberalism is). This view has no concept of original sin, and attributes the human malaise, insofar as it is recognized at all, to inadequate education, economic or social disadvantage, or some kind of disease (e.g., "mental illness" or alcoholism). Now, lack of social or economic advantage, as well as all kinds of disease, are certainly evils (of a sort), but to see these as the grounds of the human malaise mistakes the result for the cause. Curing diseases, and solving the problems of educational, economic and social deprivation have never solved the problem of evil as such; healthy, educated, and advantaged people are certainly as capable of causing pain and suffering to others as are the disadvantaged. Indeed, it is an observable fact that many of the worst evils of the twentieth century have been created and perpetuated by the most educated and most socially and economically advantaged. Some might want to say that these people have been sick, and that was the reason for their behavior. But they have not been organically or physically sick. If by "sick" is meant "affected in some way so that they are morally deficient," then this is no doubt true, but it is misleading; "sickness" has become a surrogate for what religionists mean by "affected by original sin." In other words, "sick" has then come to mean "morally depraved." It seems to me that a great deal of confusion in the psychiatric and psychological fields comes about because of this attempt to subsume "morally depraved" under the term "sick," thereupon treating this sickness as if it were similar to organic or physical disease.

As stated above, it may seem that the view that human beings are under the shadow of original sin demeans human value. If it were not the case that human beings are ontologically flawed, it would be a diminution of their value to claim otherwise. But since there are very good reasons to conclude that there is indeed a flaw at the core of human existence, then it demeans human value to claim otherwise because the denial of this flaw denies any reasonable possibility of rectifying it, and forces us to attribute evil to mistaken (and hence mistake-making) causes. We need both a doctrine of sin (to fit the "facts") and a doctrine of salvation (to provide a remedy for these observed "facts"). Bourgeois liberalism fails because it has no doctrine of sin, and Marxism fails because (among other reasons) its doctrines of the "fall" and salvation are mistaken. Both therefore make the situations that they are supposed to understand and solve even worse. Evil is not primarily a matter of structures (economic, political, social) but of the human heart, out of which structures are created. It is also not a matter of race or gender; all races and both genders are equally affected by the ontological flaw. One result of the denial of original sin (or of the assertion of mistaken views of it) is the rise of racism and sexism. The assertion of an adequate doctrine of original sin is necessary, I believe, to avoid sexism and racism, in addition to all the other reasons.

If all this is so, then having a proper or adequate doctrine of original sin provides a better and higher view of human existence than having no view of sin. An adequate doctrine of original sin enhances human well-being and human value because it conforms to observable experiences or "facts," and it provides the necessary grounds for a realistic solution. This avoids false consciousness, much like the situation in which a doctor, observing a patient with cancer, enhances the value and well-being of the patient more by admitting the existence of the cancer and attempting a cure than by denying its existence.

Having concluded that a view of original sin enhances human value, we must examine the question of just what view gives the right account of the origin and nature of sin, and especially the view that gives the correct solution to it. The wrong view of sin, or the wrong solution to it, will almost certainly be at least as problematic—and as demeaning to human well-being—as having no view at all. Therefore, although it may be a good stance for ecumenical dialogue, it is not a good philosophical or moral position to avoid presenting what one thinks is the best view and arguing for its superiority over other views, even though it may be disturbing to proponents of those other views.

Above I stated that I do not accept Niebuhr's account of original sin. Through the centuries, theologians (Christian and non-Christian) have given numerous explanations of sin; two typical views are that sin is an affliction of the will or that sin is concupiscence. If I understand Niebuhr correctly, his account parallels those views. In my judgment, the Unification account is a fuller or better view than any other I have encountered. No complete account of the Unification view will be provided here, but I will present and comment on some reasons why it is the best view.[9]

According to Unificationism, the original sin occurred when

the archangel Lucifer seduced the first woman, Eve, into an illicit or forbidden spiritual sexual relationship. This was the spiritual fall, and in this fall the archangel became Satan. Eve, in turn, seduced the first man into an improper (because it was premature and not sanctioned by God) physical sexual relationship with her. This was the physical fall.[10] As a result, the position of God as head and parent of the human race was taken over (at least partly) by Satan.[11] The fundamental result of the fall, then, is the separation of humanity, and especially the human heart, from God. Unificationism is a federal theology—what is true of the parent or leader is true of the children or followers—so all human beings inherit from the original parents of the human race this condition of fallenness.[12] Consequently, we can say that one result of the Unification account of sin is that sin is universal; there is no person who does not exist under the shadow of original sin, and consequently there are no grounds for any false hubris, any sexism, any racism, or any other claim that somehow some people are better than others.

A second result of the Unification account is that human beings are fallen—separated from God—both physically and spiritually.[13] In the Unification view, every entity has both *Sung Sang* and *Hyung Sang;* these come from God and both originate in and parallel the divine *Original Sung Sang* and *Original Hyung Sang*. In the fall, both the human *Sung Sang* and *Hyung Sang* were at least partly taken over—or *infected,* if one prefers that terminology—by Satan. So both the inner dimension of the human—intellect, emotion, will, along with ideas, concepts, laws, mathematical principles, and so on, all centering on heart—as well as the physical or bodily dimension are all infected by sin.[14] Thus, both those who locate the human malaise in the physical dimension and those who locate it in the mental or spiritual dimension are partly correct, but only partly. They are equally incorrect in failing to see that the other dimension is problematic as well. Unificationism partly agrees with those theologians who root sin either in disorders of the will or in concupiscence (or both), but also disagrees with them because they have not seen the full dimensions of sin, according to the Unification view.

A third result of the Unification view is that there is a genuine recognition of the real existence of Satan and of the demonic.[15] This may not seem to be an advantage to those who have given up belief in the real existence of Satan and other demonic entities, but to those who know differently it is useful to have an account of sin that also accounts for the origin of Satan and accounts for the hold this being has been able to maintain over human existence and human affairs. Those spiritualists who claim to have real experience of the existence and activities of Satan can also find confirmation of their experience in the Unification account of sin.

A fourth advantage of the Unification view is that it provides a better grounding for a solution to the problem of theodicy. There is no way that God can be both completely good and completely powerful if evil exists. Many attempts have been made to solve this problem. I do not claim that Unificationism solves it, but that it provides a better basis for solving it than other views. In the Unification view, God gave power and responsibility for human maturation and perfection to human beings, and this responsibility is not abrogated even in the face of impending sin.[16] It also remains even after the fall has occurred; humans have at least partial responsibility to undo the results of the fall.[17] Unificationism, therefore, draws back from declaring God to be totally powerful—God cannot intervene in such a way as to abrogate human responsibility—while retaining the declaration that God is wholly good. In this way, the Unification view offers the possibility for a better solution to theodicy than any theology or soteriology that attributes complete power to God (as do, for example, Calvinism and Augustinianism).

A fifth plus of the Unification view is that it holds that the fall occurred (and indeed was made possible) when the original humans were imperfect, but sinless.[18] Imperfection, then, is the occasion and possibility for sin, but not its cause, and sin is not the same as absence of perfection. Those views that have sin as a fall from perfection (e.g., Augustine's view) imply that even that which is perfect can sin. In the Unification view, once perfection is attained, sin is impossible. Therefore, there is the possibility that sin can eventually be completely done away with, without the fear that it might reappear in a perfected being. Another way of saying it is: in the Unification view, perfection is really perfect, without possibility of defect or sin. (But note also that the Unification view of perfection does not require that the perfect being not have any other defects or limitations; such a view of perfection is unrealistic and mistakes perfection of love for other kinds of completeness, which are not so important.)

A sixth advantage of the Unification view is that it parallels universal human experience of the power of love and the universal temptation to seduction and misuse of love. The Unification view shows the force of the misuse of love and of the lack of proper love. In this view, even murder has its roots in lack of love and in improper love (i.e., Cain's murder of Abel resulted from Cain's lack of love for his brother Abel, Abel's lack of love for his brother Cain, and the inability of fallen Adam and Eve to give proper love to their children). The evidence of scenes of seduction similar to Lucifer's seduction of Eve, and Eve's seduction of Adam, with attendant results, is all around us in human life, both historically and today. The Unification account of the fall shows why these facts are so universal and so destructive. But it also shows that they must be avoided if goodness is to prevail in human affairs. This is something that almost no other account of sin can forcefully address: *Why* should seduction be avoided? Is it just that parents, elders, and the churches and other institutions say so, or are there convincing reasons for these strictures and warnings? If the Unification account is correct, then indeed human life and well-being are denigrated far more by failing to assert and insist on these facts about the fall and original sin and its consequences than by knowing and stating them.[19]

A seventh point to be made for the Unification view is its superiority to any form of the *felix culpa* view. In the latter, human value is subordinated to a whim or caprice, or at least a power play, on the part of divinity; human happiness on a fall. In the Unification view, however, the fall is an unmitigated disaster; no one has any *real* (as opposed to *apparent*) interest in it. God did not benefit from the fall; Lucifer did not benefit—he became Satan, forced to "eat dust" as a result (Gen. 2:14–15)—and human beings became separated from God and goodness. Therefore both God and human beings have a primary interest in solving sin. One of the results of sin, however, is that human perception of reality is beclouded so that humans may fail to recognize their real interest. So one result of the fall was the beginning of human deception and the perpetuation of self-deception through the disordering of human self- and God-perception. Fallen humans have a primary interest in solving their own self-deception and their deception by Satan and the demonic forces. God also has a self-interest in having the problem of the fall solved because it is only in that way that the divine reasons for creation can be fulfilled. Even Satan, in the Unification view, must eventually be saved from sin because that is the only way that the divine purpose for creation (which includes a purpose for goodness for Lucifer as well) can be brought to fruition.[20] This divine purpose for creation, in the Unification view, is a purpose or design for only goodness. Sin and the fall constitute an unmitigated disruption of that purpose for goodness. (One could claim, I suppose, that the Unification view implies that the fall occurred because the divine purpose for having humans be responsible superseded the divine purpose for not having sin occur. But the Unification view implies, I believe, that it is not sin that God desired but human creativity. Sin came about because of the misuse of this freedom and creativity, and not because of its existence as such.) In any event, Unificationism is very clear in asserting that as a result of the fall, God, as well as humanity, has become miserable.[21]

The Unification solution to sin is also a better view than others, I believe, because it is more complete. In the Unification view, the fundamental problem of sin is a disordering of the human parentage—Satan has usurped the position of parent of the human race that is supposed to be held by God. This problem is perpetuated by all human parents from Adam and Eve on because all are born under the condition of the fall. The fundamental solution to sin, then, is to have a new set of parents who are fully connected with the divine—as Adam and Eve were before the fall but could not be by themselves afterwards. In Unification theology this divine parent is the Messiah, one who comes to restore humans to the divine by restoring the position of Adam and Eve.[22] So the function of the Messiah is, first, to restore a bride, then to have a divine family, and to restore the rest of humankind to God by having them become the children of the messianic family.[23] In Unificationism, salvation is restoration. This restoration includes restoring everything that was lost in the fall—faith in God and unity among all human beings and between humans and the natural order, centered on the divine purpose and will.[24] The Unification account of this process of salvation or restoration is a better one, I believe, because it is more complete and provides a better description of what is required of humans, of God, and of the Messiah than any other view. It offers, therefore, a better hope. This may seem a more fragile hope than what is offered by the hope of the Marxist revolution or of bourgeois education and economic advancement, but I think otherwise. Those other views either do not take sin seriously enough, and therefore offer no hope of salvation (you can't cure a patient unless you are aware he or she is sick, unless you just happen to get lucky), or they try to solve a symptom (evil economic or political or social structures) without solving the underlying problem that produces the symptoms. The Unification view, I believe, offers a realistic and hopeful solution to both the underlying problem and (eventually) to all the symptoms.

A major task that remains is to compare the Unification view of original sin and its solution with the views of other religions. In this paper, I have made some comparisons with some major Christian views. Similar comparisons must also be made with Buddhism, Hinduism, Confucianism, Islam, and so on. I am not knowledgeable enough of any of these religions to make this comparison, although, from the little I know, it seems that Unificationism does offer something more or better. But investigation of these questions must await another occasion and other more informed scholars.

Notes

1   See Nelson Goodman's *Fact, Fiction and Forecast,* 4th ed. (Cambridge: Harvard University Press, 1983), for an account of virtuous circles.

2   Cf., for example, John Rawls, *A Theory of Justice* (Cambridge: Harvard University Press, 1971). For a critical reading of Rawls from a more or less Marxist point of view, a reading that shows that Rawls cannot succeed on the basis of the principles he has adopted, see Robert Paul Wolff, *Understanding Rawls* (Princeton: Princeton University Press, 1977). Rawls has nothing to say about the processes of birth, maturation, family life, and so on; he seems to assume that all human beings are professionals between the ages of about 21 and 60.

3   Reinhold Niebuhr, *The Nature and Destiny of Man* (New York: Scribner's, 1941 & 1964), 2 vols.

4   Ibid., vii.

5   Ibid., 4ff.

6   Ibid., 5.

7   Ibid., 24.

8   Ibid., 24, 25.

9   For the Unification view, see *Divine Principle,* 2d ed. (Washington, D.C.: Holy Spirit Association for the Unification of World Christianity [HSA-UWC], 1973), esp. 65–98. See also Young Oon Kim, *Unification Theology* (New York: HSA-UWC, 1980), esp. 89–125. The papers by

Jonathan Wells and Young Oon Kim in this volume also contribute to an understanding of the Unification view, as do those by Durwood Foster and Gene James.

10 *Divine Principle,* 69–80.

11 Ibid., 73.

12 On Unificationism as a federal theology, see Herbert W. Richardson, "A Brief Outline of Unification Theology," in *A Time for Consideration* ed. M. Darrol Bryant and Herbert W. Richardson (New York: Edwin Mellen, 1978), 134.

13 See *Divine Principle,* 218, where it is asserted that both spiritual and physical rebirth are necessary.

14 Concerning Unification ontology, especially its view of *Sung Sang* and *Hyung Sang* and *Original Sung Sang* and *Original Hyung Sang,* see Sang Hun Lee, *Explaining Unification Thought* (New York: Unification Thought Institute, 1981), chaps. 1, 2, and 3.

15 See the paper by Young Oon Kim in this volume on this topic. See also her *Unification Theology,* 107–9.

16 See *Divine Principle,* 95–97.

17 See *Divine Principle,* 106, 221–30, 237–38. See also *Unification Theology,* 69–74. Reverend Moon often speaks of this responsibility in speeches to members.

18 See *Unification Theology,* 121; *Divine Principle,* 80–83.

19 See *Divine Principle,* 75, 76, "The Root of Sin."

20 This does not occur in *Divine Principle,* but Reverend Moon has occasionally mentioned it in speeches to members.

21 See the excerpts from Reverend Moon's speeches in the section entitled "God's Heart," in *The Way of Tradition* (New York: HSA-UWC, 1980), 1:43–81.

22 See [Chung Hwan Kwak], *Outline of the Principle: Level 4* (New York: HSA-UWC, 1980), pp. 55, 56.

23 Ibid., 97–99.

24 This constitutes restoration of the so-called Three Great Blessings. On this, see *Outline of the Principle: Level 4,* 22–26.

13 Sin and Society
M. DARROL BRYANT

Christianity is a vision of the unfolding of human life from and to God. Reflection upon the constitutive elements of that vision—creation, fall, redemption, sanctification, and consummation—has led to a variety of accounts or interpretations of the meaning of that vision for our life together in the world. Often presented in fierce and uncompromising opposition to one another, those rival intra-Christian accounts nonetheless bear the marks of family resemblance. Fundamental to all readings of the Christian vision is the conviction that human life is inexplicable simply in relation to itself. Rather, the Christian vision requires that we understand the unfolding of human life in all its dimensions in relation to its transcendent source and end. Moreover, despite the variations of interpretation, there is a pervasive conviction that human life is flawed, broken, or disordered. Thus our life together, sustained by the providential dispositions of God, is marked by the condition of sin.

In the modern era, the attempt to relate the Christian vision to the unfolding of a culture that increasingly understands itself in autonomous terms has often led to the eclipse of traditional teachings on sin. The reasons for this are, I believe, related to assumptions that emerged in the Enlightenment.[1] Central here is the belief in human perfectibility such that the problems of human life will finally give way to the transformation of that life through the restructuring of society by the progressive enlightenment of reason, science, and technology. The success of this social project has placed Christian theologians on the defensive, especially in relation to a teaching that our humanity is flawed, broken, or wounded in such a fundamental way that it will not be overcome by *any* form of social engineering or transformation.

Given the Enlightenment worldview and the success of the cultural project it has undergirded, what are we to make of the traditional Christian teaching that all human life is fundamentally flawed since the fall? Since the Enlightenment there have been several responses within the family of Christian traditions to this dilemma. Here, however, I want to focus on that reinterpretation of the Christian teaching on sin that I will call the "socio-political"—the type of response that we find in Walter Rauschenbusch, the great American theologian of the social gospel, and in Gregory Baum, the Canadian exponent of political theology. While I have considerable sympathy for these positions, I do believe that they also embody a fundamental mistake that skews the doctrine of sin. But before turning to a critical analysis of their views, I want to say something about my understanding of the thrust of traditional Christian teaching on this point.

Of all the teachings of the Christian faith, the teaching on sin, original and consequent, has always struck me as the most self-evidently true. The truth of this teaching I have never doubted. But the context for my sense of the reality of sin is not, in the first instance, a particular confession, nor a certain theological reading of this teaching, nor a particular exegeses of certain biblical texts. Rather, the context that has always been central for me in affirming the truth of this teaching is the context of everyday life. The belief that life is flawed by sin has always seemed to me a primal realization that simply comes with our experience of life in the world. Even prior to the reflection upon the everyday world is the experience of a "basic fault"—in an almost geological sense—that pervades our life together. It is this "fault" that manifests itself in our lives and our life together that provides the experiential touchstone for reflection on this teaching and for adjudicating second-order differences in theory.

But Christian doctrines of sin do not, to my knowledge, proceed in this commonsense way. Rather, this teaching is usually presented at a much higher level of abstraction: in creeds and confessions, in systematic treatises, and in learned exegeses of biblical texts. Within the Christian community, the teaching on sin is mediated through the liturgy and through preaching. In this way it enters more directly into the life of Christians as a way of rendering more explicable the life we daily live and suffer. Theologians should, I believe, take the context of daily life more seriously in their reflection on sin as the concrete context in which lives unfold and should know in part the mystery of sin, redemption, and the hope for the consummation of all things. In this respect, I find myself in complete agreement with Sharon MacIsaac, who in her fine study on *Freud and Original Sin,* argues that "it is important for a profound and substantial theology of original sin that the experiential starting point be the focus. That theology has been weakened and even trivialized by overspeculation, by a shift of emphasis onto hypothetical and deductive elements on the periphery of the central message."[2] The central message, I would argue, concerns the disorder that pervades our humanity in all its multiform dimensions.

Yet the distance between daily life and reflection upon sin is evident when one reads the classic literature on the doctrine of sin. Here one encounters a wide variety of theoretical accounts of sin and its origins. Usually these accounts are presented as rival theories—and in a sense they are. The differences between the accounts are buttressed by appeals to different exegeses of scriptural sources, differing philosophical accounts of human nature, different theological criteria. But one can ask whether or not the rival accounts are genuinely contrary to one another so that the affirmation of one requires the denial of another. Must one choose between an Irenaean view of sin as immaturity, an Augustinian view of sin as turning away from the good, an Anselmian view of sin as dishonoring, a Thomist view of sin as irrationality, a Calvinist view of sin as idolatry? Viewed from the perspective of the multiformity of our life in the world, we need not regard these differing accounts as mutually exclusive accounts of the reality of sin and its origins.[3] Rather we might more fruitfully view them as attempts to specify the reality of the "basic fault" in relation to differing spheres, dimensions, and aspects of our common—and fallen—experience of life in the world. If we were to examine these various accounts of sin, as it were, *from below* and trace their rootage in determinative experience, then we might well arrive at a richer understanding of the Christian teaching on sin. In other words, I would argue that *the decisive theoretical difference is not between different Christian accounts of sin and its origins, but between accounts of human life that acknowledge a "basic fault" and those that do not.*

Christian doctrines of sin are, then, attempts to grasp and penetrate, in a synthetic and resonant image and theory, the basic fault that underlies and pervades the disorder of human life together in the world. For example, Canon I of the Council of Orange states that "if anyone denies that it is the whole man, that is, both body and soul, that was 'changed for the worse' through the offense of Adam's sin . . . he is deceived."[4] Likewise, a similar emphasis on the universality of sin is found in the Westminster Confession where we read that humankind became, due to sin, "wholly defiled in all the faculties and parts of soul and body."[5] Generations of theologians have, then, devoted themselves to attempts to specify these convictions and beliefs in terms of the effect and extent of the fall, the degree of damage to human nature, the way sin manifests itself in the mind, the soul, and the body. And we have much to learn from these accounts. But the *teaching* concerning a fundamental disorder that pervades humanity will always outrun the theological specifications of that teaching.

For many theologians in the modern world, the traditional vocabulary in which the Christian teaching on sin was articulated has become problematic. Overtones have overwhelmed groundtones. But the thrust of the traditional teaching is, to my mind, clear. When Georges Florovsky, the contemporary Orthodox historian and theologian, wrote that "original sin was not just an erroneous choice, not just an option for the wrong direction, but rather a refusal to ascend toward God, a desertion from the service of God" he stood in continuity with that longer tradition.[6] But that longer tradition often assumed a worldview that stands in marked contrast to the worldview that characterizes modernity. In the Enlightened world, the traditional teaching, with its emphasis on the universality and pervasiveness of sin in all aspects of life, increasingly falls on deaf ears, or ones that find this teaching an affront to their efforts to remake the world in their own image.

In *The Language of Faith*, Samuel Laeuchli observes that there is a significant shift in the language of sin from the New Testament to the Apostolic Fathers. Whereas in the New Testament "sin is seen as a breach in the relationship between God and man," the Apostolic Fathers see sin as "primarily 'doing bad'."[7] These two ways of speaking about sin—as a broken relationship and as discrete acts—have persisted in the Christian traditions. Down to the present day, we find some Christian thinkers focusing their attention on questions of theological anthropology, while others focus their attention on discrete actions. While these emphases can be related to one another by arguing that our actions manifest the broken relationship between God and humanity, it must be acknowledged that these different emphases have often confused the discussion of sin. Here I am arguing for an understanding of *sin as a condition,* a condition that arises from a break in communion between God and humankind. The result of that break is a disordering within the very nature of humanity. Often such a view is criticized from within the Christian circle as leading to pessimism about human beings. Such a criticism would be justified, in my view, if it were not for the following remedy.

In the long history of reflection upon our wounded and fallen humanity, the conviction has persisted that such an affirmation must be linked to the simultaneous longing for redemption within the human heart. In theological terms, the doctrine of sin must always be correlated with a doctrine of redemption and consummation. Without this linkage, there is a tendency for the teaching on sin as a condition of all human beings to lead to an undesirable pessimism. But this has been avoided historically through an insistence that the consciousness of sin as a basic fault that disorders human life be dialectically linked with a consciousness of a redeemed humanity that God is forming in the very midst of this fallen world. At issue is the grounding of hope for the restoration of humanity and not any denial of the dignity of human beings.[8] Against this background, then, let me turn to the analysis of the perspectives on sin and society found in Rauschenbusch and Baum.

In *A Theology for the Social Gospel,* Walter Rauschenbusch calls for a radical reformulation of the Christian faith in terms that will be adequate to the new historical situation. At the heart of Rauschenbusch's enterprise was a desire to understand the Christian faith in social terms. He contrasted his "social gospel" with "the individualistic gospel." As he wrote, "the individualistic gospel has taught us to see the sinfulness of every human heart and has inspired us with faith in the willingness and power of God to save every soul that comes to God. But it has not given us an adequate understanding of the sinfulness of the social order and its share in the sins of all individuals within it."[9] Thus at the very core of his work is a concern to grasp the social meaning of sin.

Using the insights of recent historical criticism and of theological liberalism, Rauschenbusch argues that the "traditional doctrine of the fall has taught us to regard evil as a kind of unvarying racial endowment which is active in every new life . . ."[10] Such a view does not allow us to grasp adequately the way in which sin pervades the very structures of society and, more importantly, tends to undercut efforts to change those structures. Nonetheless, Rauschenbusch contends that his view of sin is basically a traditional view, namely, that sin is selfishness which "furnishes an excellent theological basis for a social conception of sin and salvation."[11] However, he argues further that we must then turn to society to see sin since "sin is not a private transaction between the sinner and God."[12] Sin then is manifest in society because here it is that we "put our hands on social groups who have turned the patrimony of a nation into the private property of a small class, or have left the peasant laborers cowed, degraded, demoralized and without rights . . ."[13] In this way Rauschenbusch sought to turn attention of his readers to those sinful social structures that are larger than individuals. Moreover, rather than arguing for a biological transmission of sin from generation to generation, Rauschenbusch contended that we should look to the ways that a sinful social environment affects the life of a new generation. Thus sin takes the form of "super-personal forces of evil" that stand counter to the kingdom of God.

Contrary to some critics of Rauschenbusch, it should be clear that he has a very strong doctrine of sin. Sin is selfishness both in the human heart and in human society. The selfishness that is in the human heart leads to the creation of social structures which legitimate that selfishness, becoming selfishness writ large. The question that then arises is the remedy for sin. In Rauschenbusch's view, the antidote to the kingdom of evil is the kingdom of God, which is "humanity organized according to the will of God."[14] In social terms this involves the creation of social institutions that are not selfish: "the redemption of society from political autocracies and economic oligarchies; the substitution of redemptive for vindictive penology; the abolition of constraint through hunger as part of the industrial system; and the abolition of war as the supreme expression of hate . . ."[15] If these changes in social institutions were to be accomplished, would sin then be abolished?

Seen from the perspective outlined above, Rauschenbusch's position could be seen as an attempt to specify the meaning of sin in the social order. But in the process he breaks with the traditional teaching on sin as a basic fault that arises from the disruption of the relationship between God and the creature. This fault cannot be overcome by the reorganizing of social structures. That does not mean that we cannot or should not attempt to create more humane or just social institutions. Rather, my point is that Rauschenbusch has confused two orders: the ontological and the historical. It seems to me that the traditional teaching on sin was articulated within a worldview that affirms a metaphysical or ontological understanding of human nature. In the wake of the Enlightenment, such views have increasingly come under attack. Instead, the post-Enlightenment world has come to believe that man is a creature of time alone.

Rauschenbusch, albeit ambivalently, shares that assumption. Thus within his perspective there is, it seems to me, a tendency to historicize the doctrine of sin so that it is open to an historical remedy. As I indicated earlier, I find much to admire in Rauschenbusch: his passion for justice and his critical analysis of social structures. But at the same time, his analysis of sin often leads to the mistaken conclusion that the alteration of social structures will overcome sin. Thus, once a link between sin and society is established, the tendency is to believe that the alteration of those so-called "sinful" social structures will alleviate the problem of sin. While we certainly know that social structures are open to change and that history attests to their being transformed, it seems much more difficult to show that with their transformation sin is overcome. Rather, sin as that condition of turning away from God will have its way—regardless of the social structures.[16] While the transformation of structures certainly addresses itself to the issues of justice in the world, it does not touch the issue of sin in the sense of "basic fault."

The same set of problems is encountered in more recent expressions of political theology. Gregory Baum, in his distinguished work *Religion and Alienation,* argues that "the notion of sin in theological teaching and religious practice has become excessively individualistic."[17] We have, he argues, "forgotten the social dimension of sin." And what is that? In Baum's view the social dimension of sin is dehumanizing social institutions, or better, "the structure of evil, built into society, which wounds people, distorts their inclinations and prompts them to do evil things."[18] But social sin, unlike personal sin, is not, Baum argues, rooted in deliberation and free choice, but rather it is "committed out of blindness."[19] Baum offers his analysis of social sin in the context of an interpretation of the great sociologists—Marx, Toennies, and Weber—whose insights, he argues, should be incorporated into our theological thinking. Baum's analysis of social processes is considerably more sophisticated and nuanced than is Rauschenbusch's. The personal-social dialectic of sin is, Baum argues, considerably illumined by sociologists' understanding of the relationship between consciousness and society. With the insights that sociology provides, we can distinguish, Baum argues, four levels of social sin: (1) "the injustices and dehumanizing trends built into the various institutions ... which embody people's collective life," (2) "the cultural and religious symbols that reinforce and legitimate unjust institutions,"

(3) "the false consciousness created by these institutions," and (4) "the collective decisions, generated by the distorted consciousness, which increase the injustices in society and intensify the power of the dehumanizing trends."[20] Baum's analysis of social sin is rich and often helpful in understanding the dynamics of contemporary society.

But when we ask Baum to spell out the implications of his analysis for Christian practice, then we can see the dangerous consequences of his view. For Baum, we currently find ourselves in a cultural crisis where the Christian is faced with a basic option. The question for Christians, Baum argues, is "whether they should regard it as their religious duty to shore up the inherited social consensus and the cultural values that are being questioned, or whether they should join the critical forces in society and work for the re-creation of social life in greater accord with the future promises."[21] Thus Baum's analysis of social sin leads him to a basic political option: for what is or for what might be. Baum's analysis of the current situation leads him to opt for "future promises." But is this not to oversimplify the multiform situation in which human beings find themselves? Are we not daily being asked to maintain or let go of the past—to say yes or no to the demands of the future? Can this multiform situation be transformed into an ideological option where we say once and for all *yea* or *nay* to society? Surely the question that Baum poses is overdrawn and oversimplified. Moreover, it leaves unclear the basis for determining the "dehumanizing trends in society." Are they *ipso facto* whatever is? Or, to ask the question from another side, are there not social structures that testify, if you will, to the redemptive presence of God in society to sustain and conserve human life and keep it human? It is the upshot of Baum's analysis of the structures of society that whatever is, is so bound up within the "structure of evil" that it is virtually impossible to even imagine what a healthy or humanizing institution of society would look like. But when sin is understood in social terms, rather than as a condition of our humanity that arises out of the disruption between God and humankind, then are we not committed to a view of society that cannot see it as a gift given, in part, to rescue us from our fallen condition? In other words, there are traditions within Christian theology that argue for the remedial function of society precisely in its capacity to lift us beyond ourselves to a more inclusive humanity. What happens to this tradition in the face of Baum's analysis of sin?

What is surprising in those options within modern theology that have emphasized a doctrine of social sin is the absence of a constructive statement on the place of social institutions in social life. While their analyses of present institutional forms are often insightful, one is often left with the impression of a wholesale judgment against the present social order, that all social institutions are so permeated by "sin" that they do not merit our continued stewardship and reforming loyalty. Is not the analysis of social institutions then so overlaid with an ideological grid-that we have difficulty recognizing our experience of social institutions in their descriptions? Such questions seem irrelevant to the analysis of society in North America that Baum offers. In his view, the "critical" Christian must stand over against the present order, choosing either the "reformist" or "radical" option: "the first option urges Christians to join people in the existing institutions struggling for the introduction of some public ownership into the economic system and social change on various levels of society, while the second option makes Christians seek a more radical life . . ."[22] Thus his analysis of social sin leads to a full politicization of the Christian faith. Faith, hope, and love require a distinctive political form if they are genuine.

Here, then, we see the consequences of a thoroughgoing socio-political account of sin. Underlying both the perspectives analyzed here is a commitment to a basically historicist reformulation of Christian teaching on the fall and sin. Once sin is understood in socio-political categories, then the remedy for sin comes to be viewed in increasingly political terms. The overcoming of sin is an historical process of substituting "unselfish" institutions for those "selfish" institutions that constitute the reality of sin in society, or in creating "humanizing" institutions to replace "dehumanizing" structures. Thus the Christian faith is politicized.[23] And, at least in principle, we may look forward to the overcoming of sin. Sin as the condition of our fallen humanity is eclipsed. Such a profound reformulation of the Christian teaching on sin shows itself, upon analysis, to be consistent with the assumptions of the Enlightenment worldview, in which humanity is now set free to remake itself in its own image.

An understanding of sin as a condition of our humanity arising from a break in the communion between the creature and God certainly has implications for our understanding of society. But those implications are different than what arises when the teaching on sin is explicated solely in socio-political categories. We have seen how the socio-political categories tend to overwhelm the theological categories, thus transforming Christian faith from a vision of human life in its unfolding from and to God into a political option within the field of historical power. Nevertheless, there is something proper about the modern attempts to understand the social meaning of sin. But those attempts become skewed when the *theo*logical assumptions are not maintained. In a word, though sin is certainly *manifest* in the life of humankind and in our societies, it is not the transformation of social institutions that rectifies sin. Rather sin as a condition of our humanity will continue to pervade our life together in society. This does not mean, as indicated before, that we should not seek to transform unjust social institutions and social forms that are inadequate to their tasks. But we should not believe that those new institutions will rescue us from sin.

Even in that necessary task of determining which institutions are in need of alteration, it is unclear to me that the category of "social sin" is of much help. Rather, it is often the case that the labeling of an institution or system as "sinful" precludes the discriminating analysis of social institutions required. There are, for example, those who would label the institution of marriage as "sinful" because it encourages *qua institution* attachment to another particular person to the exclusion of others and limits this type of relationship to people of opposite sexes. Likewise, the current tendency to speak of very complex economic systems such as "capitalism" or "socialism" as sinful or not sinful is more an exercise in ideological abstraction than it is anything else. Christian thinkers would do well, in my view, to resist the temptation to indulge in ideological portrayals of our life in society.[24] Indeed, it is here that the possibility of sin resides. The more pressing need, in my view, is an attempt to see the life of societies in the context of the divine economy, whose traces we may see in retrospect with sufficient clarity through prayerful contemplation within the circle of faith, so that it may give us orientation toward the future. But even that option must be pursued with great humility, since we first live in the future before we can know it.

As argued above, sin is dialectically linked with redemption. We therefore find ourselves in the midst of a fallen world where the redemptive work of God unfolds. And that redemptive work includes, I believe, the lifting up of human historic and social life into the life of God.

Society is in this perspective a gift of God that involves, in Burke's wonderful statement, the cooperative efforts of the living, the dead, and the yet unborn.[25] This perspective recognizes the fact that society both precedes the present generation and requires the cooperative efforts of those who come after us. Thus we are lifted beyond the circle of our own narcissism. And in the give and take of our exchange with the dead and unborn as well as with our own generation, we transcend that mark of sin that Augustine described as the tendency of the self to turn in upon itself. Within that intergenerational context, social institutions serve to provide a form for the addressing of the multiple social tasks that it is the obligation of every generation to address. While social institutions live and die, they are not nearly so amenable to the will as some assume. Rather, only in critical moments in the life of society do they become subject to significant transformation. In the lifting of the lives of persons beyond themselves, society, as the spiritual partnership of the "dead, the living and the yet unborn," testifies to its redemptive function in the divine economy. But every generation must be vigilant in its efforts to keep its intergenerational life, institutions, and social processes open to the divine imperatives that are their transcendent grounds. Sin is a mystery in human life—an inexplicable turning away from the good that corrupts our intergenerational life and institutions. Society, in this perspective, does not just unfold in relation to itself, but in relation to the eternal, divine ordering of all things. Thus we can not only judge a society in relation to the competing claims of one power grouping or another, but also can see the whole of society's life in the light of the divine claims of justice and unity.

Such a view of the relationship between sin and society requires, however, that we recover the tradition of sin as a condition arising from the disruption of that most primal and fundamental of all "societies," that of God and his creatures. It is this tradition that has been most called into question by the reduction of reality to what the human being makes in time and the success of the Enlightenment worldview. The perfecting of humanity through social engineering or political transformation is a belief that cannot be reconciled with the Christian vision, even when that view is draped in the language of faith. The bigger challenge to Christian thinking is to demonstrate anew the meaning of its vision of the unfolding of life from and to God in terms of the historic and social life of humankind. Here we might learn anew that the one we encounter in the midst of our daily life is not only another human image, but the One in whose image we were made.

Notes

1   In setting my discussion within the context of the impact of the Enlightenment worldview on the doctrine of sin, I want to make it clear that I do not reject the great social achievements of the Enlightenment. The contributions of the Enlightenment to modern political institutions, in terms of the doctrine of human rights and its positive support of science and technology in the life of humankind, merit our continuing loyalty and gratitude. My critique of the Enlightenment centers on the underlying assumptions of human perfectibility and autonomy, assumptions that have frightful consequences. Both of these assumptions cannot be sustained within the context of classical Christian theology. They can, however, be transformed and humanized by faith in ways analogous to the Christian appropriation of the traditions of the ancient world. In this process the classical Christian understanding of humanity as fallen is crucial. Why? It is not in order to say no to the emancipated consciousness of the Enlightenment, but in order to restore a sense of the *limits* of human improvement and the *limits* of autonomy. What is lost in the Enlightenment is, in my view, this sense of limits. When humanity is viewed as "perfect" within itself, then we lose the capacity to think about the question of human life and society against the backdrop of the transcendent vocation of all humanity to God. Moreover, we fail to recognize the theological grounds of the life of humanity—the work of God in creation, redemption, and sanctification. And we must ask, it seems to me, about the limits of science and of the dialectical relationship of rights and obligations in society. But such questions cannot be adequately handled on the basis of the assumptions of human perfection and autonomy. Here the Canadian social philosopher George Grant has been very instructive for me. See his *Technology and Empire: Perspectives on North America* (Toronto: Anansi, 1969), *Time as History* (Toronto: CBC, 1974), and the collection of essays on Grant edited by Larry Schmidt, *George Grant in Process* (Toronto: Anansi, 1978).

2   Sharon MacIsaac, *Freud and Original Sin* (New York: Paulist Press, 1974), 1.

3   What I am suggesting here is a "meta-theological" approach to the

doctrine of sin, namely, a recognition that *all* doctrines of sin are attempts to specify the nature and consequences of sin in relation to differing dimensions of the *multiform* life of humanity. Thus differing doctrines of sin may, upon analysis, be shown to address themselves to differing dimensions rather than to the same human condition. It would seem for example, that Luther, Calvin, Irenaeus, Thomas, and Augustine are not addressing themselves to the same human situation, but to differing *aspects* of a common condition. Thus a full Christian account of sin would require all these views, rather than one to the exclusion of another. Similarly, when viewed from below, the Unification teaching on sin is, in my view, an important attempt to specify the meaning of sin for familial and intergenerational life. Rather than concentrating on inward, psycho-spiritual consequences of the fall (for example, pride or faithlessness), the Unification teaching focuses on the disordering of family life that arises from sin. This more relational and institutional understanding of sin is a helpful corrective to the overly individualistic specifications of sin that characterize Protestant Christianity. But we are not confronted with a choice at this point—either the Unification view or another—but rather with an expansion of our understanding of the consequences of sin for a particular order of human life. Thus, while I am not inclined to accept the overstatements of the Unification account, I do find the emphasis on "lineage" and how sin distorts family life from generation to generation an important insight. Moreover, the relational understanding of sin emphasized in the Unification teaching is one that I find helpful.

4   *Creeds of the Churches,* ed. John H. Leith (Garden City, N.Y.: Anchor Books, 1963), 38. The thrust of the dogmatic and confessional statements of the Christian churches is toward the universality of sin, but the specification of sin is left open. That is, the creeds operate at a level of generality greater than that found in the work of particular theologians.

5   Ibid., 201. Other statements could have been selected here, and this selection is simply illustrative. How the "wholly" in this statement should be understood is, of course, a matter of controversy.

6   Georges Florovsky, *Creation and Redemption* (Belmont, Mass.: Nordland, 1976), 85. In the longer tradition, theology assumed a metaphysical component that has increasingly come into question in the modern era. The historicist assumptions of modernity stand in conflict with the longer tradition at this point.

7   Samuel Laeuchli, *The Language of Faith* (Nashville: Abingdon, 1962), 102.

8   Often objections to Christian doctrines of sin are stated in terms of a defense of the dignity of human beings. But I find that the issue escapes me. For a moving portrayal of sin in an intergenerational context see John Steinbeck's remarkable novel, *East of Eden*. Here the stature and

dignity of the characters is precisely rooted in the awareness that they could be something more than they are. Doesn't an understanding of the truly tragic dimensions of life assume a doctrine of sin?

9   Walter Rauschenbusch, *A Theology for the Social Gospel* (Nashville: Abingdon, 1945), 5.

10   Ibid., 43.

11   Ibid., 47

12   Ibid., 48.

13   Ibid., 50.

14   Ibid., 142.

15   Ibid., 143.

16   Reinhold Niebuhr makes a similar point when he argues that sin has "no history." See *An Interpretation of Christian Ethics* (Cleveland: Meridian Books, 1956), 65–93. Niebuhr's life and work make clear that a strong doctrine of sin need not undercut a persistent commitment to social justice.

17   Gregory Baum, *Religion and Alienation* (New York: Paulist Press, 1975), 197.

18   Ibid., 199. For Baum there is, as well, a psychological and trans-generational dimension to social sin. But that too is understood in an historical environmentalist context rather than pointing to an ontological condition.

19   Ibid., 200.

20   Ibid., 202–3.

21   Ibid., 212.

22   Ibid., 222. There are, of course, other dimensions to Baum's position than those I have focused on here. But the point of my analysis has been to uncover the link between a view of social sin and the tendency to politicize faith. It is quite another thing to argue that the actions and beliefs of Christians have political consequences.

23   Faith is politicized when the "real" content of faith is identified with political commitments rather than the relationship between the believer and God. Moreover, when the content of faith is circumscribed by the historical field of power within which we live, faith loses its transcendent *telos*. We are, as Rosenstock-Huessy asserts, creatures who have a "triple citizenship": in heaven, in society, and on the earth. See my account of Rosenstock-Huessy's great work, *Out of Revolution: Autobiography of Western Man* (Norwich, Vt.: Argo Books, 1969) in "Revolution and World Pluralism," *The Ecumenist* 10, no. 3, (1972): 38–41.

24   For a nonideological interpretation of society, one that focuses on

speech as "the life-blood of society," see Eugen Rosenstock-Huessy, *Speech and Reality* (Norwich, Vt.: Argo Books, 1970).

25 "I understand society as a spiritual community involving the intergenerational partnership of the 'dead, the living and the yet unborn'" (Burke). Thus society is to be chiefly understood as the intergenerational life of humankind centered in the regeneration and recreation of humankind in relation to its destiny. Central to these multiform processes is the transmission of spiritual values, faith, hope, and love. Here the family looms large as do the other communities in which we participate. Society is secondarily understood as social structures for the ordering of political, economic, and social affairs, though there is a dialectical relationship between these dimensions—the spiritual and structural—of society. In understanding society in this way, I am clearly at odds with those understandings of society found in Rauschenbusch and Baum. The failure to recognize the primary spiritual functions of society—the reproduction and regeneration of humankind in its multiform spiritual types—has, in my view, led to great confusion and to a misplaced debate about "left-wing" vs. "right-wing" Christianity. For Christianity there is something prior to the political. And that something prior is the spiritual recreation and regeneration of the sons and daughters of God in their multiform human types.

14 The Opposite of Sin Is Love
CARL SKRADE

Because of death all men have sinned.
ROMANS 5:12

Christianity is not about moving from vices to virtue but from virtue to grace.
LUTHER

Sin and neurosis are two ways of talking about the same thing—the complete isolation of the individual, his disharmony with the rest of nature, his hyperindividualism, his attempt to create his own world from within himself.
ERNEST BECKER

In the attempt to explain what sin is, it may first be useful to note briefly what sin is not, that is, to indicate views of sin which are inadequate. To crowd these rejected views together into a sentence, all shades and variations of moralistic, legalistic, and privatistic understanding of sin as sins, caused by a demonic being and inherited from Adam, are inadequate.[1]

Legalist and moralistic views of sin as violations of laws do not seem to be true to either the basic Christian source, the Bible, or to life. Sin (like righteousness and justice) is a relational rather than legalistic concept, however much the legalistic understanding has pervaded Western cultures.

A good biblical illustration of the relational nature of sin and of righteousness may be found in the potent little story of Judah and Tamar in Genesis 38. Old Judah, having lost two sons and not willing to risk a third, tries to dump his daughter-in-law, Tamar, for whom, via marriage, the concrete and physical and real locus of meaning has become life in the tribe of Judah.

But Tamar is not about to be dumped and, if we grant a willing suspension of disbelief, in order to maintain her relation to her chosen locus for the potential of meaning, she disguises herself as a whore and lures her father-in-law into her tent and her bed. Believing that a bird in the hand is worth two in the bush, Tamar rejects Judah's time payment plan and receives, in earnest for a lamb to be delivered later, Judah's signet and cord and staff—that is, his signature and seal. Judah's friend, Hirah the Adullamite, returns with the lamb (and lust?) but finds no lady of the night—and thus no signet, cord, or staff.

As the story proceeds, Tamar is found to be pregnant. Judah, now that it serves his purpose of being rid of her, wants justice—a legalistic justice. But as she is brought forth to be stoned, Tamar has the next to the last word, saying, "Father-in-law, would you like back your signet and cord and staff?" The last word is Judah's: "She is more righteous than I . . ."

Biblically, neither righteousness nor justice nor sin are contained within law or moral code. If Jesus and Paul had agreed with the generally accepted conviction that the health and meaning of relations could be safeguarded by rules and regulations, then they would not have had much to do or say other than to make, perhaps, a few adjustments in those laws. Paul could still be a Pharisee and Jesus could have joined with them or with the Essenes. Clearly, Jesus' running battle with the Pharisees focuses neither on their supposed hypocrisy nor on his claims of a virgin mother nor the ability to walk across the water. Their controversy is quite simply over the role of law in the meaning of being. For the Pharisees life circumscribed by law is the way to meaning; over against this stands Jesus' repeated shattering of this claim as, for example, in his jarring refrain, "Moses said unto you . . . but I say . . ." Moses as prototype and symbol for the legalistic approach is rejected.

The trouble with a legalistic approach, however rigid and thorough, to both sin and meaning is that, as Bultmann has said: "Law claims a man so far as his conduct can be bound by formulated percepts. Beyond these it leaves free play to man's self-will. Jesus' belief is on the contrary that the human will has no freedom before God, but is radically claimed by Him . . . formal obedience to the law as such is no radical obedience, though of course true obedience can exist in fulfillment of the law."[2]

Legalistic understandings of sin and obedience and righteousness ask too little and are too limiting before the all-demanding and all-consuming relation of God and man.

The quote from Luther, with which I have begun this paper,

implies the same. As difficult as it is for us well-conditioned bourgeoisie to entertain, an understanding of sin which does not include the potential sinfulness of all virtues, as well as all vices, will leave the depths of brokenness untouched, to play more or less seriously with symptoms but never to touch the roots of human alienation.

One should note the inadequacy of what I have labeled privatistic understandings of sin. By such an understanding I mean a view of sin which denies or obscures the radical unity and interdependence of humankind and replaces it with a thoroughgoing individualism. "Me-ism" translated into an understanding of sin goes beyond the laudable goal of emphasizing individual responsibility, into a perverse kind of egocentricity which sees the individual as the sole and self-contained cause of brokenness within the self, between self and others, and between self and God. While each of us certainly is responsible for contributing to the brokenness, we take ourselves with a misplaced seriousness when we see ourselves as the sole cause and center of the brokenness, just as we can take ourselves with a misplaced seriousness when we make our faith or our righteousness the locus of salvation, of the healing of brokenness. As Tillich has said, sin is our fate as well as our guilt. We experience an interdependence in brokenness.

Just as we are claiming too much for ourselves when we subscribe to a privatistic view of sin, we are seeking to escape too much when, dualistically, we see the origins of sin and brokenness in a demonic being, a devil, a satan. As shall be developed further below, to subscribe to such a view is untrue to both the Bible and life. The personification of the demonic in the Bible varies with the time and with the type of theology under concern. In Job 1–2 and Zechariah 3:1–9, Satan is a son of God and a sometime adversary of human beings, but not God's adversary. In the varying stories of the Davidic census in 2 Samuel 24:1–25 and in 1 Chronicles 21:1–30, one sees conflict and struggle in ancient Israel over the nature of evil and over the role of Yahweh as cause or observer or vindictive avenger of sin.

In the New Testament, growing out of apocalyptic thought and out of the traumas of the times, Satan does appear as an independent agent competing with God for the allegiance of people. Examples include Mark 1:12–13, Matthew 4:1–11, Luke 4:1–13, and the Apocalypse. Yet however vital these symbols and the insights borne by these personifications of the demonic are, both for the Christian kerygma and for the truth about reality, the biblical writers stop short of using dualism and the demonic to absolve humanity of responsibility for either the fate or the guilt of sin.

Varied explanations of the origin of sin are offered in the biblical period as one moves through the Old Testament and the intertestamental literature and into the New Testament. An excellent survey of these varied positions is offered by S. J. DeVries in his essay "Sin, sinners" in *The Interpreter's Dictionary of the Bible*. This article and its bibliography are recommended to the reader wishing to pursue the matter of biblical views of the origin of sin beyond the scope allowed here.[3]

However, a few brief quotes from DeVries's essay may be helpful at this point. He notes that:

The only passage in the Old Testament in which temptation to sin is ascribed to Satan is 1 Chronicles 21:1, where he is said to have incited David to number Israel (cf. 2 Sam. 24:1).

The Old Testament writers were more concerned to trace the origin of sin "existentially" in human life than to indulge in historical and cosmological speculations. The notion that it arises either from creatureliness as such or from sexual generation does not appear in the Old Testament.

According to Hebrew writers, sin comes from the corrupt heart of man. Here at the center of his being, the sinner is at odds with his Creator.... There is a depth of iniquity in the human heart.... It is from this evil heart that all sin arises (Gen. 6:5, cf. 8:21).[4]

The heart is not so much the seat of the intellect as of the will, and it is man's will that has become corrupt and perverse. [I will examine the matter of will further below.]

Thus sin's essence lies, not in isolated acts of transgression, but in the depth of man's being. As he fell into sin through an inordinate use of his will (Genesis 3), that same will, with its organ, the heart, has become so warped through estrangement from God that it henceforth gives rise to all sorts of evil. Thus sin becomes a fateful and tragic *habitus* leading at last to complete destruction.... It has become his very nature to sin.

I will examine the matter of nature further below; at this point I would like to note that the thrust of DeVries's comment here is, as many have noted, that the problem is not sins, but Sin.

To a great extent, the New Testament gives the Old Testament answer to the question of sin's origin. Paul ... makes the principle of sin which lies in the heart responsible for the unruliness of the desire of the flesh.

Indeed so perverse is the heart of man that the very prohibitions of the law which are intended to keep the desires in check rather than to arouse them (Rom. 7:7–8) instead do provoke them.

As Jesus declared, sin lies deep in the corrupt heart of man.

Without in any sense lessening the force of the above, DeVries accurately adds that "The New Testament inherits from intertestamental Judaism a belief in demonic temptation as a source of sin . . . closely associated with the notion of cosmic evil forces." DeVries continues: "When the question of the ultimate origin of sin is raised, it is evident that the New Testament possesses a definite historical theory. . . . It is . . . to Adam's sin in Eden that mankind's depravity is traced . . . in Rom. 5:12–19 Paul blames Adam. . . ."

However, I don't believe that the matter is quite so clear and simple as DeVries's last comment might indicate. The New Testament speakers and writers are, like all people, children of their time; this symbolism and this view of the demonic can be assumed of them. However, lest we return to pop views of the demonic and of dualism and slide back into the easy "outs" provided by the moralistic views of sin that only further the brokenness, let us turn our attention to that most powerful biblical myth of both the origin and nature of sin, Genesis 2:4b–3:24. In conjunction, let us examine further that early Christian interpretation of it given by Paul in Romans 5:12. I will seek to draw out an understanding of what it is that constitutes sin as Sin, a radical brokenness which is both our fate and our guilt, for which we are responsible, and from the power of which Christianity claims there is release.

Somewhere, as part of an adjunct to a survey of the role of rationalism in Western thought, I once wrote scores of pages on the history of interpretation of the Adam and Eve story in Genesis 2–3. Due to the scope of this paper, we all are mercifully spared that material. However, I would like to indicate two streams of interpretation of this powerful old story, one of which I affirm as giving clear insight into the origin and nature and consequences of sin, and the other of which, though more common in our culture, I reject as misleading at best.

The two streams of interpretation are sometimes labeled the Augustinian and the Irenaean. Whether either interpretation correctly represents either of these great scholars of the early church, I will leave for the specialist; however, the labels are familiar and therefore may be tentatively useful. An overly simplified sketch of the two different interpretations follows. According to the Augustinian version, life in the garden of Eden was perfect, whole, complete. God established the prohibition, but human beings violated this prohibition by "playing God without God," establishing or attempting to establish one's own boundaries, seeking meaning on one's own terms. Thus to sin is to violate the will of God. This is the sin of Adam and Eve and it is the original sin. Perfection is lost, human nature is totally corrupted, fallen, and this sin and its consequent guilt and fallenness are transmitted even as a congenital heart defect might be to all of Adam's descendants. "In Adam's fall we sinned all." Typical if not inevitable concomitants of this view (understandable, perhaps, if we remember the Augustinian controversies with Pelagius and the way in which these controversies have been interpreted down to us) are the convictions that to violate the will of God is to violate the law of God, that this fallen nature is incapable of good, and that salvation must finally involve release-removal from this time and place of fallenness to a perfect beyond, "a great Henceforth."

I do not mean to caricature or belittle this view of the origin, nature, and consequences of sin which, if not Augustinian, is at least common in Western culture. Rather, I wish to explain my preference for what I have labeled the Irenaean view, which seems to disclose more depth of meaning and possibility both in Scripture and life. According to this view, life in the garden was in process toward perfection but was not perfect, complete, final. God was about the business of moving time and nature toward God's shalom. No guilt was attached to the finitude or the incompleteness; the processes themselves were saturated with and caught up within the sacred. The sin of Adam and Eve was likewise that of attempting to play God without God, to run life on their own terms, to establish their own boundaries of meaning. Their sin was the violation of the will of God. Adam and Eve attempted to turn the processes of nature and history to ends of their own choosing, under their own control. However, this wrong choice made by Adam, while bringing in corruption and mortality, did not bring with it inherited guilt nor did it destroy the truth of human nature which belongs, inviolably, with God. Consequently, the Irenaean view has profound implications both concerning human nature and concerning the potential for meaning in time and history.

In entering into contest with the will of God, it was the will of the human being (more about this later) that was the loser. Perfection was not lost, both because creation was still only in process and because perfection belongs to God, not to humans. As the human being attempts to move the processes in his or her own impossible directions, he or she can succeed only in his or her bent for self destruction, but cannot, ultimately, alter the purposes and processes of God. People apart from God do not lose God, but rather reject their own true selves. Sin is *not* original, but is the obscuring (not obliteration or loss) of the original union with God in an "omnipotence fantasy that one dealt one's own cards and could do with them whatever one pleased, as if there were no limits, no finitude, no continuity in the structures of time."[5]

The awful choice which we as Adam and Eve have taken is the choice to reject the awesome freedom with which God has "burdened" us—the freedom to unfold within God's boundaries, boundaries which include birth and death and finitude and grace and interdependence with the earth and all others. We as Adam and Eve seek to exchange the space and freedom of the boundaries which God gives for restrictive boundaries of our own choosing: the boundaries of pretended independence or of selective dependencies oft unconfessed, and the boundaries of life on our own terms, based in our very own systems of good and evil. Life on our own terms, as Scripture knows, brings not life at all, but death, qualitative and quantitative, figurative and literal, along with the loss of the possibility of meaning. Via our knowledge systems of good and evil we would be as gods (Peter Damian says the original sin is the plural declension of the word God), immortal; but instead, we find only that death turns in on us, perversely, before its time, dominating all our efforts.

Perhaps the curious contrast between the tree of life and the tree of the knowledge of good and evil can be clarified in a comparison with Freudian ideas on the clash between a life instinct and a death instinct in each self and society at the very borders shared by the biological and the psychological. Building on Freud and Rank and Kierkegaard, Ernest Becker argued that, seeing no way out of this dualism, we opt for life, but life on our own terms, repressing death and doing whatever is necessary to maintain the *causa sui* immortality projects via which we would guarantee our self-defined "life." However, with frightening clarity, he noted that death does not go away simply because we repress it, but rather returns to dominate all we do, issuing in death-oriented selves and societies. The ancient Yahwist and Freud (at least according to interpreters/

extenders of his thought like Rank and N. O. Brown and Ernest Becker) share the conviction that the drive for life controlled on our own terms, whatever those terms, is at the root of human brokenness and leads inevitably to self-destruction, varying only in its degrees of gaudiness.[6]

A couple of illustrations, one corporate and one individual, may help to support these contentions. Since it is more comfortable to point to others and the past, let us look at Nazi Germany. Perhaps these ideas of the ancient Yahwist and of this stream of Freudians can offer insight into what sin is in general and as manifested specifically in the Nazi era. Building on von Clausewitz and Bismarck and World War I theory and experiences, the Nazis knew that they needed to stay out of a two front war if they were to have much hope of success; thus the nonaggression pact with Stalin was needed if the Nazi dream of a thousand year Reich of Aryan shalom, based in a Nazi system of, yes, good and evil, was to succeed. But Hitler broke the nonaggression pact. And an insane death-worshipping third front was opened as the Nazis instituted *Nacht und Nebel,* the final solution: the extermination of the Jews, and gypsies, and communists, and Christians who took their Christianity too seriously, and whoever else that bad luck or malice brought under their lethal sweep. Most, if not all, at the very least could have been exterminated "in good time" after the war—if winning the war really was the goal. Those executed would have gladly chosen almost any alternative, any labor, even being cannon fodder on the eastern front, to the death camps. Also, this Nazi death effort required massive quantities of men, munitions, supplies—all withdrawn from the war effort to serve death, which, rather than victory, became the *telos*.

In choosing to structure life on the basis of a system of good and evil, *any* system, we choose death, and death becomes God; "that is this generation's thought of thoughts."[7] Sin is *all* that we do in playing God without God, all that is done, including not only our "vices" but also our "virtues." Through sin, we would guarantee and secure the future on our own terms, exchanging "the glorious liberty of the children of God" for that bondage to our systems of good and evil which issue in death, figurative and literal.

Perhaps we can illustrate that same impossible and lethal detour from the will of God, that detour which we call sin, when we think of the common to banal contests we typically make of human relations. For example, most adults know what it means to fall more or less madly in love and have a relation bordering on the ecstatic and lasting anywhere from a few minutes to a few months—only to have what began so beautifully end so badly. Perhaps again we have a manifestation of sin, as the relationship deteriorates into a contest over, as Jaoulin says, who will be Pharaoh and who will be Hebrew. The relation becomes a contest over which individual's system of good and evil will form the ground rules for this particular relation. The story is as old as Adam and Eve, as grating as ashes in the mouth, as real as the moment. Such contests "work out" only in the sick pairings of sadist and masochist.

As Ernest Becker has noted, sin is neurosis, undetected or acceptable as long as it adheres to the socially dominant systems of good and evil, but perhaps most tragic when most "virtuous." Let us consider Becker's summarization of this insight:

Here Rank and Kierkegaard meet in one of those astonishing historical mergers of thought: that sin and neurosis are two ways of talking about the same thing—the complete isolation of the individual, his disharmony with the rest of nature, his hyperindividualism, his attempt to create his own world from within himself. Both sin and neurosis represent the individual blowing himself up to larger than his true size, his refusal to recognize his cosmic dependence. Neurosis, like sin, is an attempt to force nature, to pretend that the *causa-sui* immortality project really suffices. In sin and neurosis man fetishizes himself on something narrow at hand and pretends that the whole meaning and miraculousness of creation is limited to that, that he can get his beatification from that. . . .

Sin and neurosis have another side: not only their unreal self-inflation in the refusal to admit creatureliness but also a penalty for intensified self-consciousness: the failure to be consoled by shared illusions. The result is that the sinner (neurotic) is hyperconscious of the very thing he tries to deny: his creatureliness, his miserableness and unworthiness. The neurotic is thrown back on his true perceptions of the human condition which caused his isolation and individualism in the first place. He tried to build a glorified private inner world because of his deeper anxieties, but life takes its revenge. The more he separates and inflates himself, the more anxious he becomes. The more he artificially idealizes himself, the more exaggeratedly he criticizes himself. He alternates between the extremes of "I am everything" and "I am nothing." But it is clear that if one is going to be *something* he has to be a secure part of something else. There is no way to avoid paying the debt of dependency and yielding to the larger meaning of the rest of nature, to the toll of suffering and the death that it demands; and there is no way to justify this payment from within oneself, no matter how mightily one tries.[8]

One suffocates in self-imposed games of self-justification and self-condemnation.
    A further illustration of a similar understanding of sin, humorous and insightful, is offered by Anne Herbert in her memorable little commentary on Genesis 2–3:

In the beginning, God didn't make just two people; he made a bunch of us. Because he wanted us to have a lot of fun, and he said you can't really have fun unless there's a whole gang of you. He put us in Eden which was a combination garden and playground and park and told us to have fun.

At first we did have fun just like he expected. We rolled down the hills, waded in the streams, climbed on the trees, swung on the vines, ran in the meadows, frolicked in the woods, hid in the forest, and acted silly. We laughed a lot.

Then one day this snake told us that we weren't having real fun because we weren't keeping score. Back then, we didn't know what score was. When he explained it, we still couldn't see the fun. But he said we should give an apple to the person who was best at all the games and we'd never know who was best without keeping score. We could all see the fun of that, of course, because we were all sure we were best.

It was different after that. We yelled a lot. We had to make up new scoring rules for most of the games. Others, like frolicking, we stopped playing because they were too hard to score.

By the time God found out what had happened we were spending about 45 minutes a day actually playing and the rest of the time working out scoring. God was wroth about that—very, very wroth. He said we couldn't use his garden anymore because we weren't having fun. We told him we were having lots of fun. He was just being narrow minded because it wasn't exactly the kind of fun he originally thought of.

He wouldn't listen.

He kicked us out, and he said we couldn't come back until we stopped keeping score. To rub it in (to get our attention, he said), he told us we were all going to die and our scores wouldn't mean anything anyway.

He was wrong. My cumulative, all-game score now is 16,548 and that means a lot to me. If I can raise it to 20,000 before I die, I'll know I've accomplished something. Even if I can't my life has a great deal of meaning because I've taught my children to score high and they'll be able to reach 20,000 or even 30,000.

Really, it was life in the garden that didn't mean anything. Fun is great in its place but without scoring there's no reason for it. God actually has a very superficial view of life and I'm certainly glad my children are being raised away from his influence. We were lucky. We're all very grateful to the snake.[9]

To sin is to make life into a series of scorekeeping contests, tally systems for schemata of goods and evils. Through these systems we would make life behave and guarantee world and future before God and man, on our terms, within our own boundaries. Thus we would maintain, usually more by our virtues than by our vices, our impossible merit-mongering flights from the God of grace.

Let us return to the contrast between the Irenaean and Augustinian understandings of sin. While they concur in viewing sin as human attempts both through vices and virtues to play God without God, and to create and impose and sustain self-justifying *causa sui* immortality projects which lead to meaninglessness and destruction, the significance of the sin of Adam and its consequences are understood quite differently. For Augustine, the consequences are inherited guilt and a sin of nature; the human being is corrupted in his or her very nature. For the Irenaean stream of thought, "the wrong choice made by Adam brought in passion, corruption and mortality," but there is no sin of nature and no inherited guilt.[10]

In his masterful survey of Byzantine theology, John Meyendorff clarifies the issues thus:

"Nature," therefore, designates that which is, in virtue of creation, distinct from God. But nature can and must be transcended; this is the privilege and the function of the *free mind,* made "according to God's image."

Now in Greek patristic thought, only this free, personal mind can commit sin and incur the concomitant "guilt"—a point made clear by Maximus the Confessor in his distinction between "natural will" and "gnomic will." Human nature, as God's creature, always exercises its dynamic properties (which together constitute the "natural will"—a created dynamism) in accordance with the divine will which created it. But when the human person, or hypostasis, by rebelling against both God and nature misuses its freedom, it can distort the "natural will" and thus corrupt nature itself. It is able to do so because it possesses freedom, or "gnomic will," which is capable of orienting man toward the good and of "imitating God" ("God alone is good by nature," writes Maximus, "and only God's imitator is good by his *gnome*"); it is also capable of sin, because "our salvation depends on our will." But sin is always a personal act, never an act of nature. Patriarch Photius even goes so far as to say, referring to Western doctrines, that the belief in a "sin of nature" is a heresy.

From these basic ideas about the personal character of sin, it is evident that the rebellion of Adam and Eve against God could be conceived only as their personal sin; there would be no place, then, in such an anthropology for the concept of inherited guilt, or for a "sin of nature," although it admits that human nature incurs the consequences of Adam's sin.

It is obvious, therefore, that the sin of Adam must also be related to all men, just as salvation brought by Christ is salvation for all mankind; but neither original sin nor salvation can be realized in an individual's life without involving his personal and free responsibility.[11]

Perhaps a recent work by Ray Hart, *Unfinished Man and the Imagination,* can help illuminate Maximus's discussion of the natural will (cf. Thomas Merton's true self hidden with God) and the gnomic will (which via sin becomes Merton's false self, constructed on illusory fears and wishes and anchored in one's omnipotence fantasies). "By will Hart does not mean the power to make conscious decisions but an ordering principle in the self which is prior to perception and thought, influencing both."[12] The gnomic will is one's *Vorverständnis,* one's preanalytic vision, one's ordering presuppositions where society and self meet and where, usually, one acquiesces in the culturally acceptable immortality projects which provide a distorting and anesthetizing filter through which are strained all one's memories and perceptions and intentions. This will is the locus of sin, our lies, our idolatry, our rebellion, our *causa-sui* immortality projects both autonomous and heteronomous, our false selves. This will is the seat of our playing God without God, playing out our merit-based scorekeeping systems which bind us up in self-justification and self-condemnation.

This will, this fallen gnomic will, this "ordering principle in the self which is prior to perception and thought, influencing both" is, also our responsibility. We are Adam, for, as Flannery O'Connor says, "Cutting yourself off from Grace is a very decided matter, requiring a real choice, act of will, and affecting the very ground of the soul."[13] And as Jesus, "symbol-maker of the kingdom," shows in his parables, access to this gnomic will is through the imagination.

While the focus has been primarily on the Adam and Eve story in Genesis 2–3, one should also make note of the Pauline comment on this text in Romans 5:12. Paul, speaking of Adam, writes: "As sin came into the world through one man, and through sin, death, so death spread to all men because all men have sinned (*eph ho pantes hemarton*)." The interpretation of this passage was a basic matter of contention between the Augustinians and the Pelagians, and the Augustinian understanding of the passage as clear support for the notion of inherited guilt has dominated in the West. However, as Meyendorff notes, another viable interpretation not only does more justice to the Greek of the text, but also strengthens and clarifies the understanding of sin discussed above. Meyendorff comments:

In this passage (Rom. 5:12) there is a major issue of translation. The last four Greek words (*eph ho pantes hemarton*) were translated in Latin as *in quo omnes peccaverunt* ("in whom [i.e., in Adam] all men have sinned"), and this translation was used in the West to justify the doctrine of guilt inherited from Adam and spread to his descendants. But such a meaning cannot be drawn from the original Greek—the text read, of course, by the Byzantines. The form *eph ho*—a contraction of *epi* with the relative pronoun *ho*—can be translated as "because," a meaning accepted by most modern scholars of all confessional backgrounds. Such a translation renders Paul's thought to mean that death, which was "the wages of sin" (Rom. 6:23) for Adam, is also the punishment applied to those who, like him, sin. It presupposes a cosmic significance of the sin of Adam, but does not say that his descendants are "guilty" as he was, unless they also sin as he sinned.

A number of Byzantine authors, including Photius, understood the *eph ho* to mean "because" and saw nothing in the Pauline text beyond a moral similarity between Adam and other sinners, death being the normal retribution for sin. But there is also the consensus of the majority of Eastern Fathers, who interpret Romans 5:12 in close connection with 1 Corinthians 15:22—between Adam and his descendants there is a solidarity *in death* just as there is a solidarity *in life* between the risen Lord and the baptized.

This interpretation comes, obviously, from the literal, grammatical meaning of Romans 5:12. *Eph ho,* if it means "because," is a neuter pronoun; but it can also be masculine, referring to the immediately preceding substantive *thanatos* ("death"). The sentence then may have a meaning which seems improbable to a reader trained in Augustine, but which is indeed the meaning which most Greek Fathers accepted: "As sin came into the world through one man and death through sin, so death spread to all men; and *because of death,* all men have sinned . . ."

Mortality, or "corruption," or simply death (understood in a personalized sense), has indeed been viewed, since Christian antiquity, as a cosmic disease which holds humanity under its sway, both spiritually and physically, and is controlled by the one who is "the murderer from the beginning" (John 8:44). It is this death which makes sin inevitable, and in this sense "corrupts" nature.

> . . . sin remains a personal act, and inherited guilt is impossible.[14]

That is, of our own accord and of our own responsibility, we sin because we die, not vice versa. Sin is our lethal attempt to exchange the God-given boundaries of finitude, interdependence, and grace for any number of sets of boundaries, chosen autonomously or heteronomously, via which, seeking to secure life on our own terms, we become oriented to death, bound to death. In death there is both the impetus for and the wages of sin.

The focus of this paper has been an examination of sin, which I have argued is a misuse of freedom in rebellion against both God and human nature, and involves a radical corruption of the "gnomic will," the preanalytic vision out of which we see and remember and intend. This corruption involves us in an insane exchange of the wide boundaries within which God gives us freedom to be, for the restrictive and distorting boundaries chosen by an individual and/or his or her tribe. With these perverted tools we set about to fix what was not broken, and prefer botches to the wholeness towards which, nonetheless, God moves all things. While the how of this movement is beyond the scope of this paper, perhaps it would not be amiss, in conclusion, to suggest how Jesus seeks to free the bound gnomic will.

Jesus comes in full attack on sin, telling us in parables and metaphors which rattle our myths, crack open our preanalytic vision, explode outward from the very depths and center of our *Vorverständnis,* returning, restoring the potential for the union of the gnomic and the natural will, rejecting the illusory false self we would become and reuniting us with the true self we are. Not via sacrifice or supernatural negotiations or sacramental magic, but by the sword of his mouth, he makes all things new, providing both the possibility and the necessity for decision at the very deepest levels of our being—decisions as to whether or not we will reaffirm Adam's original lie or will suffer the awful rebirth of love. For God is love and the natural will of the human being is to love. And the opposite of sin is not goodness, but love. And love is not kindness, or the socially acceptable sentiment of good will, but it is the laying bare that oneness and mercy are the very nature of reality itself.[15]

For love *is* the nature of God and of the natural will of the human being; it is the loss or perversion of love which is unnatural. Thus Thomas Traherne affirms that:

> You are as prone to love as the sun is to shine; it being the most delightful and natural employment of the soul of man, without which you are dark and miserable.... For certainly he that delights not in love makes vain the universe.... The whole world ministers to you as the theatre of your love. It sustains you and all objects that you may continue to love them. Without which it were better for you to have no being. Life without object is sensible emptiness, and that is a greater misery than death or nothing.[16]

If the opposite of sin is not goodness but love and if love is "natural" to all that God creates, then the most meaningful question is: What might make us free to love, to come back to God and to our own true self? Let us recall one of the parables in which Jesus grapples with this question, not by information but by insight, his metaphor cracking through the door of imagination into our gnomic will, making it possible to see the truth about reality and, perhaps, upon seeing become new.

I have in mind the parable of the unmerciful servant in Matthew 18:21–35. Since the story is a familiar one, I will not go into the details about the servant who is forgiven for much, but who refuses to forgive another servant for little. Much more is accessible in this parable than a guilt-laden and moralistic lesson about the need to be nice. Consider Eta Linnemann's incisive concluding comments on the insight it bears.

> This ... parable brings to light something that is usually concealed

from us. We normally assign a quite different role to mercy. For us it is the great exception, the possibility of giving up a claim that one can make "by rights." To make use of this possibility is regarded as honorable and admirable—but the norm is still that one insists on one's rights. For us mercy is contained within the ordinance of justice, or it would be more correct to say within the ordinance of claims, for justice is in fact still more than claims. A claim is as it were the reverse side of justice; justice is primarily the limit that puts people in their place, and not a principle of justice on which one can take up a stand.

While the parable shows that mercy has the character of ordinance, it so opposes mercy to the ordinance of claims that a radical opposition is forced open, and only a choice of alternatives is possible. If mercy by its nature has the character of an ordinance, it cannot be an "exception," but only the "norm." In this case it is obvious that everything that now diverges from this norm cannot be an admissible exception, but can only be a failure. Here mercy is not put at our discretion as one possibility among others, but meets us as a demand. This certainly does not mean that there is no longer any such thing as justice. But it does mean that there can be such a thing as "my rights" only so far as mercy permits it. The limit of this permission is not drawn by a principle, but by the needs of one's neighbor. Otherwise it would no longer make sense to talk of mercy. The behavior of the wicked servant can appear to us to be as reprehensible as it does only because the parable introduces us to a way of looking at things that fits the ordinance of mercy. But how is it possible for us to engage in this way of thinking involuntarily, although we are used to keeping to the ordinance of claims? Someone to whom I put this question answered: "This ordinance is natural, as natural as the sun and the earth, as birds or trees!"

Can it be that the original ordering of reality becomes visible here? Our assent to the parable means that we have fallen into contradiction with ourselves. But the parable not only makes this contradiction obvious, it can also help us to overcome it. The meaning of Jesus' words is: We should risk our lives on the ordinance of mercy.

There is the truth, in front of us—this we have admitted ourselves by our involuntary agreement. Now we must afterwards match this truth with our lives—or we should have to give up the truth for our lives. After the word of Jesus has reached us, we cannot leave everything as it was and still think everything is in order.

Now here it is important to clear a misunderstanding out of the way. To venture on the way of mercy does not mean to erect a law over oneself that demands, "Thou shalt be merciful, thou shalt forgive, etc." It means rather to commit oneself to the belief that reality matches this ordinance, although appearances seem to suggest that the opposite is true. It means to question reality on whether it does not itself point a way for mercy in the place where it is needed, a way that is a way of life for the merciful, not only a list of prohibitions. Forgiveness for instance here means something other than "saying no more about it," or as it is so nicely put, "letting the grass grow over it." It means the confidence that for the other man and for me a common future is possible.

Only experience can show that mercy is the way the world is ordered, and I can get this experience only if I commit myself to it.[17]

The point of the parable is simply this: Mercy is the nature of the truth about reality. Mercy is not simply a virtue practiced more or less frequently by good people—even, perhaps, when they can ill afford to do so. Rather, mercy is reality. Because of this we object to the unmerciful servant, who is finally only asking for his fellow servant to give him what is legally due. And also because of the pervasiveness of mercy, not because of our supposed competencies (which, recurrently, do not bear much scrutiny) life and the hope of meaning are possible. As the honest, not the modest, person repeatedly relearns in work and relationship, in being itself, we indeed are Luther's beggars, utterly dependent on the ultimate triumph of mercy. Through such insights, the gnomic will is freed to move forward toward shalom.

Christianity's radical claim is that an actual release from the power of sin is possible in the present. However this release may be described, it happens, I think, precisely where the perversion of reality is rooted: in the heart of humans, in the gnomic will. "Communion in the risen body of Christ; participation in divine life; sanctification through the energy of God, which penetrates true humanity and restores it to its 'natural' state, rather than justification, or remission of inherited guilt—these are at the center of . . . the Christian Gospel."[18]

Notes

1 Somewhere Loren Eiseley says something to the effect that the greatest source of originality is reading. Both because I don't want

footnotes to exceed the paper and because I don't remember the half of what I've borrowed—let alone from whom—let me begin with the confession that while I'm stuck with the responsibility for what's bent and misborrowed in this essay, little if any is original other than perhaps this particular synthesis.

2   Rudolf Bultmann, *Jesus and the Word* (New York: Scribner's, 1958), 91.

3   S. J. DeVries, "Sin, sinners," in *The Interpreter's Dictionary of the Bible* (New York: Abingdon, 1962), 4:361–76.

4   In stressing that the locus of sin is in the human "heart," I think that one is freed from the limitation of the demonic to a demonic being, which limitation can be used as an escape from individual responsibility. Further, I think this understanding does not lessen the awareness of the reality of the demonic. Perhaps it is as Auden and Isherwood state in their play, *Ascent of F6*: "The Demon is real. Only his ministry and his visitation are unique for every nature. To the complicated and sensitive like yourself, his disguises are more subtle. . . . I think I understand your temptation. You wish to conquer the Demon and save mankind." (Quoted by Freeman Dyson, *Disturbing the Universe* [New York: Harper & Row, 1981]).

5   Tom Driver, *Patterns of Grace* (San Francisco: Harper & Row, 1977).

6   Ernest Becker, *Denial of Death* (New York: Free Press, 1973).

7   Saul Bellow, *Herzog*. For further discussion of these views, see Carl Skrade, *God and the Grotesque* (Philadelphia: Westminster, 1974), esp. chaps. 1–3.

8   Becker, 196.

9   Anne Herbert's account is from her unpublished manuscript which will be published in 1985 by Random House in *Random Kindness and Senseless Acts of Beauty*.

10   John Meyendorff, *Byzantine Theology* (New York: Fordham University Press, 1974).

11   Ibid., 143ff.

12   Robert Tannehill, *The Sword of His Mouth* (Philadelphia: Fortress, 1975), 22.

13   Flannery O'Connor, *Habit of Being* (New York: Vintage Books, 1980), 384.

14   Meyendorff, 144ff.

15   The love of which I speak here is *agapé*, the love which is the truth of God, the truth about reality, the truth of God in us. Such love is not, of course, gained by our virtuous striving but is the gift of God to which we are bound—in spite of all indications to the contrary. We are saved not by

our love but by the love of God. To love is not to be "good" but to surrender to God's dealings with us.

16   Thomas Traherne, *Second Century,* Meditation 65. See also Richard Wilbur's poem, "A World Without Objects is a Sensible Emptiness."

17   Eta Linnemann, *Parables of Jesus* (London: SPCK, 1966), 11ff.

18   Meyendorff, 146.

About the Authors

1   MAURICE BOUTIN is associate professor of philosophical theology at the Faculty of Theology, University of Montreal. He received his education at College de Saint-Laurent and the University of Montreal, and his doctorate in theology from the University of Munich in 1973. Since 1975 he has been a member of the international Colloquium on Hermeneutics (Rome, Italy) founded by Enrico Castelli. He has published articles in French, German, Swiss, American, and Canadian journals, and the book *Relationalität als Verstehensprinzip bei Rudolf Bultmann* (1974). His most recent articles appear in the journals *Foi et Vie* (Paris, 1980), *Laval Theologique et Philosophique* (Quebec, 1980), *Orient* and *Communaute Chrétienne* (Montreal, 1981–83), *Materialdienst* published by the "Konfessionskundliches Institut des Evangelischen Bundes" (Frankfurt, 1983), and *Journal of Ecumenical Studies* (Philadelphia, 1983).

2   M. DARROL BRYANT, associate professor of religion and culture at Renison College, University of Waterloo in Canada, was educated at Concordia College, Harvard Divinity School, and the University of St. Michael's College, Toronto. His work has focused on the interface of religion and society (*To Whom It May Concern: Poverty, Humanity, Community* [1969] and *A World Broken by Unshared Bread* [Geneva, 1970]), and religion and culture ("America as God's Kingdom," in *Religion and Political Society* [1974], "The Barren Twilight: Faith and History in Grant's Lament," in *George Grant in Process* [Toronto, 1978] and "Cinema, Religion & Popular Culture," in *Religion in Film* [1982]). His articles have appeared in *Dialog, Lutheran Quarterly, The Ecumenist,* and *The Anglican Theological Review*. He has edited several volumes on Unification theology and is the joint editor with Frederick Sontag of *God: The Contemporary Discussion* (1982).

3   LLOYD EBY joined the Unification Church in 1974 and graduated with the first class from the Unification Seminary in 1977. In 1978 he enrolled for graduate study in philosophy at Fordham Univer-

sity, Bronx, New York, where he is now completing his doctorate dissertation. Since 1979 he has taught Foundations in Philosophy at the Unification Theological Seminary. Prior to his becoming a Unification member, he took an undergraduate degree in philosophy at Washington University, St. Louis, Missouri, and did two years graduate study in philosophy there. Following that, he taught for two years at the State University of New York at Albany. He has travelled extensively throughout the world to seminars and workshops dealing with Unificationism, lecturing on Unification theology, Unification thought, and the Unification account of Communism, and he has written many papers on these topics.

4 DURWOOD FOSTER is professor of Christian theology at the Pacific School of Religion and the Graduate Theological Union. A United Methodist, he has taught at Duke University and Union Theological Seminary. He is the author of *The God Who Loves* (1971).

5 GENE G. JAMES is professor of philosophy and coordinator of the Religion and Society Program at Memphis State University, Memphis, Tennessee. He received his B.A. from Wake Forest University and doctorate from the University of North Carolina. He has lectured widely both in the U.S. and abroad and is the author of numerous articles on social ethics and related fields.

6 YOUNG OON KIM came to the United States as one of the first Unification Church missionaries in the West and has been on the faculty of the Unification Theological Seminary since its founding in 1975. Her books are: *Divine Principle and its Application* (1960), *Unification Theology and Christian Thought* (1975), *World Religions: A Trilogy* (1976), *Unification Theology* (1980), *An Introduction to Theology* (1983), and *The Types of Modern Theology* (1983).

7 PAUL MOJZES is professor of religious studies at Rosemont College, Rosemont, Pennsylvania. He is a native of Yugoslavia, educated at Belgrade University, Florida Southern College, and Boston University. He is the co-editor of the *Journal of Ecumenical Studies* and the editor of *Occasional Papers on Religion in Eastern Europe*. He is the author of *Christian-Marxist Dialogue in Eastern Europe* and editor of *Varieties of Christian-Marxist Dialogue* as well as

the writer of numerous articles. He is a member of the United Methodist Church.

8   SULAYMAN S. NYANG, a Gambian Muslim scholar currently living in the United States, is a specialist on African and Middle Eastern Affairs. He has written articles on African, Middle Eastern, and Islamic issues for many scholarly journals. He has also contributed chapters in many books dealing with his area of specialization. His latest book is *Reflections on the Human Condition* (1984). He is the editor-in-chief of the *American Journal of Islamic Studies*.

9   SARAH E. PETERSEN, eleven-year Unification Church member, is completing an M.T.S. from Harvard Divinity School. Her interests are business ethics and women's issues. A concern for the effect of theology on attitudes toward women led her to research this paper dealing with early Christian history. She graduated Phi Beta Kappa from the University of California at Berkeley in European nineteenth century history and literature, and is currently living with her husband, Charles Wheeler, in Washington, D.C.

10   J. DEOTIS ROBERTS is an ordained Baptist minister who has served as theologian and theological administrator. He was, for many years, Professor of Theology at Howard University, School of Religion. He served at Virginia Union's School of Theology as Dean and was President of the Interdenominational Theological Center in Atlanta, where he also taught. He has recently been appointed Distinguished Professor of Philosophical Theology at Eastern Baptist Theological Seminary and is the founding President of the Foundation for Religious and Educational Exchange, Inc. He has published widely and was editor of Howard University's *Journal of Religious Thought*. His works entitled *Liberation and Reconciliation* and *Roots of a Black Future* have been acclaimed. He is also widely known for his studies on Christian Platonism and Pascal.

11   HANS SCHWARZ is professor of systematic theology and contemporary theological issues at the University of Regensburg, West Germany. A member of the American Lutheran Church, he taught at the Gregorian University in Rome, and he taught for thirteen years at Trinity Lutheran Seminary, Columbus, Ohio. His several books include: *The Christian Church: Biblical Origin, Historical Transformation, and Potential for the Future* (1982).

12 CARL SKRADE (Ph.D. in New Testament, Union Seminary, Richmond, Virginia), whose interests are primarily in Synoptic Studies and in Religion and Culture, is a professor of religion at Capital University in Columbus, Ohio. He is, with John C. Cooper, the co-author of *Celluloid and Symbols,* a study of theological thesis in "secular" films. He is also the author of *God and the Grotesque,* a study of the experience of the *mysterium tremendum et fascinans* as evidenced in contemporary arts. The focus of his current research is the use of metaphor in the parables and aphorisms of Jesus.

13 THOMAS WALSH is a Ph.D. candidate in theological ethics at Vanderbilt University and is currently working on his dissertation: "An Examination of the Communication Ethics of Jürgen Habermas and Karl-Otto Apel as a Resource for Theological Ethics." A ten-year member of the Unification Church, Mr. Walsh has written a number of essays that deal with the social teachings and ethics of the Unification movement. Published to date is one article on the sexual ethics of the Unification movement: "Celibacy, Virtue, and the Practice of True Family," in *The Family and the Unification Church* (1983).

14 JONATHAN WELLS has been a member of the Unification Church since 1974. He graduated from Unification Theological Seminary in 1978, and is currently completing a Ph.D. in theology at Yale Graduate School. He has lectured and written extensively on Unification theology and its relation to the Christian tradition.

Index

Abel, 82, 145
Abraham, 19, 52, 75
Abrahamic theology, 53–55
Adam, 2, 3, 5, 18, 25, 33, 37–39,
    43–48, 53–55, 58, 62, 64–68,
    70, 74, 75, 77, 79, 80, 88–92,
    94, 95, 99n43, 103, 108, 109,
    112, 114, 116, 126, 145, 146, 151,
    164, 168–70, 172, 174–78
Age of Reason, 26, 88
Albright, William F., 34n5
Alexander, Samuel, 101
Ali, Maulana Muhammad, 59
Allah, 53–60
Anselm, St., 78, 84n11
Anselmianism, 151
Anthony, St. 24, 33, 36n28
Antichrist, 74
Apocalypse, 166
Apostolic Fathers, 152
Aquinas, St. Thomas, 26, 161n3
Arianism, 24
Aristotelianism, 23, 138
Ars, Curé d', 33, 36n28
Ascent of F6 (play), 181n4
Assembly of the World's
    Religions, 76
Athanasianism, 24
Athanasius, 17, 26
Athenagoras, 39
Attis, mystery cult of, 23
Auden, W. H., 181n4
Augustine, St., 67, 68, 70, 71, 102,
    109, 161n3, 174, 177
Augustinianism, 144, 151, 168, 169,
    174, 176

Babylonian Exile, 16
Barnabas, Epistle of, 24–26
Barnard, Leslie, 39, 40

Barth, Karl, 7, 27–29
Barthes, Roland, 14
Bathsheba, 16
Baudelaire, Charles, 21
Baum, Gregory, 150, 153, 155–57,
    162n18, n22
Beck, Lewis White, 12n27
Becker, Ernest, 164, 107–73
Beelzebul, 22, 23
Belial, 22
Berger, Peter, 123–24
Bergson, Henri, 101
Bible, 22, 28, 91, 107, 111, 112, 164,
    166
    See also New Testament; Old
    Testament; *specific books*
Bismarck, Otto von, 171
Black Mass, 32
Bonhoeffer, Dietrich, 7
Boston University School of
    Theology, 112
Boutin, Maurice, 13–20, 183
Bromley, D. W., 84n16
Brown, Norman O., 171
Brunner (author), 27
Bryant, M. Darrol, 149–63, 183
Buddhism, 77, 147
Bultmann, Rudolf, 13, 15, 20n6, 23,
    27, 165
Burke, Edmund, 157, 163n25
Bushnell, Horace, 110
Burrick, George, 111

Caelestius, 109
Caesar, 30
Cain, 2, 17, 75, 82, 145
Calvin, John, 26, 128, 161n3
Calvinism, 122, 123, 144, 151
Cambridge University, 101
Canaanites, 17

Catholic Church, 26, 27, 35*n*16, 75, 115, 133
   exorcism rites of, 30–32
   Fathers of, 48
Chadwick, Henry, 43
Chosen, The (Potok), 133
Christ, *see* Jesus Christ
Christ (Schillebeeckx), 27
Christian Faith, The (Schleiermacher), 109
Chronicles, First Book of, 166, 167
Clark, Francis, 70
Clausewitz, Karl von, 171
Clement of Alexandria, 24, 37, 42–48
Cobb, John, 77
Codex Sinaiticus, 24
Confucianism, 147
Constantine, Emperor, 24
Corinthians, First Book of, 177
Council of Orange, 151
Creation, 18
   Purpose of, 97

Damian, Peter, 170
Darwin, Charles, 6, 69, 101
Darwinism, 108
David, King, 6, 8, 16, 17
Davidic census, 166
Day of Judgement, 56, 60
Dead Sea Scrolls, 25, 34*n*5
DeVries, S. J., 167–68
DeWolf, L. Howard, 112–14
Dialogue with Trypho (Justin), 28, 39
Diaspora, 52
Discourse on Christian Nurture (Bushnell), 110
Divine preservation, humanity in context of, 6–8
Divine Principle, 6, 21, 26*n*29, 62–64, 67, 73–85, 87, 88, 92, 94, 96, 124–26
Dominicans, 27, 32

East of Eden (Steinbeck), 161*n*8
Eastern Fathers, 176
Eby, Lloyd, 133–48, 183–84
Egyptian Christianity, 24
Eiseley, Loren, 180*n*1
"Elders, the," 16
Elert, Werner, 6
Eliot, T. S., 21
England, 6
Enlightenment, the, 26, 108, 109, 149, 154, 160*n*1
Enoch, 34*n*5
Ephesians, Book of, 26
Essenes, 165
Ethic of responsibility, 124–31
Eu, Hyo Won, 62
Eusebius, Bishop, 17, 24
Evangelical Faith (Thielicke), 29
Evangelical Protestantism, 106, 108
Eve, 3, 5, 17, 18, 25, 33, 37–41, 43–45, 48, 53, 58, 62, 64–68, 70, 74, 75, 77, 79, 80, 88–92, 94, 95, 103, 108, 112, 114, 116, 126, 143, 145, 146, 168–70, 172, 175, 176
Evil, problem of, 86–99
Exhortation to the Greeks (Justin), 38
Exodus, Book of, 17

Fall
   biblical notion of, 1–6
   in *Divine Principle*, 73–85
   factual acceptance and practical meaning of, 13–20
   liberal Protestant understandings of, 106–18
   misognyny and, 37–51
   original sin and nature of, 101–3
   and problem of evil, 86–99
   Unification account of, 62–72
Ferguson, John, 47
Fichtner, Johannes, 11*n*12, *n*18
Florovsky, Georges, 152, 161*n*4
Floyd, William Gregory, 42–44

INDEX

Foester (author), 22
Foster, Durwood, 73–85, 184
Fouth Lateran Council, 35n16
Freud and Original Sin (MacIsaac), 150
Freud, Sigmund, 78, 137, 170
Freund, Gerhard, 14
Fromm, Erich, 3, 11n13
Fundamentalists, 36n29

Gabriel, 41
Galatians, Book of, 45
Garrigou-Lagrange, Reginald, 32–33
Gaster, T., 22
Genesis, Book of, 2, 3, 5, 14–19, 22, 39, 44, 48, 63, 64, 67, 70, 73, 75, 111, 145, 164, 167, 168, 173, 176
Germany, 6
Gnosticism, 4, 24, 43–47
God, Man and Evil (Buttrick), 111
Goodenough, Erwin, 38–40
Grant, George, 160n1
Greco-Roman philosophy, 23, 28
Greek Fathers, 177

Haag, Herbert, 20n10, 22–23
Hamburg, University of, 29
Han, Hak Ja, 84n17
Hardon, John A., 21
Harnack (author), 27
Hart, Ray, 175
Hartshorne, (author), 27
Heavenly Providence, 82
Hegel, George Wilhelm Friedrich, 2, 110, 136
Heinisch (author), 43
Herbert, Anne, 173–74, 181n9
Hering, Jean, 43
Hitler, Adolf, 29, 171
Hick, John, 87, 95
Hinduism, 147
Hirah the Adullanite, 165

Hobbes, Thomas, 137
Hodge, Charles 36n29
Holocaust, 115
Holy Ghost, 74
Holy Scriptures, 35n16
Holy Spirit, 9
Hostage to the Devil (Martin), 30
Human potential, limits of, 8–10
Human value, original sin and, 133–48
Humanism, 108
Humanity in context of divine preservation, 6–8
Huxley, Julian, 11n9
Hyung Sang, 143

Iblis, 55
Ignatius, St., Epistles of, 24–26
Imam of the Muslim, 54
International Conference on the Unity of the Sciences, 76
International Cultural Foundation/ New ERA, 82
International Religious Foundation, 82
Interpreters Dictionary of the Bible, The, 167
Irenaeanism, 151, 168, 169, 174
Irenaeus, 27, 39, 42, 70, 71, 161n3
Isaiah, Book of, 17
Isherwood, Christopher, 181n4
Isis, mystery cult of, 23
Islam, 133, 147
  concept of sin in, 52–60
Israel, ancient, 6, 16–19, 126, 166

James, Gene G., 86–99, 184
Jaoulin (author), 172
Jeroboam, 17
Jerome, St., 17
Jesuits, 21, 27, 30
Jesus, (Schillebeeckx), 27
Jesus Christ, 7–9, 17, 19, 38, 48, 54,

66, 74, 77, 79, 87, 108, 165, 168, 175–77, 179
  birth of, 41
  and concept of sin, 53
  crucifixion of, 90, 126
  and Satan, 21–28, 30, 32, 33, 34n1, 38, 43
  teachings of, 107, 111
Job, Book of, 86, 166
John the Baptist, 75, 82
John, Gospel of, 17, 22, 66, 177
Josephus, 40
Judah, 16, 165–65
Judaism, 17, 44, 47, 73, 133
  angels in, 38–39
  concept of sin in, 52–53, 58, 167, 168
  Satan in, 22–26, 34n5, 39–40, 43
Judas, 22
Judea, 16
Judges, Book of, 52
Jung, Carl, 3, 78
Jung, Leo, 34n2
Justin Martyr, 37–43, 46–48

Kant, Immanuel, 8, 13–14, 20n1
Kierkegaard, Soren, 70–71, 77, 80, 170, 172
Kim, Young Oon, 21–36, 77, 89, 90, 92, 99n43, 127, 184
King, Martin Luther, Jr., 104
Kings, First Book of, 16–17
Kittel (author), 34n4
Kliever, Lonnie, 129
Köhler, Ludwig, 10n1
Kolakowski, Leszek, 29
Küng, Hans, 35n16
Künneth, Walter, 7

Laeuchli, Samuel, 152
Lamech, 2
Language of Faith, The (Laeuchli), 152
Lee, Sang Hun, 97

Leith, John H., 161n4
Lindsey, Hal, 33
Linnemann, Eta, 178–80
Living Word, The (Wingren), 27
Lord's Prayer, 22
Love as opposite of sin, 164–82
Lucifer, 17, 21, 33, 65, 66, 68, 70, 81, 82, 98n3, 143, 145
Luke, Gospel of, 17, 22, 23, 102, 166
Lund, University of, 27
Luther, Martin, 6, 8, 24, 26, 161n3, 164, 165

MacIsaac, Sharon, 150–51
McLaughlin, Eleanor, 42
Mann, Thomas, 29
Mark, Gospel of, 22, 166
Martin, Malachi, 30
Maritain (author), 27
Marx, Karl, 78, 155
Marxism, 29, 106, 108, 111, 115–16, 123–24, 127, 136, 138–41, 146, 147n2
Mary, 37, 41
Matthew, Gospel of, 1, 23, 166, 178
Maximus the Confessor, 175
Mead, George Herbert, 128
Mennonitism, 133
Merton, Thomas, 175
Messiah, 146
Meyendorff, John, 174–77
Misogny, 37–51
Mithra, mystery cult of, 23
Mojzes, Paul, 106–18, 184–85
Monogenism, 67–69
Monophysitism, 24
Moon, Sun Myung, 62, 79, 84n17, 125, 126
Mosaic Law, 24
Moses, 18, 19, 75, 165
Muhammad, 54, 56, 57
Muslims, *see* Islam

Nag Hammadi gnosticism, 24
National Socialism, *see* Nazism
Nature and Destiny of Man, The (Niebuhr), 135
Nazism, 29, 80, 11, 171
Nestorianism, 24
New Ecumenical Research Association, 116
New Testament, 22, 24, 26–28, 32, 34n5, 35n16, 88, 107, 151, 166–68
New York Times book review, 21
Nicene Creed, 24
Niebuhr, H. Richard, 119, 120, 126, 128–30
Niebuhr, Reinhold, 27, 104, 109, 127, 135–38, 142, 162n16
Nietzsche, Friedrich, 137
Northern kingdom, 16–17
Nyang, Sulayman S., 52–61, 185

O'Connor, Flannery, 176
Old Testament, 2, 19, 22, 107, 167
Orange, Council of, 151
Origen, 25
Original Sin
  human value and, 133–48
  nature of fall and, 101–3
Outline of the Principle: Level 4, 124–26
Ovid, 14

Pantaenus, 42
Parousia, 8, 26
Parsons, Talcott, 121
Pascal, Blaise, 14
Patriarchs, 19
Paul VI, Pope, 21
Paul, St., 8, 9, 24, 25, 44, 45, 47, 165, 167, 168, 176
Pelagianism, 176
Pelagius, 169
Pensées (Pascal), 14
Personal sin, 103–4

Persian period, 22
Peter, St., 22, 25
Petersen, Sarah E., 37–51, 185
Pharisees, 23, 165
Philippians, Book of, 9
Philo of Alexandria, 25, 38, 40, 41, 43, 44, 48
Photius, Patriarch, 175, 176
Pilgrim Fathers, 6–7
Plato, 42, 136
Platonism, 23, 38, 42
"Politics as a Vocation" (Weber), 127
Pontifical University, 32–33
Positivistic Naturalism, 108
Potok, Chaim, 133
Preservation, divine, 6–8
Priestly tradition, 16
Prince of Evil, 44
Protestantism, 27, 33n2, 26n29, 75, 133, 161n3
  liberal, understandings of the fall in, 106–18
Puritans, 6

Quasten, Johannes, 42, 45, 47
Quran, 53–57, 59–60

Rahner, Karl, 27, 68
Rank, Otto, 170–72
Rationalists, 109
Rauschenbusch, Walter, 111, 150, 153–55
Rawls, John, 147n2
"Reality of the Demonic, The" (Thielicke), 29
Reformation, 26, 115
Rehoboam, 16–17
Religion and Alienation (Baum), 155
Religion Within the Limits of Reason Alone (Kant), 13–14
Renaissance, 101, 136
Responsibility, ethic of, 124–31
Resurrection, 76, 81

Revelation, Book of, 17, 22, 30
Richardson, Herbert, 66
Ricoeur, Paul, 70
Ritschl, Albrecht, 74
Roberts, J. Deotis, 100–105, 185
Romans, Book of, 8, 45, 164, 168, 176–77
Romanticism, 109
Rosenstock-Huessy, Eugen, 162n23
Reuther, Rosemary, 42

Salvation
  personal sin and, 103–4
  social sin and, 104–5
Samaritans, 39
Samma'el, 17
Samuel, Second Book of, 166, 167
Satan, 17, 38–40, 43, 44, 46, 65, 66, 74, 77, 79–83, 87–89, 94, 95, 98n3, 116, 143–45, 166, 167
  in Islam, 54, 60
  as reality or symbol, 21–36
Satan Is Alive and Well on Planet Earth (Lindsey), 33
Satanism, 21, 32
Satanology, 24, 26, 35n16
Schillenbeeckx, Edward, 27
Schiller, Friedrich, 2, 3
Schleiermacher, Friedrich, 27, 74, 75, 109–10, 128
Schluchter, Wolfgang, 123, 127
Schmauss, Michael, 35n16
Schwarz, Hans, 1–12, 185
Semites, 53
Septimus Severus, 42
Septuagint, 39
Seven Hells, 55
Sharia, 54, 57, 58, 60
Shechem, 16
Shupe, A. D., Jr., 84n16
Shrine of the New Being, 30, 31
Sin, 100–101
  Islamic concept of, 52–60
  love as opposite of, 164–82

  personal, and salvation, 103–4
  social, and salvation, 104–5
  and society, 149–63
  See also Original sin
Sin in Inheritance (Freund), 14
Sister Mary Ignatius Explains It All for You (play), 133
Sixth Commandment, 6
Skrade, Carl, 164–82, 186
"Social Gospel," 108, 111
"Social Psychology of the World Religions, The" (Weber), 121
Social Sin, 104–5
Society, sin and, 149–63
Sociology, Weberian, 120–24
Solomon, King, 16, 17
  Wisdom of, 34n5
Sontag, Frederick, 95–96, 99n36
Spencer, Herbert, 101
Stalin, Josef, 171
Steinbeck, John, 161n8
Stoicism, 23, 38
Stromata (Clement), 46
Suffering, 119–32
  of God, and ethic of responsibility, 124–31
  and sociology of theodicy, 120–24
Sufism, 54–55
Sung Sang, 143
Synoptic Gospels, 40
Synoptic traditions, 22
Syrian Christianity, 24

Tamar, 164–65
Targum of Pseudo-Janathan, 17
Tatian, 40
Teilhard de Chardin, Pierre, 2, 27
Temple, Archbishop William, 35n15
Tenbruck, Friedrich, 122
Tennant, F. R., 101
Tertullian, 39
Theodicy, 120–24
Theological Investigations (Rahner), 27

Theology of the Social Gospel, The (Rauschenbusch), 153
Thielicke, Helmut, 29–30
Thomism, 32, 151
Three Ages of the Interior Life, The (Garrigou-Lagrange), 33
Tillich, Paul, 27, 80, 84n20, 109, 166
Toennies (author), 155
Torah, 53
Tower of Babel, 2
Traherne, Thomas, 178
Trajan, Emperor, 25
Transcendentalism, 108, 109
Trent, Council of, 35n16
Troeltsch (author), 27
Twelve Patriarchs, Testaments of, 34n5
Unfinished Man and the Imagination (Hart), 175
Unification Theology (Kim), 125
Unitarians, 110
Universal Man, 54

Van Dusen, Henry P., 111

Vatican II, 27, 35n16
Vindication of Liberal Theology, The (Van Dusen), 111
Virgin Mary, *see* Mary

Walsh, Thomas, 119–32, 186
Weber, Max, 119–24, 126–28, 155
Welch, Claude, 110
Wells, Jonathan, 62–72, 77, 186
Wesley, John 85n24
Westminster Confession, 151
Whitehead, Alfred North, 101
Williams, Colin, 85n24
Wingren, Gustav, 27–28
Wolff, Robert Paul, 147n2
Wol-li Kang-ron (Eu), 62
World War I, 171
World War II, 29, 115
Wycliff Bible Encyclopedia, 33n1

Yahwist tradition, 2–5, 16–19, 170, 171

Zechariah, Book of, 166
Zimmerli, Walther, 10n1
Zoroastrian dualism, 22, 34n5

BT 710.S65 1985

circ   Society and original sin :
Bergen Community College Library

3 5936 000 038 632

**Library and Learning
Resources Center
Bergen Community College**
400 Paramus Road
Paramus, N.J. 07652-1595

Return Postage Guaranteed